AF477528

International Political Economy Series

General Editor: **Timothy M. Shaw**, Professor of Political Science and
International Development Studies, Dalhousie University, Halifax, Nova Scotia

Titles include:

Pradeep Agrawal, Subir V. Gokarn, Veena Mishra, Kirit S. Parikh and Kunal Sen
POLICY REGIMES AND INDUSTRIAL COMPETITIVENESS
A Comparative Study of East Asia and India

Roderic Alley
THE UNITED NATIONS IN SOUTHEAST ASIA AND THE SOUTH PACIFIC

Dick Beason and Jason James
THE POLITICAL ECONOMY OF JAPANESE FINANCIAL MARKETS
Myths versus Reality

Mark Beeson
COMPETING CAPITALISMS
Australia, Japan and Economic Competition in Asia-Pacific

Deborah Bräutigam
CHINESE AID AND AFRICAN DEVELOPMENT
Exporting Green Revolution

Steve Chan, Cal Clark and Danny Lam (*editors*)
BEYOND THE DEVELOPMENTAL STATE
East Asia's Political Economies Reconsidered

Abdul Rahman Embong
STATE-LED MODERNIZATION AND THE NEW MIDDLE CLASS IN MALAYSIA

Dong-Sook Shin Gills
RURAL WOMEN AND TRIPLE EXPLOITATION IN KOREAN DEVELOPMENT

Jeffrey Henderson (*editor*)
INDUSTRIAL TRANSFORMATION IN EASTERN EUROPE IN
THE LIGHT OF THE EAST ASIAN EXPERIENCE

Takashi Inoguchi
GLOBAL CHANGE
A Japanese Perspective

Dominic Kelly
JAPAN AND THE RECONSTRUCTION OF EAST ASIA

L. H. M. Ling
POSTCOLONIAL INTERNATIONAL RELATIONS
Conquest and Desire between Asia and the West

Pierre P. Lizée
PEACE, POWER AND RESISTANCE IN CAMBODIA
Global Governance and the Failure of International Conflict Resolution

Ananya Mukherjee Reed
PERSPECTIVES ON THE INDIAN CORPORATE ECONOMY
Exploring the Paradox of Profits

Cecilia Ng
POSITIONING WOMEN IN MALAYSIA
Class and Gender in an Industrializing State

Ian Scott (*editor*)
INSTITUTIONAL CHANGE AND THE POLITICAL TRANSITION IN HONG
KONG

Mark Turner (*editor*)
CENTRAL–LOCAL RELATIONS IN ASIA–PACIFIC
Convergence or Divergence?

Fei-Ling Wang
INSTITUTIONS AND INSTITUTIONAL CHANGE IN CHINA
Premodernity and Modernization

International Political Economy Series
Series Standing Order ISBN 0–333–71708–2
(*outside North America only*)

You can receive future titles in this series as they are published by placing a standing order.
Please contact your bookseller or, in case of difficulty, write to us at the address below with
your name and address, the title of the series and the ISBN quoted above.

Customer Services Department, Macmillan Distribution Ltd, Houndmills, Basingstoke,
Hampshire RG21 6XS, England

State-led Modernization and the New Middle Class in Malaysia

Abdul Rahman Embong
Professor in Sociology of Development
Institute of Malaysian and International Studies
Universiti Kebangsaan Malaysia

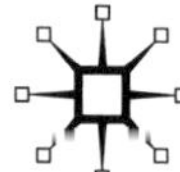

© Abdul Rahman Embong 2002

All rights reserved. No reproduction, copy or transmission of
this publication may be made without written permission.

No paragraph of this publication may be reproduced, copied or
transmitted save with written permission or in accordance with
the provisions of the Copyright, Designs and Patents Act 1988,
or under the terms of any licence permitting limited copying
issued by the Copyright Licensing Agency, 90 Tottenham Court
Road, London W1T 4LP.

Any person who does any unauthorised act in relation to this
publication may be liable to criminal prosecution and civil
claims for damages.

The author has asserted his right to be identified
as the author of this work in accordance with the
Copyright, Designs and Patents Act 1988.

First published 2002 by
PALGRAVE
Houndmills, Basingstoke, Hampshire RG21 6XS and
175 Fifth Avenue, New York, N. Y. 10010
Companies and representatives throughout the world

PALGRAVE is the new global academic imprint of
St. Martin's Press LLC Scholarly and Reference Division and
Palgrave Publishers Ltd (formerly Macmillan Press Ltd).

ISBN 0–333–96881–6 hardback

This book is printed on paper suitable for recycling and
made from fully managed and sustained forest sources.

A catalogue record for this book is available
from the British Library.

Library of Congress Cataloging-in-Publication Data
Abdul Rahman Embong
    State-led modernization and the new middle class in
    Malaysia / Abdul Rahman Embong.
        p. cm. — (Series in international political economy)
    Includes bibliographical references and index.
    ISBN 0–333–96881–6
    1. Middle class—Malaysia. 2. Civil society—Malaysia.
    3. Democratization—Malaysia.
    I. Title. II. Series.

    HT690.M3 A23 2001
    305.5′5′09595—dc21
                                                    2001034809

10   9   8   7   6   5   4   3   2   1
11   10 09 08 07 06 05 04 03 02

Printed and bound in Great Britain by
Antony Rowe Ltd, Chippenham, Wiltshire

Dedication

In memory of my late father, Haji Embong Ahmad, and my late mother, Hajah Munah Ismail, who did not have the opportunity to see the transformation of their home village or the emergence of the new Malay middle class; and in farewell salutation to Professor Ishak Shari (1948–2001): lifelong friend and collaborator, gone too soon; Director of IKMAS at UKM 1997–2001, his memory and vision live on in the scholarly work that he inspired.

Contents

List of Tables

Foreword

Professor Hans-Dieter Evers

This book deals with a topic which is currently very widely debated among social scientists, but as yet little researched in terms of empirical studies. The study is based on extensive questionnaire surveys and field observations carried out in the Klang Valley, in Kota Bharu and in Kuala Terengganu. It is therefore a major contribution to the sociological literature on Southeast Asia. Furthermore, the book is extremely well written and argued and will therefore be well received by specialists and students alike. The first two chapters in particular are among the best pieces I have read on the middle class in Southeast Asia. As the research questions have been clearly defined, the presentation of data and the analysis follow smoothly.

In this analysis the author follows the tradition of classical German sociology based on Max Weber and Karl Marx. This is sufficient to define the middle class as a macro-sociological phenomenon. In his micro-sociological analysis the leading trends of current class analysis of the French school (Bourdieu and others) as well as post-modern theory are not utilised. This shows up especially in the chapter on lifestyles in which the emphasis is centred on consumption, whereas meaning, distinction and the symbolic value of consumer items are not discussed. Recent studies on the lifestyle of Southeast Asian middle classes (such as Chua Beng-Huat on Singapore, Solvay Gerke on Indonesia, results of the Murdoch University research project super-vised by Robison) could have been taken as a lead. On the other hand, the author's analysis of the new Malay middle-class family is excellent. He shows that the nuclear family with all its problems has come into being but that it is embedded in a wider kin network. As this book is supposed to show the interrelation between industrialisation and the middle class, the impact of new technologies – such as mobile phones and e-mail – could have been stressed more to show how these networks are maintained.

Another lucid argument concerns intergenerational mobility and the formation of the middle class which shows that the Malay middle class is really predominantly 'new'. The author has thus succeeded in proving the so-called 'first-generation middle-class' thesis. He has also presented data to counteract Joel Kahn's thesis that the new Malay middle class is mainly the creation of government service. In the Klang Valley in particular, only a small part of the new middle class is employed in the public sector. This appears to be quite different from the situation in Indonesia, where recent studies have shown that up to 80 per cent of the new middle class depend on government employment. The impact of these findings on democratisation and civil society are aptly discussed in a later chapter. In the discussion on *Melayu Baru*, that has been hotly debated in Malaysia for some time, another question shows up. The author has, perhaps quite rightly, concentrated on the middle class (with some data in his survey on the working class). It would be interesting to add further thought to class relations, i.e. the social context in which the middle class emerges. Is the *Melayu Baru* really a middle-class person, or is the reference group rather the successful Malay politician old and new style, the new Malay tycoon or the modern Malay farmer after all?

The impact of industrialisation is mainly analysed in terms of job creation. The culture of industrial work, gender relations between female workers and male supervisors, ethnic relations between workers and managers etc. probably have an impact on middle-class values, lifestyles and the family. I admit that these issues are very difficult to analyse but further studies on this subject will undoubtedly benefit from Rahman's study.

Last but not least, the economic crisis, the sudden downturn in job opportunities, the increase of social insecurity, and the new political movements of the past few years are touched upon in Chapter 8 and in the last chapter of the book. The survey data, of course, refer to the period before the crisis, but follow-up data have been collected and have led to a reflection on the fate of the new Malay middle class.

Professor Rahman's book is one of the first major studies on the new middle class in Southeast Asia. His findings are highly significant, original, and make worthwhile reading. I am certain that this book will be received with great interest by the scholarly community working on Southeast Asian societies and stimulate further debate on the social and political role of the new Asian middle class.

PROFESSOR HANS-DIETER EVERS
Department of Southeast Asian Studies
University of Bonn, Germany

Preface

This study of the state-led modernization and the new middle class in Malaysia is the result of the research I carried out for several years in the 1990s. The study – focusing on the new Malay middle class – first traces the evolution of the Malaysian class structure, and shows the role of the state as well as capitalist development in promoting structural changes and the formation of the modern classes, particularly the new Malay middle class. From this macro-historical perspective, the study presents detailed analyses of the characteristics and the socio-economic and political roles of the new Malay middle class and its likely role in Malaysia in the twenty-first century. The study is based on the empirical investigations (surveys, interviews and observations) I conducted between 1995 and 2000, with a substantial part of it being based on a survey of 284 new Malay middle-class respondents conducted in 1996–97 in the metropolitan Klang Valley (Kuala Lumpur and Petaling Jaya), and two provincial towns in the east coast states of Peninsular Malaysia – Kota Bahru in Kelantan and Kuala Terengganu in Terengganu. Nevertheless, the political twists and turns in Malaysia following the 1997–98 Asian financial and economic crises – the most significant event being the political crisis triggered by the sacking of Anwar Ibrahim, Malaysia's former Deputy Prime Minister and Mahathir's heir-designate from the Cabinet and the ruling UMNO – marked a turning point in Malaysia's history, which saw a sea-change in the politics of the new Malay middle class. These developments are far too important to be left unaddressed. This made me postpone the publication of this manuscript though it was largely completed in January 1999. I needed time to assess the new developments in the hope of making the necessary revisions and incorporating the post-crisis developments into the book. Ill health, however, delayed the completion of the manuscript until more than a year later. I am glad that I eventually managed to incorporate some aspects of the post-crisis developments, particularly in Chapters 8 and 10 of this book.

This study of the new Malay middle class has come to fruition via a circuitous route. In my days as a young lecturer in the early 1970s, I studied and wrote about the peasantry, the working class and intellectuals in the midst of change. Peasants, fishermen and worker-squatters were the most popular themes in the research and writing of that period, when

Malaysia was still primarily an agricultural country and was just embarking upon the process of rapid urbanization and export-led industrialization under the New Economic Policy (1971–1990). During this period, studies of the middle class were scarce. However, things have changed since then as the various chapters in my study attempt to show. Malaysia has become a modern and rapidly industrializing country, with bustling cities and towns. Unlike during colonial times, the peasants and workers of yesteryear have produced many children who no longer continue their parents' occupations as literate or better peasants, fishermen or workers, but have instead become middle-class professionals, managers, administrators as well as entrepreneurs, who are playing important roles in Malaysia's development. Besides their roles in economic and social developments, their role in politics and democratization too has become important. This makes a comprehensive study of the new Malay middle class both timely and necessary.

Social scientists, including sociologists, have conducted research and presented findings and 'discoveries'. But have they produced anything new? The words of the well-known American sociologist Robert K. Merton cross my mind when reflecting on this issue. He reminisced that a sociologist is regarded as someone who spends thousands of dollars discovering something which everyone already knew; but if he discovers something which was not 'known', then there is a refusal to believe the findings, since 'common sense' decrees that it cannot be true. I do not know if the findings and conclusions of my study fall into Merton's category of stating the obvious, or of making 'unbelievable' claims. I leave it to the wise judgement of the reader to decide which.

ABDUL RAHMAN EMBONG
Institute of Malaysian and International Studies (IKMAS)
Universiti Kebangsaan Malaysia
Bangi, Selangor, Malaysia

Acknowledgements

This book is based on my doctoral dissertation submitted to the Institute of Postgraduate Studies and Research at the University of Malaya in January 1999. Although my doctoral study was self-financed, I was fortunate to have obtained several research grants that contributed to this work. I am grateful to the Faculty of the Social Sciences and Humanities, Universiti Kebangsaan Malaysia (National University of Malaysia or UKM) for a modest grant awarded in 1996, to study Malay professionals, and to the Malaysian Ministry of Science, Technology and Environment for the Intensified Research in Priority Areas (IRPA) grant to study the Malaysian middle class in 1997. In 1996, I was the principal researcher for Malaysia in a comparative study of the Southeast Asian middle classes sponsored by the Program for Southeast Asian Area Studies (PROSEA), Academia Sinica, Taipei headed by my colleague and friend, Professor Michael Hsiao. I must thank Michael for this opportunity. I was also director of a collaborative research project to study the impact of the Asian crisis on the Malaysian and Indonesian middle classes financed by the Toyota Foundation in 1998–99 for which I am grateful. All these studies helped enrich my knowledge about the middle class which I used in various ways in writing this book.

I would like to put on record that though I was a sociology lecturer at UKM for about four years in the early 1970s, after having obtained my first and second degrees from Leicester and London in the United Kingdom, I was out of academia and the country for almost two decades from 1975 to 1992, and only rejoined in 1993. I am very much a self-taught person, and am greatly indebted to many colleagues and friends for my intellectual and academic life. I would not have undertaken and completed this study had it not been for the encouragement and support of numerous friends, whose names are too many to be listed. A few, however, need to be mentioned, in particular, my former schoolmate and friend, Jomo K.S., a well-known economics professor at the Faculty of Economics and Administration, University of Malaya whose unflagging support as my doctoral supervisor is most appreciated. Thanks are also due to my first supervisor, Zawawi Ibrahim, with whom I started when I registered in 1995, but he later moved from the University of Malaya to take up the appointment of Professor in Anthropology at Universiti Malaysia Sarawak (Unimas) in January 1998. My colleagues and friends – Ishak Shari, Halim Ali, Norani Othman, Sumit Mandal, Diana Wong, Khoo Kay Jin, Shamsul

A.B., Rajah Rasiah, Hairi Abdullah, Abdul Samad Hadi, Rustam Sani, Kamaruddin Said, Rahimah Aziz and many others – at Universiti Kebangsaan Malaysia and elsewhere, with whom I have worked and traded ideas, criticisms, recycled jokes, and so on are a source of inspiration that propelled me to complete this work. I also had the privilege of regular exchanges with the distinguished sociologist, Professor Syed Hussein Alatas, former Vice-Chancellor of the University of Malaya, whose sharp mind and ideas provoked my thought and imagination. The intellectual exchanges with well-known scholars from abroad such as Clive Kessler from the University of New South Wales, Australia, Han-Dieter Evers from Bielefeld University, Germany, James Mittelman from the American University, Washington, DC, and Bob Hefner from Boston University, USA – all of whom at one time or other had made their debut at UKM, have also been very stimulating. I am also indebted to Ku Shamsul Bariah from the University of Malaya and Timothy Shaw from the Dalhousie University, Canada for their insightful comments on an earlier draft of this book.

My Old Boys' network from the Federation Military College (now Royal Military College), Sungai Besi – particularly Hamzah Pilus, Shaharuddin Bahaudin, Mazlan Hashim, Yahya Yaacob, Michael Tan, Wan Salleh and Azzat Kamaludin – and other old friends, especially Albert Foo and Adi Satria, have been very helpful in their own way in facilitating my research. I also would like to place on record a big *terima kasih* to Nor Hayati Sa'at, now a research officer at the Institute of Malaysian and International Studies (IKMAS), Universiti Kebangsaan Malaysia, where I am currently attached, for her untiring assistance from the time I embarked on this study till the present. Salwani Ismail's technical assistance in the final preparation of the manuscript is also appreciated.

I am also very fortunate for having by my side Suraya, who has always given me staunch support and encouragement in her own simple ways. Her constant reminder to complete the manuscript in time finally made me dash for the finishing line. I am also thankful to Azrian, our only child, whose distraction and inquisitive mind, not befitting his age, often provided me welcome relief from the otherwise onerous task of poring over materials and writing drafts of this book.

Finally, to the respondents in this study, I am eternally grateful. I am particularly indebted to all those persons with whom I have conducted wide-ranging interviews for their valuable time and for sharing with me their thoughts and observations.

Glossary

Balik kampung
Literally meaning 'return to home village', a cultural practice of returning to the home village or town during cultural festivals, and other occasions to visit parents and relatives

Bumiputera
Literally meaning 'sons of the soil', referring to Malays and other indigenous groups in Malaysia

Dakwah
Muslim missionary activity to spread the message of Islam.

Folk urbanites
Modern urban-dwellers whose lifestyles are relatively modest, with a strong family and community orientation, rather than being cosmopolitan, individualistic and isolated from kin and community. Culturally, 'folk urbanites' – though living in modern urban settings – tend to operate within the domain of their cultural values and religious practices.

Gotong royong
Mutual help, a traditional form of cooperation among Malay villagers, especially when performing tasks involving a lot of physical labour.

Haj
Pilgrimage to Mecca to fulfill Islam's fifth pillar performed in Zulhijjah, the twelfth month of the Muslim calendar.

Hari Raya (Haji)
Also known as *Hari Raya Idiladha,* a Muslim celebration held on the 10th of Zulhijjah, the month Muslims perform their pilgrimage to Mecca.

Hari Raya (Puasa)
Also known as *Hari Raya Idilfitri,* a Muslim celebration held after the end of the fasting month of Ramadan.

Homogamous marriage
Marriage within the same social group; for example, members of the new middle class marrying other members of the same class.

Kampung

Malay word for 'village'.

Kampung-like urban community

A community or a local social system in an urban setting whose members generally have characteristics of 'folk urbanites'. The social relationships established within such a community are normally *surau*-based, with members knowing each other personally and practising *gotong royong* or mutual help, especially when holding important social functions.

Kenduri

Feast held by Malays to celebrate important social occasions such as wedding, circumcision, house-warming, or any other event.

Klang Valley

The most industrially developed and advanced region in Malaysia, in which Kuala Lumpur and its suburb Petaling Jaya are located.

Melayu Baru

Literally meaning 'the New Malay', a term first used by Prime Minister Dr Mahathir Mohamad in his address to the UMNO General Assembly in 1991 to call for the creation of a new work culture among Malays in keeping with his industrialization drive and the creation of a Malay capitalist class and a new Malay middle class.

Melayu Lama

Literally meaning 'the Old Malay', a term used to contrast it with *Melayu Baru*.

Merdeka

Malay word for 'independence'.

New Economic Policy

A policy implemented following the communal riots of 13 May 1969 in Malaysia meant to redress ethnic socio-economic imbalances. During its implementation over a twenty-year period (1971 to 1990), it was supposed to achieve the two-pronged objectives of reducing poverty irrespective of ethnic group and restructuring society to eradicate the ethnic identification of economic activities.

Ontological security

Security of living and existence.

Rumah terbuka
Literally meaning 'open house', a traditionally-based modern cultural practice of opening the house for guests to celebrate the *Hari Raya* festival. It is also used to refer to the practice of hosting guests to celebrate other major festivals.

Reformasi
Literally meaning 'reform', this term became a popular rallying call in Malaysia following the downfall of Indonesia's Suharto in May 1998. In public discourse in Malaysia, it is often associated with the protest movement led by Anwar Ibrahim against Prime Minister Mahathir Mohamad.

Surau
Muslim community prayer-house which is smaller than a mosque.

Tahlil
A thanksgiving feast among Malays and Muslims usually organized to remember deceased parents, relatives or friends.

Umrah
Pilgrimage to Mecca peformed outside the *haj* season.

Warak
Fervently religious.

List of Abbreviations

APU	Angkatan Perpaduan Ummah (Movement for the Unity of Believers)
BA	Barisan Alternatif (Alternative Front)
BN	Barisan Nasional (National Front)
DAP	Democratic Action Party
FOMCA	Federation of Malaysian Consumers' Associations
GDP	gross domestic product
GNP	gross national product
ISA	Internal Security Act
KEADILAN	Parti Keadilan Nasional (National Justice Party)
MCA	Malaysian Chinese Association
MIC	Malaysian Indian Congress
NDP	National Development Policy
NEP	New Economic Policy
NGO	non-governmental organization
PAS	Parti Islam Se-Malaysia (Pan-Malaysian Islamic Party)
PRM	Parti Rakyat Malaysia (Malaysian People's Party)
Semangat '46	Parti Melayu Semangat '46 (Spirit of '46 Malay Party)
UMNO	United Malays National Organisation

1
Introduction

Class formation and the new middle class

In a paper published almost three decades ago, Hans-Dieter Evers (1973: 108–31) argued that the framework of a theory of class formation and class conflict could be used to analyse a major trend in the modernization of Southeast Asia – that is, the emergence of new social positions and class formations. In his opinion, by the early 1970s Southeast Asian societies had already developed, or were in the process of developing, a rather specific type of class structure and this class structure and its inherent conflicts provided the framework within which political activities and economic efforts would have to take place. He contended that the dynamics of class formation itself will influence if not determine future social, political and economic developments in the area.

To my mind, this observation, made at around the time when Malaysia – an important country in the Southeast Asian region – had just begun to implement its New Economic Policy (NEP) (1971–90) and rapid industrialization, was not only insightful but has also been borne out by subsequent historical developments. Today, when class formations and conflicts have crystallized with the emergence and expansion of the capitalist, the middle and the working classes in Malaysia and other Southeast Asian societies, class theory from either the Marxist or the Weberian tradition, or from a convergence of both, still has a heuristic value and relevance.

My study, shaped to some extent by both the Marxist and the Weberian traditions of class analysis, is of the new Malay middle class in Malaysia. Together with their non-Malay counterparts, the new Malay middle class, comprised of managers, professionals and administrators, has become very visible in Malaysian towns and cities over the last three decades, a period during which Malaysia has experienced rapid modernization, industrialization and economic growth. Members of this class work in comfortable air-conditioned offices and often in very large organizations, commute daily to work in air-conditioned cars, and live mostly in suburban housing estates. As managers, professionals and administrators, they are playing important roles in Malaysia's development and modernization. In addition, being relatively affluent, they have become an important market for various types of consumer products and have become trendsetters for certain lifestyles. Being highly educated, they are expected to be important social and political forces in promoting modernization and the growth of democracy and civil society, as well as standard-bearers for modern culture and civilization throughout Malaysia.

Although modern classes in Malaysia emerged about a century ago with the development of colonial capitalism, this rapid growth and expansion is a post-independence phenomenon connected to the state-led policies of modernization – namely the implementation of the NEP and export-led industrialization. Based on official statistics, over the three decades between 1970 and 2000, several major changes in the occupational patterns can be seen: there has been an increase in the proportions of managerial, professional and administrative workers from 5.9 per cent in 1970 to 15.2 per cent in 2000; the proportion of clerical, sales and service workers has risen from 21.9 per cent in 1970 to 33.9 per cent in 2000; and that of production workers from 27.3 per cent in 1970 to 32.8 per cent in 2000. On the other hand, the proportion of agricultural workers fell sharply – from 44.8 per cent in 1970 to 18.1 per cent in 2000, a drop of 26.7 percentage points over the three decades (for further details, see Chapter 3). This shows that the proportions of those groups which make up the new middle class in the workforce, that is, those in the professional, managerial and administrative categories, have increased considerably. The most significant proportional increase is in the managerial and administrative category, which went up by four times, from 1.1 per cent in 1970 to 4.2 per cent in 2000, while the proportion of professional and technical workers increased by 2.3 times, from 4.8 per cent to 11.0 per cent during the same period.

When comparing the three major ethnic groups (Malays, Chinese and Indian), the most noticeable increase in the proportion of managers, professionals and administrators has been among the Malays/Bumiputera.[1] In the Malay/Bumiputera workforce, the proportion of managers, professionals and administrators increased from 4.9 per cent in 1970 to 16.7 per cent in 2000; among the Chinese, it increased from

7.1 per cent to 17.1 per cent, while among the Indians and others, the observed increase was comparatively small, from 6.1 per cent to 8.2 per cent (see Chapter 3). In fact, if we examine *only* the proportions of managers and administrators (excluding professionals) in the workforce of the respective ethnic groups, the proportion of Malay/Bumiputera managers and administrators increased sixfold – from only 0.5 per cent in 1970 to 3.0 per cent in 2000, compared to the 3.9 times increase in the proportion of Chinese managers and administrators from 1.9 per cent to 7.5 per cent, while among Indians and others, the proportion of managers and administrators remained constant at 1.4 per cent over this 30 year period. In absolute terms, Malay/Bumiputera managers and administrators increased by 18 times, from only 7556 in 1970 to 135 900 in 2000; Chinese managers and administrators increased tenfold, from 19 721 in 1970 to 197 400 in 2000, while Indian (including other) managers and administrators increased by almost the same proportion, from 4076 in 1970 to 39 300 in 2000. In short, the number of managers and administrators in all the major ethnic groups – though still a tiny minority in the total workforce – increased in absolute terms over the period, with the increase within the Malay/Bumiputera community being the most noticeable. For professional and technical workers category, in absolute terms, the number increased by nearly six times – from 136 814 (4.18 per cent of the labour force) in 1970 to 975 800 (11.0 per cent of the labour force) in 2000; in this category, the fastest increase was also recorded among Malay/Bumiputera professionals – from 64 439 in 1970 to 620 700 in 2000, an increase of 9.6 times. The number of Chinese professionals and technical workers also increased, although at a slower rate, by 4.7 times from 54 041 to 252 800, while for Indians and others, the increase was by 5.6 times from 18 333 to 102 300 during the same period.

As recently as only thirty years ago, Malay society had been predominantly rural and agricultural, with only a small proportion involved in the modern economic sector, and its middle class mostly comprised of government administrators. The emergence of a modern and influential class of Malay managers, professionals and administrators – or the new middle class as they are referred to in the literature – reflects the extent to which Malaysian society has undergone modernization and social transformation. This class is still in the process of formation and expansion as Malaysia enters the twenty-first century. Thus, a study of the new Malay middle class – an exercise which has not yet been comprehensively undertaken (see Chapter 2) – is not only timely, but also important to serve as a window on this historic transition.

Objectives and scope of the study

As in the West[2] and East Asia,[3] the new middle class in Malaysia has attracted a number of Malaysian as well as foreign scholars, who over the years have conducted research and produced numerous writings on the new middle class. As will be shown in detail in Chapter 2, although aspects of the Malaysian middle class have been studied since the 1960s, the adoption of a broader approach in its research and writings is quite recent, taking shape mostly since the late 1980s and early 1990s. Empirically, while the few middle-class studies of the 1960s and 1970s focused on the most important and powerful middle class of that period – that is, the Malay government administrators in Kuala Lumpur and its suburbs – later studies have broadened their scope to include the middle class working in both the state and the private sectors, the middle class of various ethnic groups, and the middle class in the metropolitan area of the Klang Valley, as well as in provincial towns.

My study of the new Malay middle class in Malaysia is one of a number of recent studies of the middle class in Malaysia. Although this study focuses on the new Malay middle class, its main purpose is to offer a comparative perspective. Unlike earlier studies, which were conducted mainly in the metropolitan area of the Klang Valley – that is, around Kuala Lumpur and Petaling Jaya – or in other urban centres in the more developed West Coast states, my study compares the new Malay middle class in the Klang Valley with the new Malay middle class in two provincial towns – Kota Bharu in Kelantan and Kuala Terengganu in Terengganu. At the same time, the study also draws comparison between the new Malay middle class and the new Chinese and Indian middle classes as well as the Malay working class.

This study examines the new Malay middle class against the backdrop of state-led modernization. Thus, the choice of the metropolitan Klang Valley as the research site – although ostensibly replicating some of the earlier studies that have chosen it as their site – is necessary, especially for comparative purposes. Living in the most multi-ethnic, modern and advanced region both economically and socially, and also the region which seats the national capital, the new middle class in Kuala Lumpur and Petaling Jaya is expected to be more affluent and modern, with urban lifestyles and cosmopolitan outlooks, than their counterparts elsewhere in the country. Being the most industrially developed region, over the last several decades the Klang Valley has attracted large numbers of migrants, especially Malays, from rural areas and smaller towns, who have come in search of higher education, better job opportunities and a generally better standard of living. It is in the Klang Valley that one can find the modern, multi-ethnic classes – the capitalist class, the various middle-class fractions and the working class – that serve as a yardstick for comparison.

Kota Bharu, the capital of Kelantan, and Kuala Terengganu, the capital of Terengganu – both on the East Coast of Peninsular Malaysia – have been chosen as suitable research sites for comparison with the Klang Valley for a number of reasons. First, as mentioned above, and as will be shown in more detail in Chapter 2, most studies of the middle class thus far have been Klang Valley-centric or mainly focused on the more developed West Coast states. Thus, a comparative study of the new Malay middle class in the two provincial towns and the Klang Valley is in order to offset any over-concentration on the latter. Second, besides having predominantly Malay populations, which are still basically rural and agricultural despite having experienced some degrees of modernization, urbanization and industria-lization, these states have been neglected for some time in terms of development. As a result, Kelantan had the second highest levels of poverty, while Terengganu had the third highest, in Malaysia in 1995.[4] Compared to the more modernized, industrially developed and urbanized West Coast states, the two East Coast states thus stand on the lower rungs of the developmental ladder, and this has had particular impacts upon the characteristics of the new middle classes in these areas. Conducting a study of the new middle class in both states helps to demonstrate empirically that despite being less developed, both states have also produced a new middle class of their own just like the West Coast states.[5]

Third, politically the UMNO-led Barisan Nasional (BN) and the Islamic opposition party, Parti Islam Se-Malaysia (PAS), compete intensely with each other to win the support of Malay voters in both Kelantan and Terengganu. A study of the new middle class in the two provincial capitals is thus especially interesting because, over most of the post-independence period to date, Kelantan has been ruled by PAS, while Terengganu had experienced PAS rule for a brief period after the 1959 general election, and was captured again by PAS in the general election held in November 1999. A comparison between the metropolitan new Malay middle class and its provincial counterparts is of interest, not only theoretically, but also empirically, since it provides an opportunity to examine the internal differentiation within the new Malay middle class based on geographical area, levels of development and political inclinations.[6]

While the above comparison gives us an idea of the extent of horizontal differentiation – that is, differentiation within the same class of the same ethnic group, this study – wherever possible and appropriate – also makes inter-ethnic comparisons between the new Malay middle class and its non-Malay counterparts. Such a comparison allows us to see the internal differentiation within the new Malaysian middle class of various ethnic groups, and to assess the extent to which it has developed similar or dissimilar characteristics independent of ethnicity.

However, the social transformation over the last three decades has also brought about social inequalities within Malay society, expressed in the form of class inequalities with the emergence of the Malay capitalist, middle and working classes. In this study, comparison is also made between the new Malay middle class and the working class, but because of data limitations, this is part of the study is confined to the Klang Valley. This comparison allows us to examine the extent of class inequality and its impact upon class boundaries – that is, whether class boundaries have crystallized over the last three decades within Malay society, or whether Malay society is still very much culturally homogeneous in nature despite increasing economic differences.

Methodology and sample

This study combined several methods in order to obtain the data to facilitate analysis. The main method used was the survey by administering questionnaires, containing mostly closed questions, with some open-ended ones. The survey of the new Malay middle class was conducted in 1996 and 1997, with follow-up studies undertaken in 1998 and 1999, at a time when Malaysia experienced both economic and political crises. The total survey sample consisted of 284 respondents – 108 in the Klang Valley, 80 in Kota Bharu and 96 in Kuala Terengganu. This study does not claim to be representative since its sample was captured by using the purposive 'snow-ball sampling' technique.[7] The purposive sample is obtained by means of capturing from a group in the population those whose occupations can be taken as proxies for new middle-class jobs. Since they could be identified by their professional positions, respondents were approached mostly in their workplaces, although some were approached in their homes after making appointments if they could not be interviewed during office hours.

The researcher adopted the purposive 'snowball' sampling for two reasons. First, since the objective of the study is to examine the new middle class of managers, professionals and administrators, it is better to focus on respondents who occupy such positions. This can be done better by going to their workplace where their professional positions are easily identifiable. Although such an approach lacks representativeness, the strength of this technique is that the researcher can obtain a sample that meets his criteria. Second, while random sampling has the advantage of representativeness, it is more appropriate for a research team, rather than a single researcher. A researcher on his/her own would face lots of practical problems if he/she were to administer questionnaires by approaching respondents in their homes, because the middle class values privacy, and would normally be reluctant to open their doors to strangers.[8] In their offices, middle-class respondents are more approachable and willing to cooperate once the purpose of the study is clearly explained to them.

To complement the survey data, the researcher conducted a series of in-depth interviews with 30 informants who occupied important positions in their respective organizations. Most of the interviews were conducted in 1996 and 1997, while the rest were carried out during and after the 1997–98 economic and political crises. The researcher also made observations through day-to-day interactions with members of the new middle-class, personal participation in new middle-class family functions (such as *Hari Raya*, *tahlil* (or thanksgiving prayers) and weddings), social gatherings (such as 'Old Boys" dinners), and group meetings of Malay professionals and managers on various issues. The political crisis following the sacking of Deputy Prime Minister Anwar Ibrahim in September 1998 and the intense political manoeuvrings during and after the 1999 general election provided a great opportunity for the researcher to assess at first hand the changes and transformation in the attitudes and stances of the new middle class. These interviews and observations enabled the researcher to grasp those qualitative dimensions of the new middle class that could not easily be captured in surveys, namely, how informants – through their narratives, reflections, opinions and metaphors – engaged in the social construction of the new middle class.

Besides relying on primary data, the researcher also made use of secondary materials in the form of statistics culled from official documents and other publications – this provided especially useful for the macro-level historical analysis. At the same time, the researcher also undertook a careful reading of newspapers, magazines and materials posted on various websites to capture the views and sentiments among the new middle class following the economic and political crises and their aftermath faced by Malaysia in 1997 and 1998.

The concept of the middle class

Class, particularly the middle class, is a highly contested concept in the social sciences. It is not only elusive but also difficult to define, which makes research on class, especially the new middle class, a very complex and demanding task. Our task becomes even more formidable because among scholars, a 'war' on the issue of class has been raging not only between the Marxist and Weberian traditions, but also between those who uphold class or stratification analysis and those who dismiss it as largely irrelevant to a sociological understanding of the contemporary industrialized societies (and, by extension, industrializing societies). Criticisms of class as a concept and as an analytical tool have come from various quarters, including, of late, from the postmodernists. However, scholars who have been researching class maintain that it is a useful concept that has not been exhausted, and that class analysis has a promising future. Arguing that class analysis should be 'brought back in' (Levine and Fantasia 1991), the scholars have not only defended class analysis, but have also shown its continued relevance in sociological inquiry today by making a continuing research programme in trying to understand social inequality in advanced societies as well as societies of the Third World.[9]

My study of the new Malay middle class adopts the position that class and class analysis are useful analytical tools in the sociological understanding of Malaysian social transformation and social inequality. Following the Marxist tradition, class in this study is taken to mean the social formation defined in terms of its position in relation to ownership of the means of production. Thus, the capitalist class is the class that owns the means of production and commands power over labour, while the working class is the one that has neither capital nor high qualifications and sophisticated skills, but has labour power to sell to the capitalists in return for wages.

While defining the concepts of the capitalist class and the working class is relatively easier if one adopts the Marxist tradition, defining the middle class is more complicated, partly because Marxist analysis used to see societies in rather dichotomous terms, paying little attention to the class 'in the middle'. To operationalize the concept of the middle class in this study, I have to rely on both the Marxist and Weberian traditions, particularly the works of the neo-Marxists, namely Wright (1985, 1991, 1994, 1999) and neo-Weberians, namely Goldthorpe (1980, 1982), Edgell (1993) and Marshall (1988, 1997). However, utilizing the analytical tools derived from both traditions is not an unproblematic exercise. As cautioned by various scholars (Marshall 1988, 1997; Edgell 1993, Abercrombie and Urry 1984), there is an unbridgeable epistemological gap between the Marxist and Weberian frameworks for the society generally; while Marx's philosophy emphasized practice, Weber insisted on the logical and methodological separation of fact and value, and advocated a value-free sociology. However, our concern here is not their divergent political and ideological standpoints. Though the competing intellectual traditions have made research into class more complicated, it should be acknowledged that these traditions have made sociology a very lively and dynamic discipline. Despite their divergent starting points, there is strong evidence to suggest that scholarly works in both traditions have today tended towards a convergence, especially when they come to the question of operationalizing the concept of class (Edgell 1993: chs 2 and 3; Marshall 1997). In fact, their respective accounts of class mechanisms appear to be not wholly dissimilar (Marshall 1988: 14), something which can clearly be seen in the works of both neo-Marxists and neo-Weberians.

Let us deal briefly with how neo-Marxists and neo-Weberians formulate the concept of the middle class today. Wright, a neo-Marxist, argues that the Marxist tradition stresses ownership of the means of production and class exploitation, and sees class as a fundamental determinant of social conflict and social change, with the non-owning class launching struggles against the owning class. Taking what he calls the 'maximalist' position on class,[10] Wright (1991, 1999) explains the problem of the 'middle class' from the Marxist perspective, by using the concept of 'contradictory class location' in an attempt to provide a systematic theoretical status to non-proletarian or white-collar employees. To him, the middle class occupies a contradictory class location because, on the one hand, it is on the side of the bourgeoisie vis-à-vis the workers, since it has authority over them and serves as an instrument of the bourgeoisie to exploit the workers; yet on the other hand, in relation to the bourgeoisie, the middle class is in a similar position to that of the propertyless workers since it also does not own the means of production. The often ambivalent political character and stance of the middle class on various issues have thus to be understood in this context.

In a life chances class concept following the Weberian tradition, the central claim is that people in the middle class control a particular kind of resource – namely high qualifications and skills – which significantly enhances their market capacity compared to people who lack this resource. Although the Weberian class concept is relational, it is not based on an abstract model of polarized, antagonistic class relations as in the Marxist tradition. Classes within the Weberian tradition are viewed as stratification categories specific to market societies. Using the Weberian theoretical insights, scholars like Goldthorpe (1980, 1982) and Lockwood (1995) advance the theory of the service class, and propose that the new middle class (or service class I and II in their schema) consists of those with high qualifications and skills, who make up 'the salariat' – that is, professional, managerial and administrative employees who share a distinctive employment status whose principal feature is the 'trust' that employers necessarily have to place in these employees whose delegated or specialized tasks give them a considerable autonomy (Lockwood 1995).

In both approaches, it is recognized that members of the new middle class – because of their relatively superior cultural and organizational assets not possessed by those from the working class – enjoy a special position because they exercise some autonomy and have their employer's trust, and at the same time, they enjoy some power over labour. However, in Wright's formulation, such trust and autonomy are given only to the extent that the new middle class performs in the interests of the bourgeoisie to exploit and exercise control over the workers. In the formulation by Goldthorpe and Lockwood, trust and autonomy are not instruments of exploitation, but are given because employers recognize that members of the new middle class have greater market capacity in performing their tasks.

Besides the new middle class, there are two other fractions within the middle class which need some brief mention here – the old middle class and the marginal middle class. In Wright's formulation, the old middle class is referred to as the petit bourgeoisie – members of a social category who own some capital to hire workers, but who themselves must work – while in Goldthorpe's formulation, they consist of members of class IV – that is, small proprietors with or without employees. However, in their analysis of the marginal middle class, there is some difference between the two formulations. In Golthorpe's class map, the marginal middle class is actually grouped under class III – that is, members of the intermediate class consisting of routine non-manual employees in administration and commerce, sales personnel, and other rank-and-file service workers. However, in Wright's class map, following his proletarianization thesis, this group of semi-autonomous workers is not distinguishable from the working class; in fact, he merged this class with the proletariat, thereby abandoning the category of semi-autonomous workers. However, since the focus of my study is the new middle class, I shall not go into details regarding the old middle class and the marginal middle class except to show their class place in the both the neo-Marxist and neo-Weberian class schemes.

What is germane from the above is that, from these two conflicting traditions, it can be seen that, in their approach to class, both traditions examine the occupational positions occupied by individuals defined by employment relations in labour markets and production units. In other words, when it comes to the actual operationalization of class, both the Marxist and Weberian traditions recognize occupations as a measure of class. In fact, occupations are a basic ingredient of all class maps (Edgell 1993: 37) constructed by researchers from both traditions. More specifically, both traditions recognize the growth of, and the significant role played by the new middle class in modern capitalist society, and that members of this class are recognized by their positions in the occupational hierarchy.

The relevance of class analysis, and the fact that the concept of class can be operationalized by examining occupations, is summed up succinctly by Marshall, one of the most prominent class theorists today. Marshall (1997: 49–50, italics added) argues that

> class analysis ... has as its central concern the study of relationships among class structures, class mobility, class-based inequalities, and class-based action. More specifically, it explores the interconnections between positions defined by employment relations in labour markets and production units in different sectors of national economies; the processes through which individuals and families are distributed and redistributed among these positions over time; and the consequences thereof for their life-chances and for the social identities that they adopt and the social values and interests that they pursue.

Marshall argues further that looking at class analysis in this way involves a commitment not to any particular class theory, but to a research programme within which different, and even rival theories may be formulated and assessed in terms of their heuristic and explanatory performance.

Main arguments of the book

My study of the new Malay middle class addresses four major questions. First, who are the new Malay middle class? Second, how did members of this new middle class come into being in Malaysia? Third, what are the economic, social, cultural and political characteristics of the new Malay middle class? Fourth, what role is to be played this class in Malaysia's future transformation? The last is very important, especially in the aftermath of the 1997–98 economic and political crises experienced by Malaysia in its critical transition in the twenty-first century.

The various questions presented above deserve some explanations and elaboration. First, as discussed above, the question of 'who are the new middle class?' (and by extension, 'who are the new Malay middle class?') is a complex one, defying precise definitions. However, a working definition is necessary so that we know who we are talking about. Thus, this study has to begin with some clarifications and operational definitions of the term 'class', including the new middle class. Following the brief theoretical discussion in the preceding section, it is argued in this study that classes in developing countries can be operationalized by using occupations as their indicator in much the same way as scholars who have been researching on class in developed countries have done. This is because in countries like Malaysia, members of the workforce can be recognized by their occupations, and most of them are employees in the same way as members of the workforce in the advanced countries.

At the same time, it should be recognized that classes – as manifestations of persistent and structured social inequalities – are historically constituted and dynamic entities, emerging in the specific historical, political, economic and cultural contexts of the society's development, and that their definitions, while universal, have also to be historically and culturally informed. In Malaysia, it is argued that although the evolution of the modern class structure began about a century ago, classes are not new phenomena in pre-colonial Malay society, which was already divided along class lines – by virtue of differences in wealth, status and political power – into the ruling aristocracy on the one hand, and the peasantry on the other, with merchants and craftsmen forming the intermediate class. What is *new* today are at least three phenomena: (i) modern classes that have emerged and expanded as part and parcel of the modernizing process in tandem with the expansion of the modern state and capitalist development, taking place most clearly since independence and more so since the beginning of the NEP period; (ii) new occupational positions, namely managers, professionals and administrators, which were rare in Malay society and in Malaysia in the earlier historical periods, but are becoming more common today, forming an important new class; and (iii) new idioms used in popular discourse, such as *orang korporat* (corporate players),[11] *orang bergaya korporat* (corporate-styled individuals),[12] *orang kaya baru* (new rich)[13] or *Melayu Baru* (New Malays)[14] to refer, in one way or another, to members of this class. Examined from this perspective, the new Malay middle class then refers to the group of Malay managers, professionals and administrators employed in both state and private sector organizations, including transnational corporations, that has objectively emerged and expanded in the process of Malaysia's post-independence state-led modernization, and which is also perceived in popular discourse as the 'newly arrived'. Imprecise although it may be, this working definition not only allows us to come up with a broad answer to the question of 'Who are the new Malay middle class?' in our study, but also directs us to the underlying historical and cultural processes that have led to the emergence of this class.[15]

Second, the question of 'How did members of this middle class come into being in Malaysia?' refers to the underlying processes leading to the making of the Malaysian middle class in general, and the new Malay middle class in particular. This question has to be answered in the light of Malaysia's political economy and sociocultural history. In this study, the author argues that the dynamics of at least two major social forces – capitalist economic development and the formation and expansion of the modern state – operating with different strengths during different historical periods over the last one hundred years, especially in the post-independence era, had transformed Malaysian society. The author disagrees with the view that onesidedly emphasizes the role of the state, underplaying, or even denying the role of capitalist development in the process of middle-class formation.[16] It is argued in the study that while the role of the state has been critical in middle-class formation, especially that of the new Malay middle class, it is the dynamics of capitalist development – guided and at times directed by the state during the NEP's 'state-as-entrepreneur' phase – that has transformed Malaysian society into what it is today. The author contends that while the state has been directly instrumental in the growth of the new Malay middle class, the state's role in the formation of the new non-Malay middle class has in the main been indirect; that since the state has generally been market-friendly, even when it was implementing the NEP's affirmative action policies, it has encouraged the growth of capitalism, which provided opportunities for the economically stronger Chinese community to produce their own new middle class. At the same time, the author argues that although the new Malay middle class has been state-created, its future development is likely to be less state-dependent, because of the neoliberal shifts towards privatization as well as because of the changing outlook and attitudes of members of the new Malay middle class.

The third question – 'What are the economic, social, cultural and political characteristics of the new Malay middle class?' – revolves around the question of the economic position and activities of the new Malay middle class, which enable them to enjoy their current class position; their social and cultural values and practices, as reflected in their work culture and ethics; and their lifestyles, family and kin relations and interactions with other members of the community. In this study, the author argues that the new Malay middle class is a 'first-generation' middle class, which is relatively affluent, has developed a new work culture and ethic consistent with the demands of a rapidly industrializing society, and has earned the trust and confidence of others in the ability of their members. Nevertheless, the new Malay middle class is not homogenous with regard to lifestyle, religious commitment or political beliefs and activities. This is because modernization is not something linear, with the resultant breakdown of tradition on the one hand and the adoption of western values and lifestyles on the other. Rather, the dynamics of modern social class formations and urban living produce a myriad of cultural forms, including a complex array of adaptations, innovations and changes. Thus, while some common patterns can be discerned among the new Malay middle class in both the metropolitan area of the Klang Valley and the provincial towns, they nevertheless tend to exhibit greater cultural varieties and nuances, especially if they work and live in a less familiar, cosmopolitan environment such as the metropolitan Klang Valley area, rather than a more familiar environment like Kota Bharu and Kuala Terengganu, which they can easily identify with. The fourth question – 'What is the role of this class in Malaysia's future transformation?' – refers to middle-class politics, namely the values, stances and practices of the new middle class with respect to expanding democracy and civil society. In this study, it is argued that middle-class politics do not follow a straightforward equation of for or against democracy and civil society. While their demand for change cannot automatically be taken to mean a demand for democracy, it is equally true to say that their insistence on maintaining the current political order does not necessarily mean support for authoritarianism. It is also argued here, based on the evidence during the 1997–98 economic and political crises and their aftermath, that despite being state-sponsored, sections of the new Malay middle class have developed critical attitudes towards the state, and are beginning to assert their ideological and political independence from the latter.

The four questions listed above lay out the intellectual terrain traversed in the course of this book. They are discussed in detail in the various chapters outlined below.

The organization of the book

To deal in detail with the key questions set out above, the book is divided into three parts. In Chapter 2 a critical review is made of studies of the Malaysian middle class that have been conducted to date. The review examines not only the theoretical and empirical thrusts of these studies, but also their foci, highlights some of their main findings, and evaluates their contributions. In the course of the review, an attempt is made to locate my own study in the context of other studies to show its significance.

The second part, which is presented in Chapter 3, offers a macro-historical analysis of the evolution of the class structure, with particular reference to middle-class formation in Malaysia from the early twentieth century to the present day. It examines the new middle class in four phases: (i) the colonial or pre-independence period, that is, prior to 1957; (ii) the immediate post-independence years until 1970, that is, the pre-NEP period; (iii) the NEP period 1971–90; and (iv) the post-NEP period from the beginning of the 1990s to the present day. The chapter engages in detail the debate on the role of the state and capitalist development in middle-class formation and expansion in Malaysia.

The macro-historical analysis in this chapter provides the background to subsequent chapters which contain micro-analysis based on my fieldwork conducted since 1996 among the new Malay middle class in the metropolitan city of Kuala Lumpur (and Petaling Jaya), and two provincial towns – Kota Bharu and Kuala Terengganu. While the first part provides the backdrop and the second part offers the macro-level historical analysis, the third part, consisting of the rest of the study, deals with the analysis and findings of the substantive study. Chapter 4 analyses the making of the new Malay middle class by examining the 'first-generation' hypothesis, which posits that the new middle class is of recent origin; it also shows that the new middle class is relatively affluent, and that it has experienced a transformation in its work culture and ethics, in keeping with the *Melayu Baru* (New Malay) concept espoused by Prime Minister Mahathir Mohamad.

Chapter 5 examines several interrelated questions concerning the impact of industrialization, urbanization and modernization on the new Malay middle-class family. It examines the pattern of marriage and parenthood among the new Malay middle class, power-sharing within the new Malay middle-class family, class reproduction, and the relationship between the nuclear family and the earlier pattern of extended kin networks. It concludes that the new Malay middle-class family, although nuclear in form, is embedded within a modified extended family framework, albeit one that is now adapted to urban conditions.

Chapter 6 builds on earlier chapters by examining several aspects of the new Malay middle-class lifestyles and culture, such as living conditions, asset ownership, consumption patterns, leisure activities, and the respondents' evaluation of their own class positions, to see if their subjective evaluations match our objective definition of the new middle-class. This chapter aims to show that the new Malay middle-class lifestyles and cultural preferences are not homogenous; and that while the more affluent sections of the new Malay middle class have developed distinctive high-status lifestyles and cultural preferences and become cosmopolitan urbanites, many still have lifestyles and cultural preferences that do not differentiate them as a distinct social category from the lower classes.

Chapter 7 examines the social culture of the new Malay middle class by looking at the processes through which the new Malay middle class attempts to establish communities within new urban environments and examining the relationship between these processes and their religious commitment and activities. It shows that the *surau* (a Muslim prayer-house smaller than the mosque) is pivotal in community-building among the new Malay middle class, and that although Malay urban communities are built by relying on certain cultural resources acquired by Malays when they grew up in their *kampung*, they also contain new, innovative elements created under changed material conditions.

Chapter 8 examines the political culture of the new Malay middle class, namely their role in the democratization process, politics and civil society in Malaysia. It focuses on the question of the civic and political consciousness of the new middle class, and the activities of the latter in civil society organizations as well as political activities, in an attempt to assess its attitudes towards democracy and state authoritarianism. The chapter shows that the new Malay middle-class politics is not monolithic, since while the majority, especially those in the Klang Valley, seems to accept the ruling Barisan Nasional government framework, and tolerates its authoritarianism, an important segment has become critical and has started to demand political change.

Chapter 9 examines the question of the new Malay middle class and *Melayu Baru*. It suggests that the *Melayu Baru* is a project aimed to achieve the transformation and modernization of Malay society, and that the new Malay middle class is an important component of *Melayu Baru*. This chapter traces the *Melayu Baru* debate historically, and shows that the current emphasis in the *Melayu Baru* discourse is biased towards the creation of the Malay capitalist and the new middle classes and industrial work ethic because of the ideological orientation of Prime Minister Mahathir, who strongly believes in the creation and expansion of Malay capitalism and the Malay capitalist class.

The study ends with Chapter 10, which draws together some of the major arguments regarding the social and political culture of the new

Malay middle class, and explores the implications of these arguments for Malaysia's social transformation, especially in the light of the 1997–98 economic and political crises in Malaysia, and subsequent developments.

2
A Critical Review of Malaysian Middle-Class Studies[1]

Introduction

Academic discussion and analysis of the middle class in Malaysia is fairly recent, starting in the late 1960s, but only really gathering momentum in the late 1990s. During the last three decades, Malaysian social science research has justifiably focused more on those pressing issues faced in the immediate post-independence years – such as development and under-development (with particular emphasis on factors impeding development of the Bumiputera), culture, Islam, ethnic relations, inter-ethnic imbalances, national unity, and so on. Most of these studies made only passing references to the middle class. The proliferation of studies on some of these themes – particularly of peasants, factory women, ethnicity and Islam – led some scholars to label it as 'an outpouring', suggesting that these studies 'in their distribution (are) far from fully representative of current trends in the Malay community' (Kahn 1996b: 49). However, the claim that 'the growth of the middle class is ... largely ignored', that 'there has been remarkably little interest among social scientists in the phenomenon', so much so that there has existed a 'yawning gap' (Kahn 1996b: 49, 67), and that the advertising industry had discovered the middle class before the academics (Kahn 1996a), has to be examined critically against the available evidence. While the middle class has not been given prominent attention by scholars in studies of the preceding decades, there was no such yawning gap, for there had been several studies of the new middle class in Malaysia even during these years. A review of the literature will bear this out.

In general, studies of the new Malaysian middle class thus far can be grouped under two broad categories. First, there were a number of earlier studies on the administrative middle class (that is, the new middle class consisting of administrators) that developed in the colonial period and the early independence years. These studies cover such themes as the origin, growth and social composition of the administrative middle class, its role during the colonial period with regard to nationalism, its ideology and role after independence and under the policy of Malaysianization (the replacement of British expatriates with Malaysians), as well as the lifestyles of the administrative middle class who replaced the British administrators. Most of these studies were carried out in the late 1960s and the 1970s.

Second, there have been more recent studies which examine the impact of post-independence state-led modernization and social tranformation, including social engineering and export-oriented industrialization, on the Malaysian social structure, with particular reference to socio-economic transformation and the growth of the new middle class. These studies examine the structural changes that have arisen as a result of rapid industrialization and economic growth, the role of the state in class formations and in the expansion of the new middle class, the ethnic composition of the new middle class, middle-class consciousness, politics and culture, as well as the impact of this class on national unity and democratization. A number of these studies also consider the critical question of the problematic of both middle-class conceptualization and theorizing.

In this chapter, I shall present a selective review of these studies, focusing in particular on the more recent ones. The main arguments and findings of these studies will be highlighted, and evaluated. At the same time, I also attempt to locate my study in the context of the other studies and show its relevance.

The contribution of earlier middle-class studies

As indicated in Chapter 1, and as will be shown in greater detail in Chapter 3, the new middle class in Malaysia, in particular the administrative middle class, had already emerged during the colonial period, from the early twentieth century, although their rapid growth and expansion only began with the NEP's social engineering and export-led industrialization since the 1970s. Malaysia's experience of class formation has been very different from that of Western Europe, where the origin and growth of the new middle class was associated with the rise of cities into autonomous principalities, as well as the rising bourgeoisie and the Industrial Revolution (Alatas 1972). In Malaysia, British colonialism not only created a plural society with the influx of Chinese and Indian immigrants from the mid-nineteenth century onwards, living alongside but separate from the indigenous Malays, but also spawned a class of middlemen or *compradors* (mainly Chinese and, to a certain extent, Indian and Arab who served as intermediaries between the foreign concerns and the local populace) on the one hand, as well as a small but growing intelligentsia on the other. While the early *compradors* could be regarded as the forerunners of today's business or capitalist class, especially among Chinese and Indians, the early intelligentsia – educated either in English or in the vernacular, and who served as junior administrators, clerks, technicians, and teachers – were the forerunners of today's new middle class – the white-collar 'salariat', consisting of managers, professionals and administrators.

The most important component of the indigenous new middle class before Malaysia's independence until the 1970s was the administrative middle class, a group with immense power and prestige vis-à-vis the rest of the population. Khasnor's (1984) study on the origin and role of this administrative class, which was conducted in early 1970s for her PhD degree in History at Monash University, was by far the most influential analysis of this topic. By sieving through historical records, Khasnor traced the origin of the Malay administrative class to the establishment by the British, in 1910, of the Malay Administrative Service (MAS) which served as the stepping stone to the powerful and prestigious British-controlled Malayan Civil Service (MCS), the forerunner of the contemporary Malaysian Administrative and Diplomatic Service (*Perkhidmatan Tadbir dan Diplomatik* – PTD). As argued by Khasnor, the scheme was an attempt by the British to reintegrate members of the traditional Malay aristocracy into the lower echelons of the British colonial administration, by becoming part of British officialdom. The key to social mobility was English education, which increasingly provided a new criterion of, and passport to, social distinction (Khasnor 1984: 5). Mainly educated at the Malay College Kuala Kangsar – initially set up in 1905 for male children of the aristocracy – the administrators came to be seen as the standard-setters for Malays drawn into the modern world, especially apparent in the then new Malay attitudes to salaried employment. In absolute terms, the Malay officers constituted only a small, but clearly bounded and highly status-conscious social group, increasing from 55 in 1916 to 78 in 1928, and 105 (including four on probation) in 1940, compared to 120 Europeans in the higher civil service positions in the Federated Malay States (the first four Malay states taken over by the British) (Khasnor 1984: 104). Those promoted into the MCS were very much smaller in number – only one in 1921, although by the eve of independence, the number had increased to

106. After independence and with the policy of Malayanization (1957–1963), and then Malaysianization (from 1963 onwards after the formation of Malaysia), the ranks of Malays in the civil service rose dramatically, to 706 in 1968, and to 1137 in 1974 (Nordin 1976: 146).

While Khasnor's 1984 study focused on the origin and development as well as the power and prestige of the administrative class, there had been three earlier studies which had examined different aspects of this class. One, by the historian William Roff (1967), was on the origin of Malay nationalism and the role of the Malay intelligentsia in the nationalist movement prior to the Second World War, while the other two – on the ideology, role and lifestyle of the Malay administrative middle class in newly-independent Malaysia – were by political scientist James Scott (1968) and sociologist Nordin Selat (1976).

Though Roff's pioneering work on Malay nationalism (1967; second edition 1994) was not focused on the middle class per se, it is related to this area since it links the origin and development of nationalism to the leading elements of the Malay intelligentsia. His study – hailed by Harry J. Benda as 'the first sociological history of modern Malay society' (see his 'Foreword' in Roff 1994: ix) – identified the politicized middle strata of three 'contending' new elites in Malay society before the Second World War: the Arabic-educated religious reformists; the largely Malay-educated radical intelligentsia; and the English-educated administrators mainly recruited from the traditional Malay ruling class (the group studied by Khasnor).

As implied by Roff, during the colonial period in Malaya, anti-colonial nationalist ideology could neither be articulated by the peasantry, owing to their narrow experience and outlook, as well as to a lack of literacy and organizational capability, nor by the feudal aristocracy who were largely allied to the colonial order. As a result, this task was taken on by others, that is, those from the educated middle strata – the intelligentsia – whose education, social position, and ideology predisposed them to nationalism. The Arab-educated reformists and Malay-educated intelligentsia espoused anti-colonial nationalism, while members of the westernized English-educated elite in the main were often the mouthpieces of conservative nationalism.

What is significant is that, for various reasons, the westernized elite was able to capture the leadership of the independence movement in the 1950s to lead the country to independence. Although Roff's study only mapped out the development of Malay nationalism until the outbreak of the Second World War, other studies show that this westernized class of administrators formed the core of the leadership of the United Malays

National Organization (UMNO), formed in 1946, and to whom the baton of power was handed over by the British in 1957.

Unlike the two historians, who used a historical approach to examine different aspects of the administrative middle class during the colonial period, Scott and Nordin focused on the post-independence administrative middle class which assumed greater power and significance after independence – in particular after the policies of decolonization and Malaysianization. Their approach was sociological, relying not only on secondary data extracted from published records and other sources, but, more importantly, on primary data obtained through their own interviews, questionnaires and observations.

Scott conducted interviews with 17 senior Kuala Lumpur-based civil servants (10 Malays, four Indians and three Chinese) drawn from a sampling frame of about 3000 officers holding Division I posts in the 1964 establishment. Scott's purpose was to examine the ideology and political beliefs of the administrators with a view to investigate the basis of democracy and the conditions under which democratic values could flourish. Defining 'personal ideology' as 'an organization of opinions, attitudes and values – a way of thinking about man and society' unique to an individual, and differentiating it from formal ideologies such as socialism or liberalism, Scott (1968: 31) hoped that through in-depth interviewing and administering psychoanalytical tests on his respondents, he could grasp the essence of their ideologies and political beliefs.

To Scott, though, this westernizing elite group of civil servants were in effect 'indigenous-aliens' whose western education and values created a great gap between them and the masses (Scott 1968: 16). Nevertheless, in new nations like Malaysia, the bureaucracy has generally had broader responsibilities than in the West. According to him, the civil service remains, often by default, the major body from which plans for a new society emanate and through which they will be executed. Given this continuing crucial role for the bureaucracy, the ideology of civil servants remains of crucial importance for the future of former colonies regardless of political changes (Scott 1968: 18–19). Making similar observations to Khasnor's, Scott observed that in a post-colonial society like Malaysia, popular acceptance of, and deference to, the westernized elite – particularly civil servants – was the rule rather than the exception.

In his study, Scott found that the basic value-orientations of the administrators were anchored in the belief that 'man is narrowly selfish and lacking in restraint, that economic life is a zero-sum game, and that only short-term gains are possible', and also 'that external control mechanisms are required to restrain man's natural rapaciousness' (Scott

1968: 247–9). As Scott put it, despite their commitment to democratic forms and ideals, these administrators felt that liberal democracy was not practicable for Malaysia. Instead, guided or 'tutelary' democracy appealed to them because its assumptions about the environment seemed to match much of what they themselves believed in or had experienced.

Hence, Scott concluded that the Malaysian administrative class was not predisposed to support liberal democracy but, instead, was more inclined to a form of 'tutelary democracy' synonymous with elite rule. According to him, this was inevitable because, on the one hand, the westernized elite group had a monopoly in education, technical skills, and experience in managing a modern state, and the masses looked to them for leadership. On the other hand, there is also the view that popular rule may tear a nation such as Malaysia apart because it arouses racial antagonisms. Thus, 'post-colonial experience has, if anything, enhanced the attractiveness of strong, paternalistic rule' (Scott 1968: 251–2).

Although Scott's analysis is fairly sophisticated and theoretically informed, and he was careful in choosing his sample, the sample was far too small to warrant the generalizations or claims of representativeness which he drew from it. Furthermore, a study of political attitudes and ideologies in isolation may not reveal much about behaviour because of the perennial discrepancy between behaviour and attitudes. As admitted by Scott, the relationship between belief and behaviour is problematic, for behaviour cannot be predicted from beliefs alone. Nevertheless, his study provided a useful insight into the attitudes and beliefs of a segment of the administrative middle class during the early independence years prior to the implementation of the NEP – a useful source for comparison with subsequent studies.

While Scott examined the ideology and political beliefs of the administrative middle class and their implications for democracy, Nordin's study (1976) attempted to provide a social map of the Malay administrative middle class, in particular their socio-economic characteristics, intergenerational mobility, and their lifestyles, including cultural values, consumption patterns, tastes, and habits.

Nordin's study was based on a slightly larger sample, consisting of 105 Division I Malay civil servants also working in the federal capital of Kuala Lumpur. Aged between 29 and 54, the majority were highly educated, with 74 per cent holding at least a first degree. They had also experienced intergenerational mobility, because two-thirds of their fathers (or guardians) had received either vernacular education or had no education at all. About one-third hailed from rural-peasant backgrounds and a similar percentage came from the families of clerks or lower-grade schoolteachers. Their humble origins could also be seen in the fact that almost half were the only university-educated children in their families. Their family and class backgrounds were markedly different from the aristocratic origins of the pre-independence administrative middle class, a fact indicative of social mobility and the changes that had taken place in the social composition of the administrative middle class in the two historical periods.

Nevertheless, despite such changes, Nordin pointed out that the post-independence Malay administrative middle class also aped the West in terms of lifestyles. All married, the majority (70 per cent) had small- or medium-sized families with two or three children; furthermore an overwhelming majority (88 per cent) had domestic servants. Relieved of domestic chores, many of the respondents' spouses could pursue their own careers. As evidence of their affluent lifestyles, 41 per cent of respondents lived in government quarters in Kuala Lumpur, and about one-half lived in their own bungalows in the surrounding suburbs. All respondents owned cars, with 40 per cent having more than one. Their reading materials consisted of English-language periodicals such as *Time*, the *Far Eastern Economic Review*, and *Newsweek*, while very few read Malay magazines. Their leisure hours were filled with social activities such as playing golf (60 per cent were members of prestigious golf clubs) or going to the cinema. The majority were well-travelled, with 95 per cent having travelled overseas. Their topics of conversation often consisted of 'shop-talk' – about promotion, golf, cars, overseas travel, and so on.

However, Nordin's study was basically descriptive. He was content to leave it empirical, with little or no attempt at strengthening it conceptually, theoretically or methodologically. Nevertheless, despite such weaknesses, it is a valuable reference as a pioneering empirical study of the post-independence Malay administrative middle class.

More recent studies: social transformation and the new middle class

While the concern of the earlier studies had generally been with the administrative middle class and basically descriptive in nature (with the exception of Scott's), more recent studies have attempted to move beyond them not only in scope but also in terms of conceptual and theoretical approaches. These more recent studies attempt to address several interrelated questions, including Malaysia's social transformation, which has resulted in the emergence of the capitalist, the middle and the working classes; the historical forces that have shaped the emergence and growth of these classes; middle-class consciousness, politics, family, lifestyle and culture; and what conceptual and theoretical models can best inform or guide the study of the new Malaysian middle class. Many of these are new research questions, which had not been specifically addressed in earlier studies.

The socio-economic transformation of Malaysian society over the last four decades, from an agricultural economy into a rapidly industrializing one, from a rural society into an increasingly urbanized society, and from a poor country into a middle income country, and their impacts on class structure and formation of modern classes, have been described in many works. Among the most prominent are Crouch (1981, 1993, 1996), Husin Ali (1984), Jomo (1986, 1999), Johan Saravanamuttu (1989, 2001), Mohd Nor (1991), Kahn (1991, 1992, 1996a, 1996b), Fatimah Abdullah (1994), Shamsul (1997, 1999), Abdul Rahman (1995a, 1995b, 1996, 1997a, 1997b, 1998, 1999), Norani Othman et al. (1996); Norani Othman (1997); Tan Poo Chang et al. (1996).[2] The recent studies, however, only appear as articles in journals or chapters in books; a single volume devoted specifically to a consideration of the Malaysian middle class has yet to be published. Some of these studies not only focused on the social transformation and the evolution of the class structure that have taken place since the implementation of the NEP and export-led industrialization, but also engaged in a more direct critical discourse on the middle class, utilizing both official statistics as well as data from field research and observations. These works, in varying ways, especially the more recent ones, present preliminary class maps of the new middle class, analyses of middle-class consciousness, politics and culture in relation to national unity and democratization, and clarifications of the term 'middle class(es)'. The divergent points of views – theoretical, methodological and empirical – expressed in the debate are not only a measure of the complexity of Malaysian class transformation, but also a reflection of the conflicting perspectives extant in the sociological literature on the middle class.

It is generally acknowledged that most studies of class, including the new middle class, have been developed following a western model, adopting either the Marxist or the Weberian tradition, or a combination of both. While acknowledging that such models are useful heuristic devices in guiding analysis, both Malaysian scholars and Malaysianists have often stressed the need to exercise caution when using them, in order to avoid the mechanical application of models to widely divergent historical conditions.

A recurrent theme in the current discourse is the general agreement that the notion of the 'middle class' is problematic and difficult to define. Thus a number of these scholars (see, for example, Kahn 1991, 1996a; Jomo 1999) opt for the usage in the plural – middle class*es* – rather than the singular to reflect not only the shifting definition of the term, but also the heterogeneity of the middle class as well as their lack of coherence, boundedness and self-consciousness. They also caution that the 'new' middle class is not really new since similar middle-class occupations – administrators, doctors, teachers, technologists, managers, and so on – though small in number, had already emerged under colonialism and before the adoption of the policy of export-led industrialization in the 1970s. They also noted that the growth of the *new* middle class has not caused the disintegration or elimination of the *old* middle class – the petit bourgeoisie – which has increased in absolute terms too (see, for example, Jomo 1999; Abdul Rahman 1995a).

Nevertheless, there is no consensus among scholars on how to approach the question of the new middle class in Malaysia. Let us take, as an example, Giddens' theoretical approach on middle-class concept-ualization (Giddens 1980) as used by Saravanamuttu (1989). In his work, Giddens develops a three-class model of society, based on what he calls 'three sorts of market capacity' – ownership of property in the means of production, which produces the capitalist or upper class; possession of educational and/or technical qualifications, which produces the middle class; and possession of manual labour power, which produces the working class. Applying Giddens' model in the Malaysian context, Saravanamuttu suggests that the middle class consists of non-manual workers and non-peasants, that is, salaried employees who possess qualifications and/or technical skills, and occupy middle-class positions by virtue of their relatively advantaged market capacity.

Kahn (1991, 1996a, 1996b) – a Malaysianist – on the other hand is very critical of Saravanamuttu's ownership approach. Labelling it as 'trying to fit the middle class into a model of class established for nineteenth century capitalism', Kahn feels that we should opt for a 'revised concept' of the middle class. To him, the middle class should not be defined by reference to the relations of production, or even in terms of cultural capital; rather, it should be defined by reference to the processes of modern state formation in both the colonial and the post-colonial periods (Kahn 1991: 56). What is significant in Kahn's approach is his stress on the importance of the state in middle-class formation and expansion. As he puts it, the Malaysian middle classes owe their existence not so much to the changing demands of capital, as to the emergence of the modern state; to him, the 'middle class' identified by Saravanamuttu did not primarily consist of middle-ranking employees of private enterprises, but rather employees of the state (Kahn 1996a: 24). Kahn feels that recognizing the role of the state is crucial because there is, for him, an important link between the constitution of power relations in the modern state and the emergence of both universalistic and particularistic political discourses among middle-class state employees. In another article, Kahn disagrees with scholars who see 'an intimate relationship between market rationality and democratisation', and others 'who look to the middle classes to carry the torch of political modernism', because to him, 'the modernist agenda [in Malaysia is] being pushed from above, and hence a modernism must perforce be authoritarianism at the same time' (Kahn 1996b: 69).

In my earlier works (Abdul Rahman 1995a, 1996), I have adopted a third position. While agreeing with a number of points raised by Saravanamuttu and Kahn, I have argued that both authors have overemphasized one side at the expense of the other, especially with regard to the question of 'What historical forces actually contributed to the expansion of the Malaysian middle class?' While Saravanamuttu emphasizes capitalist development and fails to give sufficient recognition to the important role of the developmentalist state and its impacts on middle-class politics, I suggest that Kahn overemphasizes the state and ignores the role of capitalist development and expansion. In fact, both forces – capitalist production and the role of the developmentalist state – have been crucial in the formation and expansion of the middle class in Malaysia. Besides capitalist development and the role of the state, the question of culture (that is, the possession of educational qualifications, cultural attributes and lifestyles) also needs to be taken into account in middle-class conceptualization as a means of delineating the middle from other classes (Abdul Rahman 1995a).

Related to the conceptual and theoretical problems, another contentious issue raised in the debate concerns middle-class consciousness, politics and culture – about which researchers seem to have drawn conflicting conclusions. Given the increasingly multi-ethnic character of the various classes, especially the new middle class, researchers have posed the following questions: Has the new middle class developed multi-ethnic perspectives transcending ethnic sentiments? Furthermore, has it developed democratic proclivities, becoming a new force championing universalistic values such as democracy and human rights? Answers to these questions have been varied, ranging from the affirmative to the negative, and mixtures of both.

Besides presenting theoretical arguments and providing a brief class map of the new middle class, Saravanamuttu (1989) also attempts to throw some light on the question of whether the new Malaysian middle class expresses ethnic or class-consciousness, and whether it is an agent of democratization. He is of the opinion that the multi-ethnic new Malaysian middle class should be regarded as a new force on the Malaysian political scene championing democratic ideals, and that this class is not affected by questions of ethnicity since it has transcended ethnic perspectives.[3] However, his conclusion is drawn from a skewed sample consisting of 464 respondents (60 per cent Malays and the remainder non-Malays) comprised mostly of leaders of various organizations such as professional associations, trade unions, cooperatives, and farmers associations – in short, the organized members of the new middle class. At the same time, to support his conclusion of the democratic proclivities of the middle class, he cites struggles launched by various middle-class organizations in the 1980s against issues such as the Societies Act, the Official Secrets Act (OSA) and the October 1987 mass arrests under the Internal Security Act (ISA) – which actually only represent some organized segments of the new middle class.

Although one can agree with Saravanamuttu that tendencies towards multi-ethnic perspectives exist, particularistic tendencies are also evident. In his survey of the attitudes and perceptions of members of the new middle class with regard to ethnic relations and national unity, Mohd Nor (1991)[4] draws somewhat different conclusions to Saravanamuttu. According to him, the growth and expansion on the one hand, of the new middle class, especially among Malays, gave them a new sense of confidence, enabling them to identify with and relate on an equal footing to new middle-class non-Malays, thus reducing ethnicity as a basis for collective identification and action. On the other hand, Mohd Nor asserts that due to inter-ethnic intra-class rivalries, the growth and expansion of the Malay segment of the new middle class had produced a negative reaction from among their non-Malay counterparts, who felt their interests threatened by this ascendancy and, more generally, by what they perceived as the pro-Malay policies of the NEP. Contrary to Saravanamuttu, Mohd Nor's study concludes that – although successful in transforming Malays, particularly by expanding their new middle-class component and changing the ethnic mix of the new middle class – the NEP has, in practice, made national unity more tenuous and problematic since it has 'increased and sharpened communal politics' (Mohd Nor 1991: 153).

Writing on middle-class politics and its impact on the state vis-à-vis the democratization issue, the political scientist Harold Crouch (1993, 1996) argues that rapid economic growth has made it relatively easy for the government to satisfy the material aspirations of the new middle class, thus turning the latter into a stabilizing force appreciative and supportive of the state. He points out that the rapid growth of the new Malay middle class had not been directly at the expense of the new non-Malay middle class, which continued to expand, although it certainly would have expanded faster if special measures had not been taken by the government to ensure increased Malay participation in middle-class occupations (Crouch 1993: 142). But, according to Crouch, contrary to expectations, the changing class structure and the emergence and expansion of the new middle class in Malaysia did not produce strong pressures toward full democratization.[5] In his later work, Crouch (1996) argues that on the surface, the evolution of the Malaysian class structure seems to have progressed to a point where it could have been expected to strengthen the democratic proclivities of the political system, but the middle class does not constitute a coherent force because it is sharply divided along ethnic lines. In fact, he suggests that 'it is more appropriate to examine the middle class within ethnic communities' (Crouch 1996: 192).

Kahn, however, goes beyond Crouch. Critical of the current middle-class theorizing and relying on his ethnographic observations, he argues that there is no logical reason to expect the middle classes to articulate enlightened or universalistic ideals like democracy. According to him, the new middle classes, especially the Malay component, have been particularly ethnicized, imbued with ethnic consciousness and heavily involved in the construction of ethnicity. He feels that if we want to examine the issue of middle-class consciousness, we must look at the conditions in which middle-class groups come to articulate or practise one or other of the discourses imputed to them. He maintains that members of the new Malay middle class were actively engaged in the construction of culture and ethnicity (Kahn 1992) – hence, particularistic values – and implies that they were not engaged in championing democratic issues. They had no modernist agenda, for the latter came 'from above' (Kahn 1996b: 69). Kahn also contends that 'the new Malay middle classes constitute a breeding ground for new forms of anti-Chinese sentiment' (Kahn 1994: 39).

While a number of the above studies have focused on the historical formation of the Malaysian middle class, post-independence social transformation, and middle class politics, by examining the thesis of the new middle class as champions of universal values and democracy, another dimension studied by researchers is the cultural transformation of the new middle class and their role as standard-bearers of modernity. In

1995, Norani Othman, together with three other scholars, including myself, attempted to examine the new middle class, by posing the question of whether members of the new Malaysian middle class, as products of modernization, are themselves bearers and agents of modernity. In a paper subsequently written based on the study, Norani (1997), for example, argues that in order to understand the new Malaysian middle class, one needs to take a different route – not defined by the material standards of living alone, but defined qualitatively – that is, by looking into the 'more profound and deeper change within the cultural milieu and within the world view of its bearers' (meaning, members of the middle class). The study by Norani et al. covered 586 new middle-class respondents in the Klang Valley, comprised of 60.6 per cent Malays and 39.4 per cent Chinese and Indians, with 65.6 per cent drawn from the government sector, and the rest from the private sector (including 3.4 per cent self-employed). From the study, it is found that despite their high education and their facility in at least two languages (their mother tongue and English), only a small number appears to have a sustained interest in the 'higher and finer aspects of life', while most members of the middle class have not developed a strong intellectual and cultural tradition, being lacking in strong reading habits and sophisticated cultural tastes. Many are basically consumerist in orientation, involved in material pursuits and acquiring status items as symbols of 'having arrived'. Therefore, they are rather poor bearers and agents of modernity in Malaysia. Nevertheless, in terms of attitudes and perceptions about work relations, the study found that members of the new middle class have developed cosmopolitan and rational outlooks, and they are prepared to work under bosses, irrespective of the latter's ethnicity, sex, age and level of education. Even among the new Malay middle-class component, there is little indication that they have become breeding grounds for strong anti-Chinese sentiments.

Conclusions

This chapter has shown that a number of important questions on the new middle class have been or are being addressed by scholars in their works. In the main, the studies discussed above have significantly enriched the literature on the new Malaysian middle class. They have indicated clearly that the new middle class has come to stay and that the historical trajectory of Malaysian society in future will be shaped or influenced more strongly by the expanding multi-ethnic new middle class.

Nevertheless, these and other questions, especially the problematic of middle class theorizing and conceptualization; the historical forces that have influenced the formation and expansion of the new middle class; intergenerational mobility, affluence and work culture; new middle-class family, community, religious activities, class reproduction, lifestyles and value orientations; as well as middle-class politics, democratization and ethnicity, still require further research and analysis. At the same time, to avoid the peninsular bias, the scope in the Malaysian middle class studies has to be widened to include Sarawak and Sabah. New questions such as gender and the new middle-class also need to be addressed seriously. These questions are too many and complex to be addressed effectively in one study. As the various chapters will show, my study of the new Malay middle class is a modest attempt to answer some of these questions.

3
Industrialization and Middle-Class Formation in Malaysia

Introduction

This chapter offers a macro-analysis of the evolution of class structure, with particular reference to middle-class formation, in Malaysia from the early twentieth century to the present day. The discussion is conducted against the backdrop of the structural changes that have occurred in the country during the pre- and post-independence periods, with emphasis on the post-1970s' changes and transformation. The chapter traces the evolution of the class structure, and shows the role of the state as well as capitalist production relations in promoting structural changes and the formation of modern classes, including the new middle class. The macro-analysis in this chapter provides the background to subsequent chapters which contain the micro-analysis based on field studies conducted among the new Malay middle class in the metropolitan city of Kuala Lumpur (and Petaling Jaya) (also referred to as the Klang Valley), and two provincial towns in the east coast states of peninsular Malaysia – Kota Bharu in Kelantan and Kuala Terengganu in Terengganu.

However, as discussed in Chapter 1, although the new middle class is not easy to define, many scholars, of various theoretical inclinations, have utilized occupational categories for their working definition of class. In this chapter, I also adopt the occupational approach to identify the new middle class, by using data on occupations tabulated in official statistics available since the early decades of the twentieth century. These statistics, however, only refer to occupational categories. They give statistics of different types of occupations, both white-collar and blue-collar. However, the occupational definition used here is only for the purpose of making estimates of the relative sizes of various occupational groups in the workforce, and should only be taken as a proxy of class. In this approach, we take the first two top categories – professional and technical, as well as administrative and managerial – to represent the new middle class, while those in the clerical, sales and some services categories are taken to represent the lower-middle-class occupations.[1] Two other categories – the production and related workers category, and the agricultural workers category – are used as proxies for the working class and the rural community classes respectively. The concept of the new middle class used here is in keeping with John Goldthorpe (1980, 1982) and David Lockwood (1995), who proposed that the new middle class consists of 'the salariat', consisting of professional, managerial and administrative employees who share a 'distinctive employment status whose principal feature is the 'trust' that employers necessarily have to place in these employees whose delegated or specialized tasks give them a considerable autonomy' (Lockwood 1995: 1).

Pre-independence structural changes and evolution of the class structure

Although the structural transformation and evolution of the modern class structure in Malaysia (before 1963, it was referred to as Malaya) began in the late nineteenth century and the beginning of the twentieth century, classes were not a new phenomenon in Malay society. Prior to western colonial penetration in the Malay Peninsula or Malaya, the major classes in indigenous Malay society were the aristocracy on one hand, and the peasantry on the other. Elements of a merchant class – most pronounced during the Malacca period (1400–1511) – were also already in existence to a certain degree. Whether these latter elements would have transformed themselves into a bourgeoisie and modern middle classes, and play a revolutionary modernizing role like their counterparts in the West had there been no colonization by western powers is a matter of historical conjecture, which we will not indulge in here.

While the early colonial powers – the Portuguese (1511–1641) and the Dutch (1641–1824) – only set up trading posts in Malacca, the British colonialists who first colonized Penang in 1786 eventually turned the whole of Malaya into their colony after the signing of the Pangkor Treaty in January 1874. By 1914, the Malay peninsula was organized into three administrative units under the British – the Straits Settlements (SS) comprising Singapore, Malacca and Penang; the Federated Malay States (FMS) comprising Perak, Selangor, Negri Sembilan and Pahang; and the Unfederated Malay States (UFMS) comprising Johor, Kelantan, Terengganu, Kedah and Perlis. In 1948, all of these constituent states (with the exception of Singapore) became the Federation of Malaya, which attained independence in 1957. In 1963, the federation expanded to become the Federation of Malaysia, which included Sabah, Sarawak and Singapore, but Singapore subsequently seceded in 1965 to become the Republic of Singapore. Unless otherwise stated, the historical data used in this chapter refer to Malaya (or peninsular Malaysia) without Singapore, while the data for the post-independence period refer mainly to peninsular Malaysia.

The imposition of western colonial capitalism on Malaya had long-lasting effects on Malaysian society. Malaya – a prize colony for Britain – attracted western investments, mostly in the rubber and tin industries, whose output rose from US$194 million in 1914 to US$560 million in 1930, and US$455 million in 1937, with about 70 per cent of the total being contributed by British investors (Allen and Donnithorne 1957: 200). The development of the rubber and tin industries in Malaya made the colony Britain's biggest dollar-earner (Li Dun Jen 1982). This can be seen from the value of exported raw materials from Malaya to the United States, which amounted to US$270 million in 1948, or 69 per cent of the value of all exports to Malaya's major trading partners. This gave a net surplus of US$172 million for Malaya, the biggest surplus in dollar terms compared to the dollar earnings of all other British colonies (other figures were US$47.5 million for the Gold Coast [Ghana], US$24.5 million for Gambia, and US$23.0 for Ceylon [Sri Lanka]) (Hua Wu Yin 1983: 91–92, Tables 4.1 and 4.2). As pointed out by several scholars, in the immediate post-war period, Malaya's contribution of export earnings in US dollars to British recovery was very crucial given the international balance of payments deficit faced by Britain. For example, in 1951, of the US$400 million earned by Malaya, 83 per cent was siphoned off to Britain (Jomo 1986: 147).

Several scholars have argued that while the actual 'take-off' stage of Malaysian economic growth took place in the 1970s, it was preceded by at least a half-century of quite significant change away from the classic colonial pattern (see, for example, Brookfield 1994). From available figures, it can be seen that of the workforce of 1 718 870 in 1921, 70.9 per cent were in the primary sector (agriculture, mining and quarrying), 5.9 per cent in the secondary sector (manufacturing, building and construction), and the rest (23.2 per cent) in the tertiary sector. However, by 1957, the contribution of the secondary sector to the labour force had increased to 9.6 per cent, while the primary sector had declined to 61.3 per cent. This shows that during the three-and-a-half decades prior to independence, limited industrialization had taken place (Brookfield 1994: 5).

Industrialization and developments in commerce during the British colonial period were catalytic in promoting the growth, albeit slow, of new classes in Malaya. Among these the new classes were the European bourgeoisie, a small group of European officers, Chinese *compradors* (Puthucheary 1979), Indian money-lenders, Malay junior administrators, Asian white-collar employees, and a growing (mainly Chinese and Indian) proletariat. While a small proportion among them – in particular, the Malay administrators and non-Malay white-collar and technical workers – were products of the expansion of the British colonial state, others emerged, directly or indirectly, in response to the demands of expanding colonial capitalism.

An examination of data on occupations will provide an idea of the evolution of the pre-independence class structure. In 1931, of a total registered male[2] workforce of 1.5 million, 35.5 per cent were Malays, 44 per cent Chinese, 20 per cent Indians, and 0.5 per cent were classified as Others. The majority (58 per cent) were workers in the agricultural category, while another 24 per cent were production, transportation and related workers. However, those in the clerical, sales and services categories (the lower middle class) made up 6.7 per cent, while those in the higher-grade white-collar middle-class professional and technical jobs as well as administrative and managerial employees, were very small minority (2.1 per cent).

The growth of the economy, and hence the modern classes, including the various middle-class fractions in Malaya, was very much affected by the Great Depression of the 1930s. The ravages of the Pacific War (1941–45), which involved the Japanese occupation of Malaya for almost four years, destroyed the economy further. The post-war recovery was slow, but with the boom of the early 1950s following the Korean War, Malaya's economy picked up again.

However, the argument that industrialization began during the British colonial period should be read with some caution. It should not be interpreted to mean that colonial capitalism had any interest in promoting local manufacturing or social transformation based on industrialization. As argued by Jesudason (1990), during the colonial period, manufacturing was never considered to be a major part of the Malayan economy. This can be seen from the fact that of the 108 million pound sterling of British direct investment in Malaya in 1930, 85.2 per cent was in agriculture (the plantation sector), 7.4 per cent in mining, 7.4 per cent in other sectors, but none in manufacturing. This situation continued throughout the colonial period. Only after independence did British capitalists divert a portion of their direct investment into manufacturing. Thus, we see that in 1965, of a total of £144 million of British direct investment in Malaysia, their investment in manufacturing made up 13.8 per cent, while the proportion of investment in the plantation sector dropped to 66.4 per cent (Hua Wu Yin 1983: 44, Table 2.6).

During the colonial period, the colonial state favoured an international division of labour in which colonies would produce primary commodities and the metropole, manufactured goods, a policy that had the effect of constraining local manufacturing (Jesudason 1990: 32). Furthermore, during the colonial period, incentives for industrial growth were few, and suggestions for and attempts at protection policies to encourage local industrialization were at best ignored, or at worst, resisted by the colonial state (Jomo 1986: 219). Thus, it is unsurprising that there was little growth in the size of the middle class during the colonial period. From census figures, we find that by 1947, the new middle class – those in the professional and technical, as well as the administrative and managerial categories – increased very marginally, from 2.1 per cent in 1931 to only 2.8 per cent in 1947. However, the growth of these categories was slightly more noticeable in the 1950s, when they increased to 4.4 per cent by 1957 (Hirschman 1975: 22–3).

Because of the ethnic division of labour developed by the colonial state, we find that the new middle-class occupations were mainly dominated by ethnic Chinese, Indians and Eurasians. In 1957, the majority (57 per cent) of the professional and technical, as well as administrative and managerial employees were Chinese, 34 per cent Malays, and the rest (9 per cent) were Indians and Others. If we consider only those employees occupying administrative and managerial jobs, which numbered slightly more than 25 000 in 1957, the Chinese proportion was very much higher, that is, 62.4 per cent compared to 17.6 per cent Malays, and 12.0 per cent Indians and Others. In short, the new Malay middle class at this time was still very small and weak.

Post-independence structural changes and social transformation

While colonial capitalism did result in the formation of new classes, the rapid growth and expansion of the latter, namely the new middle class, is a phenomenon largely associated with the last three decades of the twentieth century. It came mainly in the wake of the post-1970s labour-intensive industrialization and public sector expansion, which were planned and executed by a strong developmentalist state. Unlike the pre-

1970s period, when the capitalist and middle classes were mainly Chinese, and the new Malay middle class mainly comprised a small group of government administrators, the 1970s saw the beginning of the expansion of a more multi-ethnic new middle class. Besides administrators, this new middle class was mostly made up of managers and other professionals, some in the state sector, but the majority working for private industry.

The changes that had taken place, which led to the emergence and expansion of a multi-ethnic new middle class, suggest that the middle class is not a static social category but, rather, an historically constituted and dynamic one, which has emerged in the specific historical, political, economic and cultural context of Malaysia's development. The dramatic changes in the ethnic and sectoral composition of the new Malaysian middle class is closely related to Malaysia's state-led modernization and social transformation in the last thirty years.

Three major transformative processes, which had an important bearing on middle class formation and expansion, shall be highlighted here.

First, the rapid and extensive structural changes in the economy and society, especially over the last three decades, have transformed Malaysia from being basically a primary-producing agricultural economy to becoming a second-tier newly industrialized economy (NIE). Such structural transformation brought about by industrialization can be clearly seen if we compare the relative positions of the primary, secondary and tertiary sectors over the last three decades, which show the rapid contraction of the contribution of the agricultural sector to the gross domestic product (GDP). Official statistics show that while the contribution of the agricultural sector to GDP was the highest in 1970, amounting to 31.4 per cent, its share fell to 18.7 per cent in 1990, and fell further to 12.8 per cent in 2000 (Malaysia 1999: 39). This decline in the agricultural sector contrasted with the rapid expansion of the secondary sector (manufacturing, construction, and mining),[3] which increased its contribution to GDP from 23.3 per cent in 1970 to 40.2 per cent in 1990 (an increase of 16.9 percentage points), and increased further to 45.2 per cent in 2000. The contribution of the tertiary sector (various types of services) to GDP also expanded in absolute terms over the three decades, although in proportionate terms, its contribution, which was 45.3 per cent in 1970, fell slightly to 41.1 per cent in 1990, and remained at 42.0 per cent in 2000 (Malaysia 1971; 1999: 39).

Second, the structural changes outlined above brought about changes in the occupational pattern of the labour force, with a decline in the rural labour force and an expansion of the labour force in the secondary and tertiary sectors. Official figures show that the proportion of the rural labour force shrank from 54 per cent of the total labour force in 1970 to 28 per cent in 1990, and 16.1 per cent in 2000 (Malaysia 1996, 1999). By contrast, the non-agricultural labour force expanded very rapidly. For example, the proportion of the labour force in the manufacturing sector increased from 8.7 per cent in 1970 to 19.5 per cent in 1990 and 27.5 per cent in 2000, registering an average annual growth rate of 10.3 per cent during the period 1971–90. The service-sector labour force, which grew at an average annual rate of 7.6 per cent during the 1971–90 period, increased its share of the total labour force from 32.5 per cent in 1970 to 45.7 per cent in 1990 (Malaysia 1996) and 47.5 per cent in 2000 (Malaysia 1999).

Third, rapid urbanization during the last three decades had transformed Malaysia's agricultural society into a predominantly urban industrializing society. In 1970, of the 10.4 million population, only slightly more than a quarter (26.7 per cent) lived in urban areas. However, the ensuing decade saw rapid urbanization, which increased the proportion of the urban population to more than one-third (34.2 per cent) – an increase of 7.5 percentage points during the inter-censal period. A decade later, the 1991 census showed that of a total population of 19 million, the urban population had increased sharply to 50.7 per cent (Malaysia, 1995: 30–31), and 60 per cent by 2000. However, it should be noted that the sharp increase in the urban population in the 1990s has been due to three factors, viz. natural growth and in-migration, as well as the redefinition of urban areas. While in previous censuses, urban areas only included gazetted areas which had a population of 10 000 or more, the 1991 census expanded urban areas to include both gazetted areas and adjacent built-up areas with a concentration of 10 000 or more population.[4]

It should be emphasized that these transformative processes took place during a period of rapid economic growth and unprecedented affluence in Malaysia. In fact, during the economic transformation of the last thirty years, the GDP grew at an average rate of 6.7 per cent per annum. It recorded a rapid annual average growth rate of 7.5 per cent in the 1970s, but fell to 5.9 per cent in the 1980s following the 1985–86 recession. However, from the late 1980s until early 1997, the GDP grew more rapidly, recording an average annual rate of 8.7 per cent. Nevertheless, with the 1997–98 financial and economic crisis and the GDP contracting by 6.7 per cent in 1998, the GDP is expected to record an average annual growth of only three per cent for the Seventh Malaysian Plan (1996–2000) period (Malaysia 1999: 5).

Growth and expansion of the middle class

Based on the data provided in official statistics, we can provide a sketch of the evolution of modern class structure, with an emphasis on the new middle-class formation in Malaysian society. To do so, we have to consider several indicators, such as occupation (the most important indicator), which should be examined together with other variables such as educational qualification, household income, and ownership of cars and expensive household items.

We shall first begin by examining changes in the occupational structure, focusing on middle-class formation. However, discussing the new middle class by itself without alluding to the capitalist class, the petit bourgeoisie (or the old middle class) as well as the lower classes would not provide the whole class configuration (see Chapter 1 for an explanation of these terms). While it is easier to estimate the working class from official statistics, occupational categories do not provide any idea of the size of the capitalist class and the old middle class. In order to make such estimates, we have to take another route, by examining the data on the occupational status of the workforce, taking those categorized as 'employers' to be a proxy for the capitalist class, and a part of 'the self-employed', particularly those in the services category (such as in the wholesale and retail trade, catering and lodging services) as proxies for the old middle class. Again, the inconsistency in the compilation of official statistics from one census to another makes this task more difficult. For example, the population censuses for 1957 and 1970 lumped the 'employers' and 'self-employed' categories together. We thus have to rely on the data for 1947 as a base year to estimate the size of the capitalist class and the old middle class before independence, and the data for the 1980 and 1991 censuses for the post-independence period. Based on the 1947 census, 'employers' numbered some 24 220 persons, or 1.3 per cent of the working population, while by 1980, the number had increased to 150 526, or 4 per cent of the working population, registering a sixfold increase in absolute terms over three decades (Table 3.1).

By 1991, the employers' category had increased further in absolute terms to 84 169, of which over a third (34.4 per cent) were Bumiputera employers. The proportion of employers in the working population as a whole fell to 3.2 per cent in 1991 due to the rapid expansion of those in the 'employees' category. This means that the capitalist class – the rich and powerful in society – constitute only about 3 per cent of the working population, but, together with foreign capitalists, they control the country's wealth.

Table 3.1   Malaysia: distribution of employers by ethnic group, 1947–1991

Ethnic group	1947	1980	1991
Malays/Bumiputera	4 086	53 416	63 346
(%)	(16.9)	(35.5)	(34.4)
Chinese	16 718	77 459	101 837
(%)	(69.0)	(51.5)	(55.3)
Indians and Others	3 416	19 651	18 986
(%)	(14.1)	(13.0)	(10.3)
Total no. of employers	24 220	150 526	184 169
Total workforce	1 896 126	3 793 102	5 781 248
Employers as a percentage of total workforce	1.28	3.97	3.18

Source: Adapted from Jomo 1988: 322–3.
Department of Statistics (1995b: 723–31).
Notes: 1. The 1947 figures refer to peninsular Malaysia only.
2. The figures for 1957 and 1970 do not distinguish between 'employers' and 'the self-employed', hence they cannot be presented in this table.
3. Data on employers for the year 2000 is not available because the latest population census was conducted in July 2000 and the report will only be published in 2001 or 2002.

The old middle class, however, is more difficult to estimate from official statistics because the official definition of the 'self-employed' includes not only those in the informal sector such as petty merchants in retail trade and in catering and lodging services, but also farmers operating their own independent farm units. Thus, although statistics show that the 'self-employed' made up 41.2 per cent of the workforce in 1947, 26.2 per cent in 1980, and 23.7 per cent in 1991, the real size of the old middle class of small proprietors is unknown. However, if we focus on small businesses, namely retail trade and catering and lodging services, in which the self-employed small proprietors are found, we may be able to make an estimate. Official statistics from the 1980 census show that there were 210 505 working proprietors in Malaysia, or 4.5 per cent of the workforce of 4.67 million. By 1991, from a total workforce of 5.63 million, 281 180 persons (or 5 per cent) were involved in these services (Department of Statistics 1995b: 563–4). This means that the old middle class made up approximately 5 per cent of the workforce in the late 1980s and early 1990s. This shows that despite the growth of the capitalist class and the new middle class (see below), the old middle class has not disappeared, but continues to coexist alongside the other classes.

Table 3.2   Malaysia: employment according to major occupation 1957–2000

Occupational categories	1957	1970	1980	1990	1995	2000
Professional, technical & related workers	2.8	4.8	6.6	8.8	10.3	11.0
Administrative & managerial workers	1.2	1.1	1.1	2.4	2.7	4.2
Clerical & related workers	2.9	5.0	7.3	9.8	10.1	11.1
Sales workers	8.6	9.1	8.9	11.5	11.3	11.0
Service workers	8.6	7.9	9.2	11.6	12.4	11.8
Workers in agriculture, livestock, forestry, fisheries & hunting	56.4	44.8	32.1	28.3	21.0	18.1
Production & related workers	18.9	27.3	34.8	27.6	32.2	32.8
Total	100	100	100	100	100	100
	2 126 200	2 850 300	4 023 000	6 686 000	7 915 400	8 870 600

Note:
Figures for 1957 and 1970 refer to peninsular Malaysia only, while figures for 2000 are projections.
Sources: Extracted from Jomo (1988: 300–1).
Malaysia (1996: 113; 1999: 103).

As indicated above, the section of the new middle class that had experienced the most dramatic growth since the 1970s comprised of professional and technical workers as well as administrative and managerial workers. Though clerical workers also increased significantly, from 2.9 per cent in 1957 to 10.1 in 1995 and 11.1 per cent in 2000, the increase in the higher white-collar occupations is more pronounced. From being a relatively small group in the early years of independence, making up only 4.0 per cent in 1957 and 5.9 per cent in 1970 (Table 3.2), the new middle class increased significantly to 11.2 per cent in 1990, 13.0 per cent in 1995, and 15.2 per cent in 2000 – almost a fourfold increase in around forty years.

The lower-middle class (employees in clerical, sales and about half the services categories) made up another 15.8 per cent and 23.9 per cent in 1957 and 1970 respectively. Their proportion increased to 27.1 per cent in 1990, 27.6 per cent in 1995, and 28.0 per cent in 2000 (Table 3.2) – a much lower percentage increase than that of the new middle class.

During the same period, the rural classes shrank drastically, from 44.8 per cent in 1970 to about 21.0 per cent in 1995, and 18.1 per cent in 2000. However, the ranks of the blue-collar workers had grown together with the middle class. The proportion of production workers expanded from 27.3 per cent in 1970 to 32.2 per cent in 1995, and is stabilizing around 33.0 per cent in 2000 (see Table 3.2).

Nevertheless, it should be noted that although the proportion of the new middle class in Malaysia may be rising its proportion is still relatively small when compared with the proportion of the new middle class in the four East Asian 'Tiger Economies' – Taiwan, South Korea, Hong Kong and Singapore – which had undergone a phase of rapid industrialization much earlier (Rodan, Hewison and Robison 1997). For example, in neighbouring Singapore, the employers' category made up 1.9 per cent of the workforce in 1945, 3.9 per cent in 1980 and 5.9 per cent in 1993. This is a larger percentage than the employers' category in Malaysia, which stood at 3.1 per cent in 1991. Similarly, the professional and technical, as well as administrative and managerial categories in Singapore have expanded from 11 per cent in 1970 to 18 per cent in 1980 and 29.5 per cent in 1992 (Hing Ai Yun 1997: 79–118), which is proportionately far bigger the comparable figure in Malaysia, which stood at 13 per cent of the workforce in 1995.

Educational attainment is a major avenue for social mobility and an important indicator of social class formation. The increase in the number of secondary schools, colleges, and universities over the last three decades in Malaysia has been impressive. In terms of university education, from having only one university, the University of Malaya, before 1969, Malaysia today has eleven public universities,[5] several private universities[6] and many private institutions of higher learning offering degree courses through twinning as well as external degree programmes. The university student population, which numbered 52 810 in 1990, had increased to 79 330 by 1995, and is expected to increase further to 114 700 in 2000 (Malaysia 1996: 313). This number does not include the more than 50 000 students enrolled in degree level courses abroad in 1995, due to the shortage of places in local universities.

Educational expansion and the democratization of education, especially at the tertiary level, has resulted in an increase in the number of certificate-holders. There are six types of certificates issued to students who passed examinations at various educational levels in Malaysia. The certificates are the *Sijil Rendah Pelajaran* (SRP) [Lower Certificate of Education]; *Sijil Pelajaran Malaysia* (SPM) [Malaysian Certificate of Education]; *Sijil Pelajaran Vokasional Malaysia* (SPVM) [Malaysian Certificate of Vocational Education]; *Sijil Pelajaran Tinggi Malaysia* (STPM)

[Malaysian Higher Certificate of Education]; diploma/certificate, and degree (including Masters' and Doctoral degrees) (Malaysia 1995: 120).

Official figures indicate that the number of persons having qualifications has increased significantly. In the 1991 census, about 4.6 million persons, or about 42 per cent of the population aged 15 years and above, possessed educational qualifications compared to 1.9 million persons, or about 24 per cent for the corresponding age group in 1980, registering an average annual growth rate of 8.1 per cent during the 1980–91 period. What is more significant is the increase in the number of those having tertiary education qualifications. In 1980, degree-holders in Malaysia made up only 3 per cent of the population aged 15 and above, while in 1991, their number increased to 5 per cent. For diploma- and certificate-holders, the number also increased from 2 to 5 per cent during the same period. Compared with the growth rates for other types of certificate-holders, the average annual growth rates for those possessing diplomas/certificates and degrees were highest, registering 15.5 per cent and 10.7 per cent respectively during the inter-censal period (Malaysia 1995: 121). Given the strong emphasis on tertiary education in Malaysia today, the proportion of degree-holders among Malaysians will increase much faster in the future, thus further expanding the ranks of the new middle class.

The trends in class formation can also be corroborated by examining household income levels, and household consumption and lifestyles. Over the last two decades, the mean monthly household incomes of Malaysians increased significantly. For Malaysia as a whole, the mean monthly household income was only RM505 in 1976, but it increased to RM1167 in 1990 and RM2007 in 1995 (figures in current prices) – about a fourfold increase in twenty years (Malaysia 1996: 94), with an average growth rate of 9.5 per cent per annum during the period 1990–95.

Class analysis lends itself to examining income distribution reflecting the increasing class stratification. Based on data in the Seventh Malaysia Plan 1996–2000 (Malaysia 1996: 89), income inequalities reflecting class differences are sharp, especially in urban areas. There has been a decline in the percentage of 'low-income households' (defined in the Seventh Malaysia Plan as those earning less than RM1000 per month) from 61 per cent in 1990 to 36 per cent in 1995. At the same time, there has been a substantial increase in the percentage of those earning between RM1000 and RM3000 per month – referred to in the plan document as 'middle income' households. The number of such households has risen from 33 per cent in 1990 to 47 per cent in 1995, and the number of high-income households (above RM3000) has grown from 6 per cent to 17 per cent during the same period (Malaysia 1996: 89).

However, there is a widening income inequality among the three categories of households, mainly brought about by the difference in the growth rates of the rural and urban economies (Malaysia 1996: 91). The mean income of the low-income households increased by only 3.9 per cent annually during the period 1985–90, and 8.1 per cent per annum between 1991 and 1995 – the lowest growth among the three categories of households. On the other hand, the growth rate for 'upper-income' households was highest, with an average of 10 per cent per annum between 1991 and 1995, followed by 'middle-income' households, whose growth rate was 9.2 per cent during the same period (Malaysia 1996: 91). Given the already marked income difference among the three income categories in absolute terms, with the growth rate highest for the top-income households, and lowest for the low-income households, one can expect a further expansion of income differences in ensuing years. The creation of the new poor (note the swelling ranks of the unemployed to over half a million following the 1997–98 economic crisis) will certainly increase income inequality.

Such inequality and income stratification can be further seen in the ownership and consumption of certain expensive household items. An increase in household income provides households with greater purchasing power, enabling them to acquire more affluent household items whose ownership and consumption is indicative of the growth of the middle and upper classes. Since nationwide house ownership data are not readily available, data on car ownership are used to examine this phenomenon. Official figures indicate that there is a corresponding increase in car ownership among Malaysian households during the inter-censal period 1980–91. In 1980, only 19 per cent, or about one-fifth of Malaysian households, had cars, but by 1991, car ownership had increased dramatically to almost one-third of all households. Urban-dwellers reflected the change most dramatically, as shown by the fact that in 1980, only 33 per cent of all households had cars, but by 1991, this figure had increased to 46 per cent – an increase by 13 percentage points over the 11-year period (Department of Statistics 1995a: 166).

A caveat is in order here. Although in some countries, car ownership may not reflect inequality, in many developing countries, including Malaysia, car ownership does reflect it. In Malaysia, the prices of the cheapest and most economical saloon cars (Kancil and Proton Iswara) today are between RM25 000 and RM40 000. With such prices, they can only be afforded by those whose monthly earnings are well over R1500, while those on a lesser income can only afford to own motorcycles, or second-hand cars. Thus, in Malaysia car ownership – taken together with other indicators such as occupation, educational qualifications, house ownership and ownership of other assets, lifestyles, and so on – does indicate the growth of the new middle class.

From the above discussion, it is clear that the capitalist and the new middle classes have emerged and grown significantly over the last few decades in Malaysia.

The state and middle-class growth

As indicated in Chapter 1, the central question in the discussion of the new middle class in late-industrializing economies is the role of the state in social transformation and in middle-class growth and expansion. To assess the role of the state in the growth and expansion of the new middle class in Malaysia, one needs to briefly examine the nature of the Malaysian state, its historical and global context, as well as the ideology of the ruling elite.

The concept of the state is hard to grasp. As argued by Held, 'there is nothing more central to political and social theory than the nature of the state, and nothing more contested' (Held 1983: 1). Not only is the nature of the state problematic, there is also debate about its role in development. The World Bank, which was rather dismissive of the role of the state when reviewing the success of East Asian economies in the early 1990s (World Bank 1993), has lately argued for an effective state, as central to economic and social development, not only as a direct provider of growth, but also as a partner, catalyst, and facilitator of growth (World Bank 1997).

In Malaysia, a debate from different perspectives has ensued regarding the nature and role of the Malaysian state in social transformation and middle-class formation. The debate, which revolves around the relation-ship between ethnicity and class, is understandably inconclusive. Some writers maintain that the Malaysian state is a Bumiputera or an ethnic hegemonic state; the Malaysian Constitution is claimed as 'a first step toward the consolidation of a Malay State, [and] the NEP a supplemental strategy for achieving that political ideal' (Ho Khai Leong 1997: 217). Other writers, arguing from a class perspective, regard the Malaysian state as capitalist, and ethnicity as only a mask or instrument for advancing underlying material class interests (see, among others, Hua Wu Yin 1983). Various terms, such as administocrats (Chandra 1979: Chs 4 and 5), statist capitalists (Jomo 1986), and bureaucratic bourgeoisie (Brown 1994), have been used to describe the governing group or dominant class or class fraction controlling the state.

It is also argued that functioning in the interests of international capitalism, the Malaysian state must mediate the interests of the various classes and fractions (Brown 1994). State bureaucrats must employ the government machinery in ways which are responsive to various class interests, rather than simply in ways which promote their own interests. State bureaucrats attempt a 'balancing act', employing the state machinery to promote their own interests and their emergence as the dominant class, but having to compromise these interests in order to serve international capital, and to mediate among the capitalist class fractions and also between the dominant and subordinate classes more generally (Brown 1994: 210–11).[7] In short, the state would not only serve the interests of the dominant group, but would also make compromises with other groups and classes in society in order to maintain the smooth running of the system. This logic supposedly helps to explain the role of the Malaysian state in bringing about social transformation and the growth of the new middle class, especially among Malays, in the last three decades.

However, what is germane to our discussion here includes the following issues: Is the state the principal actor in middle-class formation? Or are classes, including the new middle class, the product of the expansion of capitalism? As shown in Chapter 2, Joel Kahn (1991, 1992, 1996a, 1996b) has been a proponent of the state's overriding role in middle-class formation and expansion in Malaysia. He dismisses Giddens' 'relations of production' approach, applied in the Malaysian context by Johan Saravanamuttu (1989), and also the 'cultural capital' approach of Bourdieu (1977, 1984). (For further details of the debate, see Abdul Rahman 1995, 1996.) Kahn (1991: 56) sums up his position thus:

> I have argued for a definition of the middle class which locates them primarily by reference not to the relations of production, or even what Bourdieu maintains are the relations of production of cultural capital, but to the processes of modern state formation both in the colonial and post-colonial periods [in Malaysia].

In criticizing Saravanamuttu, Kahn maintains that applying the 'relations of production' approach to Malaysian middle class studies would be tantamount to mechanically imposing western class models to Malaysian experience. Kahn maintains that the Malaysian middle classes did not so much owe their existence to the changing demands of capital, but more to the emergence of the modern state, and that the middle classes have been just as embedded in the state as in capitalist relations. In fact, he further argues that the emergence of a new middle class, at least in post-colonial Malaysia, might have as much, if not more to do with the emergence of the modern state than with capitalist development per se, and that the middle class 'is composed largely not of private, self-employed entrepreneurs, or middle ranking employees of private enterprises, but those employed directly or indirectly by the state' (Kahn 1996b: 24).

It is true that the state has played a very significant role in the transformation of the Malaysian economy and society over the last three decades. However, the nature and extent of the state's role in middle-class formation and expansion cannot be assumed, but should be clearly delineated and substantiated empirically. In Kahn's analysis, the state's role is overemphasized as though other factors, such as capitalist relations and cultural capital, are of little or no relevance in middle-class formation. A one-sided emphasis on the role of the state is not only empirically questionable, but also smacks of theoretical apriorism.

The politically dominant Malay administrators-turned-politicians or 'administocrats' were economically weak when they took over the reins of government from the British in 1957. Although they controlled the state machinery, they had limited access to wealth. Economic wealth was then concentrated in the hands of western capitalists and, to a certain extent, Chinese *compradors* (Puthucheary 1979). Since there was no correspondence between political and economic power, the Malay administocrats could not rule on their own. They therefore worked out 'consociational' arrangements with leaders of the Malaysian Chinese Association (MCA) and Malaysian Indian Congress (MIC) respectively to form the Alliance (later Barisan Nasional or National Front) to rule the country. They formulated policies and strategies to strengthen their economic base, while strengthening the bases of their support especially within the Malay community.

Despite being economically weak, the Malay administocrats holding the reins of state power enjoyed some political legitimacy, partly by virtue of UMNO's credentials in opposing and defeating the British-engineered Malayan Union in 1946, a scheme which was perceived as a direct threat to Malay interests, as well as its credentials for gaining independence, a mantle it inherited when other Malay-based parties were either banned by the British following the declaration of the Emergency in June 1948, or were rendered ineffective. However, while the state could be relatively autonomous from the dominant foreign and Chinese business groups (Jesudason 1989: chapter 7), intra-class and inter-ethnic competition and political support-building, especially from the mid-1960s, led the state to adopt a more developmentalist role and to address the 'Malay dilemma' (Mahathir 1970) by creating a Malay capitalist class and a new Malay middle class as a counterweight to the non-Malay, especially Chinese, bourgeoisie and new middle class, and by modernizing Malay society.

The role of the state in socio-economic transformation since 1957 until the close of the twentieth century can be divided into four distinct phases: first, the so-called laissez-faire period (1957–69); second, the interventionist period (1970–85); third, the period of private sector-led growth through privatization and liberalization (1986–97); and fourth, the period of reassertion of the state's role to bail out certain politically connected companies, and to serve as a catalyst to kick-start economic growth following the 1997–98 financial and economic crisis.

As indicated in the preceding section, the formation and growth of modern classes became much more pronounced after independence. To gauge the nature and extent of the state's role in social transformation and the growth of such classes, especially the capitalist and the middle classes (discussed in the next section), we shall compare the situation in the 1950s and the 1960s – prior to the implementation of the NEP and export-led industrialization – with the situation in the 1980s and the 1990s. However, it should be noted that throughout the four decades since independence, Malaysia has maintained a capitalist economic system, and at no stage in its post-colonial history had the state attempted to nationalize foreign assets, or turned the country into a centrally-planned economy. The state has maintained an open economy, which has become more closely integrated with the world economy since the mid-1980s under the impact of globalization.

As indicated above, the early post-colonial period of 1957–69 has been described as laissez-faire (Jesudason 1989), although the state – besides playing a regulatory role and providing utilities – also promoted import-substitution industrialization. Nevertheless, the state generally left the development of commerce and industry to private enterprise, both foreign and local (Rugayah 1995: 63), and only intervened, to a certain extent, by directly undertaking rural development, and developing economic infrastructure. The 'restrained role' of the state was overseen by Tunku Abdul Rahman, the first Prime Minister, who was regarded as the 'ultimate guarantor of the laissez-faire approach and the consociational political scheme [between UMNO, MCA and MIC]' (Jesudason 1989: 55). The state's relatively laissez-faire approach was regarded by some scholars as approximating to the neoclassical economist's view of economic rationality to a greater degree than economic arrangements after 1970 (Jesudason 1989: 47).

Although successful in bringing about economic growth, the state's restrained role above did not address the historical problem of the 'Malay dilemma', and, in fact, heightened the Malay sense of insecurity and vulnerability arising from their weak economic position and the perceived threats mainly from the economically stronger Chinese. During the 1957–69 period, Malaysia already had a relatively sizeable Chinese capitalist class and middle class, as well as a large Chinese proletariat. But the Malays – who constituted the majority of the population (49 per cent in 1947, 50 per cent in 1957, and 53 per cent in 1970) – made few advances in the modern economic sector, with the Malay capitalist class and middle class, as well as the working class, being small and economically weak. For example, in the employers' category, of the 24 200 employers in 1947 mentioned above, Chinese formed the majority (69.0 per cent), Indians and Others 14.1 per cent, while Malays, mainly involved in the retail business, made up only 16.9 per cent of all employers (Table 3.1). The Malay capitalist class remained weak for many years, even after independence. In 1970, of a total share capital of RM5329.2 million in peninsular Malaysia, Malay corporate ownership was a meagre 2.4 per cent (1.6 per cent owned by Malay/Bumiputera individuals, while 0.8 per cent was held by trust agencies), compared with 22.0 per cent owned by Chinese capitalists, 63.3 per cent by foreigners, and 10.0 per cent unknown.[8]

At the same time, in 1970 as in 1957, the Malays occupied only a small proportion of new middle-class jobs. For example, of the 31 353 employees in the administrative and managerial category in 1970, only 24.1 per cent were Malays, compared to 63.0 per cent Chinese (Table 3.3). The Malays were especially underrepresented in managerial and professional posts in the manufacturing sector; in 1970, only 7 per cent of the professional and managerial category in the manufacturing sector were Malays, compared to 68 per cent Chinese, 4 per cent Indians, and 18 per cent foreigners (Jomo 1986: 76). Although Malays appear to be well-represented in the professional and technical category in general, contributing 47.1 per cent of the 131 814 employees in 1970, many were in lower-rung professional and technical jobs, such as nursing and teaching.

The ethnic share ownership and occupational imbalances were compounded further by increasing unemployment and rampant poverty during that period. Unemployment and poverty cut across ethnic groups, but the proportion of unemployed and poor Malays was higher than for non-Malays. Job creation – growing at only 2.5 per cent annually – lagged behind population growth of 3.3 per cent per annum, pushing up unemployment to 6.0 per cent in 1960, while the level of underemployment also remained substantial. Although the Pioneer

Table 3.3 Peninsular Malaysia: employment by ethnic group and work category 1957 and 1970

Category	1957				1970				Percentage increase 1957–70 (%)
	Malays	*Chinese*	*Indians & Others*	*Total (%)*	*Malays*	*Chinese*	*Indians & Others*	*Total (%)*	
Professional & technical	41.0	38.0	21.0	2.8 (59 534)	47.1	39.5	13.4	4.8 (136 814)	129.8
Administrative & managerial	17.6	62.4	20.0	1.2 (25 514)	24.1	62.9	13.0	1.1 (31 353)	22.9
Clerical & related workers	27.1	46.2	26.7	2.9 (61 660)	35.4	45.9	18.7	5.0 (142 515)	131.1
Sales & related workers	15.9	66.1	18.0	8.6 (182 853)	26.7	61.7	11.6	9.1 (259 377)	41.8
Service workers	39.7	33.3	27.0	8.6 (182 853)	44.3	17.3	38.4	7.9 (225 174)	23.1
Agricultural workers	62.1	24.3	13.6	56.4 (1 199 177)	72.0	17.3	10.7	44.8 (1 276 934)	6.5
Production, transport & other workers	26.5	53.5	20.0	18.9 (401 852)	34.2	55.9	9.9	27.3 (778 132)	93.6
Total	004.3 (48.2)	759.0 (36.3)	362.9 (15.5)	2 126.2	1 477.6 (51.8)	1 043.6 (36.6)	301.4 (11.6)	2 850.3	

Source: Adapted from Jomo (1988: 300–1).
Note: Value in brackets shows absolute number employed in each category.

Industries Programme brought in foreign investment and managed to increase manufacturing's share of the GDP from 8.5 per cent in 1960 to 13.5 per cent in 1970, it created only 23 000 new jobs (Jesudason 1990: 58). Thus, the unemployment rate increased dangerously to reach 8.0 per cent in 1970. Poverty was widespread, officially estimated at 49.3 per cent in peninsular Malaysia in 1970, with Malay households constituting the majority or 74 per cent of all poor households. In other words, the policy of leaving growth and distribution to market forces had resulted in growth, but with greater inequality. Thus, class and ethnic frustrations experienced by the Malays became intertwined, and raised ethnic tensions that triggered the May 1969 riots.

Despite the state's 'restrained' role during this period, it did intervene, to a certain extent, to promote foreign investment in Malaysia, particularly by instituting the Pioneer Industries Ordinance in 1958, which tried to promote a policy of import-substituting industrialization. However, because of the capital-intensive nature of the import-substitution programme and the limited domestic market, the impact of the policy was limited. Only after the introduction of the Investment Incentives Act of 1968, the Free Trade Zone Act in 1971 – both of which spurred export-oriented industrialization – and the Industrial Coordination Act in 1975, did the transformation processes really begin to impact upon the economic and social structure as a whole. This change in the direction of Malaysian industrialization policy coincided with the implementation of the NEP from 1971, beginning with the Second Malaysia Plan (1971–75) (Ishak 1995: 13). During the Fourth Malaysia Plan (1981–85), the Malaysian state engineered another major shift in her industrialization policy, from labour-intensive to more capital- and technology-intensive industrialization, with its heavy industrialization policy. The Industrial Master Plan (1986–1995) (IMP), reaffirmed the export-oriented industrialization policy thrust of the 1970s. In sum, the NEP's twin objectives of 'restructuring' society (to remove the identification of economic activities with ethnic groups) and poverty reduction, and the export-led industrialization industrial policy transformed Malaysia into what it is today (Anuwar Ali 1995: 14–28).

Throughout the 1960s, pressure was exerted upon the government, especially by the Malays, to increase state intervention. The Bumiputera Economic Congress was first held in 1965 and then again in 1968, demanding that the government provide credit, set up banks, training facilities and other institutions to help promote the growth of the Malay capitalist class and the new middle class, as well as to modernize Malay society. As a result of this pressure, departures from the previous policy were effected from the mid-1960s, but the 'laissez-faire' period only ended with the power struggle within the ruling UMNO in 1969 after Tun Abdul Razak Hussein became the second Prime Minister (1970–76). The changes led to the introduction of the NEP, characterized by active state intervention, especially for the first decade. The NEP's two-pronged objective was formulated to achieve national unity. The NEP's target was not only to increase Bumiputera share ownership to 30 per cent by 1990, but also to restructure occupational patterns as well as the ethnic balance in student intake into tertiary institutions to better reflect the ethnic mix of the population.

State intervention in the economy as an 'entrepreneur' made a significant impact on the growth and expansion of the new middle class, especially among Malays. In implementing this strategy, the state gained control of a number of giant foreign-controlled conglomerates involved in sectors regarded as nationally 'strategic' – for example, the take-over of the plantation companies, which owned hundreds of thousands of hectares of prime land such as Sime Darby by Perbadanan Nasional (Pernas) in the late 1970s, and of Guthrie and Harrisons and Crosfield by Permodalan Nasional Berhad (PNB) in the 1980s, and earlier of the Malaysian Mining Corporation (MMC) which was involved in tin mining. It also carried out occupational restructuring, especially at the management level, in state-owned and publicly-listed companies in which the state – through its trust agencies – had a controlling interest. The state also encouraged the growth of a Bumiputera capitalist class (described in policy documents as the Bumiputera Commercial and Industrial Community), by awarding contracts, loans, training and other kinds of assistance to existing or new businessmen to help them to go seriously into business ventures.[9]

At the same time, to develop the country's human resources, the state expanded educational opportunities at the tertiary level by setting up more universities and colleges, while simultaneously the increasing intake into existing ones. With the state's generous provision of scholarships/grants to most Malay students to pursue tertiary education, this facilitated occupational and social mobility into new middle-class jobs which had previously been closed to Malays.

Under the NEP's 'state-as-entrepreneur' or 'government-in-business' strategy, government intervention in the economy occurred on a very large scale, importantly leading to the setting up of state-owned enterprises (SOEs). In 1960, there were only 22 such enterprises in Malaysia; the number had increased to 109 in 1970. However, with the implementation of the NEP from 1971, the number increased sharply to

362 in 1975, 656 in 1980, and 1010 in 1985 (Gomez 1997: 3). Some writers argue that for an economy which is fundamentally market-oriented, Malaysia's SOE sector has been surprisingly large, in fact, among the largest in the world outside the centrally planned economies (Adam and Cavendish 1995: 15). The SOEs were actively engaged in core utilities – transport, communications, water supply, energy, and finance – with a substantial proportion also in non-traditional sectors such as services, construction, and, particularly, manufacturing (Adam and Cavendish 1995: 15). The expansion of SOE participation in the commercial, industrial, and service sectors as well as in the emerging oil- and gas-based exploration sector was so rapid that the SOE sector grew at an average rate of over 100 enterprises per year in the mid-1970s. By March 1990, SOEs numbered 1158, with a total paid-up capital of RM23.9 billion (Adam and Cavendish 1995: 16–17). The significance of the state sector to the economy can be seen from the fact that in 1990 25 per cent of GDP was contributed by SOEs.

With the state playing an active role in the economy, its role as the single largest employer in the country became more pronounced. As a percentage of total employment, public sector employment grew from 12 per cent in the early 1970s to a peak of 15 per cent in 1981, before declining slightly to 12.5 per cent in 1991 (Rugayah 1995: 65). In absolute terms, state employees numbered 398 000, or 11.9 per cent out of a total workforce of 3.34 million in 1970, 692 000, or 14.4 per cent of total employment in 1980, and 850 000, or 12.9 per cent of total employment in 1990 (Rugayah 1995: 65).

However, as indicated above, from the mid-1980s, following the implementation of the 'Malaysia Incorporated' policy in 1983 by the fourth Prime Minister Dr Mahathir Mohamad, who was responsible for privatization policies, the downsizing of the public sector, and the introduction of the Privatization Master Plan in 1991, the contribution of the state sector to total employment began to decline, especially with the transfer of state employees to the private sector. According to official figures, between 1983 and 1995, over 100 SOEs were privatized. At the same time, 96 756 public sector employees, or 11.4 per cent of the total public sector labour force, have been transferred to the private sector since 1983 through privatization (Malaysia 1996: 206). This number excludes personnel from previously government-owned companies which had been privatized before this period.

The dramatic decline in the role of the state sector as a source of employment since then can be clearly seen from the following figures. During the 1970–80 period, state employees increased from 398 000 in

1970 to 692 000 in 1980, an increase of 73.9 per cent, but between 1981 and 1990, its increase was small (only 12.3 per cent). With public sector downsizing and privatization fully under way in the 1990s, public sector employment during the Sixth Malaysia Plan (1991–95) increased only marginally, from 850 000 in 1990 to 872 000 in 1995, and is expected to number 894 000 (or 9.9 per cent of total employment) in the year 2000 – an increase of only 4.7 per cent above the 1991 figure, making a dramatic drop from the high 73.9 per cent increase in the 1970s.

The important fact that needs to be stressed is that, although the state has been and still is the single biggest employer, especially during the NEP period, its contribution to total employment has varied from as high as 15 per cent in 1981 to as low as 11 per cent in 1995. Over 80 per cent of employment is contributed not by the state, but by the private sector, including the informal sector.

Second, though the state has been very significant in the formation and expansion of the new middle class – especially its Malay component – new middle-class occupations (those listed in the Grade A and B posts) are less than one-half of all public sector occupations. Most new middle-class occupations are actually outside the state sector, and the future expansion of the new middle class will be more and more determined by private sector expansion rather than by the state, given the continued thrust towards privatization and downsizing of the public sector (Abdul Rahman 1995a).

Third, as a corollary to the above, the new middle class (made up of those in the professional and technical, as well as administrative and managerial categories), which constitutes the most important middle-class fraction, has been growing very rapidly over the last three decades. Their number was in the region of 168 167 in 1970 (5.9 per cent of the total number employed), 750 200 in 1990 (11.2 per cent of the total employed), and 1.35 million in 2000 (15.2 per cent of the total employed) (Tables 3.3, 3.4 and 3.5). However, the overwhelming majority of this new middle class is in the private sector, with a relatively small, albeit significant number in the public sector.

Fourth, it has been claimed that one clear result of the NEP's implementation is that the free enterprise philosophy which the Malaysian government had previously endorsed was *discarded* in favour of massive direct state intervention aimed at creating a Malay capitalist class (Sieh Lee Mei Ling 1992: 103). However, this statement is rather sweeping. Despite active state intervention during the NEP period (1971–90), private enterprise continued, no outright nationalization ever took place of any industry, be it foreign or local. The closest was the take-over

Table 3.4 Employment by occupation and ethnic group 1990 (000s)

Occupation	Ethnic			
	Bumiputera (%)	*Chinese (%)*	*Indians (%) & Others*	*Total (%)*
Professional & technical	354.8 (10.0)	170.5 (7.8)	61.0 (6.2)	586.4 (8.8)
(%)	(60.5)	(29.1)	(10.4)	(100.0)
Teachers & nurses[1]	152.0 (4.3)	54.6 (2.5)	15.2 (1.5)	221.8 (3.3)
(%)	(68.5)	(24.6)	(6.9)	(100.0)
Administrative & managerial	47.1 (1.3)	101.9 (4.7)	14.8 (1.5)	163.8 (2.4)
(%)	(28.7)	(62.2)	(9.1)	(100.0)
Clerical workers	341.8 (9.7)	252.3 (11.6)	58.5 (6.0)	652.6 (9.8)
(%)	(52.4)	(38.6)	(9.0)	(100.0)
Sales workers	229.8 (6.5)	449.3 (20.7)	89.8 (9.2)	768.9 (11.5)
(%)	(29.9)	(58.4)	(11.7)	(100.0)
Service workers	449.6 (12.7)	208.4 (9.6)	119.6 (12.2)	777.6 (11.6)
(%)	(57.8)	(26.8)	(15.4)	(100.0)
Agricultural workers	1 305.6 (37.0)	261.8 (12.0)	323.3 (33.1)	1 890.7 (28.3)
(%)	(69.1)	(13.8)	(17.1)	(100.0)
Production workers	804.6 (22.8)	730.8 (33.6)	310.6 (31.8)	846.0 (27.6)
(%)	(43.6)	(39.6)	(16.8)	(100.0)
Total	3 533.3 (100.0)	2 175.0 (100.0)	977.6 (100.0)	6 686.0 (100.0)
(%)	(52.9)	(32.5)	(14.6)	(100.0)

Source: Malaysia (1996: 82).
Note:
[1] Teachers and nurses are a major component in the professional and technical category.

of Sime Darby in the late 1970s and Guthrie in 1981, but these acquisitions were as a result of purchases on the London Stock Exchange. In fact, while the state facilitated the growth of a Malay capitalist and the new middle classes, it also actively encouraged foreign and local private investment, remaining friendly to market forces. As such, private sector growth continued, involving Chinese capitalists. Despite extensive capital accumulation by the state in the 1970s and early 1980s, state-owned enterprises contributed only one-quarter of the GDP in 1990, while most of the rest came from the private sector.

Table 3.5   Employment by occupation and ethnic group 2000 (000s)

Occupation	Ethnic			
	Bumiputera (%)	Chinese (%)	Indians (%) & Others[1]	Total (%)
Professional & technical	620.7 *(13.7)*	252.8 *(9.6)*	102.3 *(6.0)*	975.8 *(11.0)*
(%)	(63.2)	(25.9)	(10.9)	(100.0)
Teachers & nurses[2]	246.1 *(5.4)*	61.9 *(2.3)*	28.2 *(1.7)*	336.2 *(3.8)*
(%)	(73.2)	(18.4)	(8.4)	(100.0)
Administrative & managerial	135.9 *(3.0)*	197.4 *(7.5)*	39.3 *(2.3)*	372.6 *(4.2)*
(%)	(36.5)	(53.0)	(10.5)	(100.0)
Clerical workers	552.4 *(12.2)*	321.9 *(12.2)*	110.3 *(6.5)*	984.6 *(11.1)*
(%)	(56.1)	(32.7)	(11.2)	(100.0)
Sales workers	365.9 *(8.1)*	491.7 *(18.6)*	118.2 *(6.9)*	975.8 *(11.0)*
(%)	*(37.5)*	*(50.4)*	*(12.1)*	*(100.0)*
Service workers	602.4 *(13.3)*	222.7 *(8.4)*	221.6 *(13.0)*	1 046.7 *(11.8)*
(%)	(57.5)	(21.3)	(21.2)	(100.0)
Agricultural workers	967.8 *(24.1)*	175.1 *(6.6)*	462.7 *(27.2)*	1 605.6 *(18.1)*
(%)	(60.3)	(10.9)	(28.8)	(100.0)
Production workers	1 283.0 *(28.3)*	980.0 *(37.1)*	646.5 *(38.0)*	2 909.5 *(32.8)*
(%)	(44.1)	(33.7)	(22.2)	(100.0)
Total	4 528.1 *(100.0)*	2 641.6 *(100.0)*	1 700.9 *(100.0)*	8 870.6 *(100.0)*
(%)	*(51.0)*	*(29.8)*	*(19.2)*	*(100.0)*

Source: Computed from Malaysia (1999: 78–9).
Notes:
[1] Includes non-citizens.
[2] Teachers and nurses are a major component in the professional and technical category.

   One major development during the NEP era which worked favourably for private capital was the setting up of the Kuala Lumpur Stock Exchange (KLSE) in 1973 as a separate entity independent of the Stock Exchange of Singapore (SES) – an exercise in keeping with the NEP's objectives. The establishment of the KLSE, which dramatically expanded the Malaysian domestic capital market, provided an unprecedented source of private sector funds for financing corporate expansion, quickly tapped by Chinese businessmen to expand their activities (Heng Pek Koon 1992: 129).

Despite restrictions on Chinese capital, and on the expansion of the new Chinese middle class, the NEP period indirectly conferred benefits on them as well. In fact, a section of Chinese business did not regard the NEP as hostile to them, but, rather, as a necessary move to expand Malay capital and the new middle class to 'correct' the inter-ethnic imbalance and hence create a stable sociopolitical condition. Thus, despite the state's pro-Bumiputera affirmative action efforts, the Chinese capitalist and new middle classes grew during the NEP period. The picture is clear when we examine share-ownership figures for 1990. Despite the NEP's targeted 30 per cent Bumiputera share ownership in the corporate sector by 1990, the Bumiputera share increased from 2.4 per cent in 1970 to only 19.3 per cent (well below the 30 per cent NEP target); the Chinese share did not decrease, but instead increased both in absolute as well as in proportionate terms from about 22 per cent in 1970 to 45.5 per cent in 1990, while foreign interests declined from 63 per cent in 1970 to 25.4 per cent in 1990 (Malaysia 1996: 86) – with the major portion of foreign capital involved in the manufacturing sector. Therefore, together with the state sector, the private sector has been a major engine of growth – even during the NEP period – encouraged by the government's export-oriented industrialization policy. Capitalist production relations have not only been vital for capital accumulation and production, but also in providing employment opportunities, including the creation of many new middle-class occupations. The growth and expansion of the massive private sector required a large number of professional and technical workers, as well as managers. In fact, the majority of those in the managerial category, which numbered over 370 000 in 2000 – or 3.8 per cent of the total number employed – were in the private sector. Of this number, only slightly more than one-third (36.5 per cent) were Bumiputera (mainly in the state sector), while Chinese managers and administrators made up 53.0 per cent, mostly in the private sector (Table 3.5).

Conclusions

This chapter has offered a macro-historical analysis of the evolution of the class structure, with particular reference to middle-class formation, in Malaysia from the early decades of the twentieth century to the present day. It has shown that unlike earlier periods, when the new middle class in Malaysia tended to be dominated by those of Chinese origin, the new

Malaysian middle class today is multi-ethnic in composition, with the new Malay middle class constituting an important component. It has emphasized the need to examine both the role of the state and capitalist production relations in the formation and expansion of the new middle class in Malaysia.

While the state has played a crucial role in creating the Malay capitalist and new middle classes (Muhamad Ikmal 1995), for a major segment of the new non-Malay middle class, the state's role has ranged from being indirect to being insignificant. The state has also instituted pro-business policies, and created a stable environment conducive to business and has been a major source of business expansion, especially for privatized infrastructure development projects implemented actively since the mid-1980s.

Nevertheless, this chapter has argued that the state's role in the formation and expansion of the new middle class, though crucial, should not be overemphasized. Since the state has neither opted for nationalization, nor discarded the free enterprise system – even during the NEP period – the development of capitalist relations of production has continued unabated. Thus, the latter have also played a very significant role in creating the new middle class.

It should be noted that although the majority of the new middle class may not owe their existence and growth to the state, the policies and programmes of the latter are crucial in influencing their political attitudes and orientation. For example, the liberalization and deregulation policies embarked on by the state since the late 1980s have paid political dividends, because the predominantly Chinese urban constituencies voted overwhelmingly for the ruling BN in the 1995 and 1999 general elections.

However, the new Malaysian middle class – which is more multi-ethnic in composition today – is still in the process of formation and has yet to consolidate itself. By indulging in certain consumption patterns and lifestyles, some segments, especially those in the upper-income brackets, exhibit a tendency towards status differentiation, for example, by their choice of exclusive residential areas, possession of status items such as luxury cars, country club membership, foreign travel, and so on. This cultural dimension, which is becoming increasingly important as an expression of middle-class 'lifestyling' (Gerke 1995), will be discussed in detail in Chapter 6.

4
The Making of the New Malay Middle Class

From the macro-historical analysis in Chapter 3, we now proceed to examine the new Malay middle class in detail, basing our analysis on an empirical study, carried out in 1996 (with follow-ups in 1997, 1998 and 1999), of 284 respondents in the metropolitan Klang Valley, and in two provincial towns – Kota Bharu in Kelantan, and Kuala Terengganu in Terengganu. Table 4.1 shows the basic profiles of respondents in terms of sex, age, marital status and geographical origin. Of the total, 108 respondents (38 per cent) were taken from the Klang Valley, 80 (28.2 per cent) from Kota Bharu, and 96 (33.8 per cent) from Kuala Terengganu. In terms of sex, slightly over two-thirds, or 69.4 per cent, were male. In terms of age, young respondents (aged 30 and below) made up 29.2 per cent; those aged 31–40 years old made up the largest group, totalling 42.2 per cent; those aged 41–50 came to 23.6 per cent; and the oldest group (aged 51 and above) accounted for just under 5 per cent. The proportion of young respondents was highest in the Klang Valley sample (one-third of the sample was made up of those in that age group), while in Kota Bharu and Kuala Terengganu, their proportions were slightly smaller (about one-quarter each).

In terms of marital status, 81.3 per cent were married, 16.9 per cent single, and another 1.8 per cent were either widowed or divorced. Because the Klang Valley sample had the largest proportion of young respondents, it is not surprising that it also had the largest percentage (22.2 per cent) still remaining single. In the sample, those born in rural and urban areas were equal in proportion. However, those who were natives of the urban centres made up 44.5 per cent, while the majority (55.5 per cent) consisted of migrants from elsewhere.

Table 4.1   Basic profile of respondents

	Klang Valley (*n* = 108)	Kota Bharu (*n* = 80)	Kuala Terengganu (*n* = 96)	All respondents (*N* = 284)
Sex				
• Male	74.1	67.5	65.6	69.4 (*n* = 197)
• Female	25.9	32.5	34.4	30.6 (*n* = 87)
Age (years)				
• 30 & below	33.3	27.5	26.0	29.2 (*n* = 83)
• 31–40	35.2	38.8	53.1	42.2 (*n* = 120)
• 41–50	27.8	26.3	16.7	23.6 (*n* = 67)
• 51 & upper	3.7	7.5	4.2	4.9 (*n* = 14)
Marital status				
• Married	74.1	87.5	84.4	81.3 (*n* = 231)
• Widowed/ divorced	3.7	–	1.0	1.8 (*n* = 5)
• Single	22.2	12.5	14.6	16.9 (*n* = 48)
Origin				
• Urban	57.4	52.5	39.6	50.0 (*n* = 142)
• Rural	42.6	47.5	60.4	50.0 (*n* = 142)
Urban natives/ migrants				
• Born in urban centre studied	34.0	50.0	51.0	44.5 (*n* = 126)
• Migrated from outside	66.0	50.0	49.0	55.5 (*n* = 158)

Source: Survey data 1996 and 1997.

The making of the new Malay middle class: an explanatory note

This chapter considers the making of the new Malay middle class based on this sample, by examining the socio-economic transformation that members of this class have gone through compared to their parents, and how they have established themselves as new middle-class urbanites today. In the literature on class, especially on the new middle class, a distinction – borrowed from Marx – is often made between the 'fact of class' (or class in itself), and 'consciousness of class' (or class for itself) (Abercrombie and Urry 1984). The first refers to how classes, including the new middle class, come to be formed and consolidated materially, while the second refers to subjective aspects of class consciousness expressed in their members' lifestyles, their self-evaluation of their own class position, their ideology, political consciousness and activities, and so on. Based on this analytical distinction, this study attempts to, first, analyse how the new Malay middle class came to be formed materially, by examining the socio-economic conditions which have enabled members of this class to occupy and strengthen their current class position. The making of the new Malay middle class is examined by comparing the class positions and educational levels of parents with those of respondents to observe intergenerational mobility, followed by an analysis of the respondents' occupations, incomes and assets, and work culture. This chapter attempts to demonstrate that the new Malay middle class is a 'first-generation' middle class, which is relatively affluent compared to their parents and other classes in society, especially the Malay working class. In this discussion, attempts are made, whenever possible, to compare the new *Malay* middle class with the new *Malaysian* middle class as a whole, and also with the Malay *working* class.

However, in order for the new middle class to be fully formed and differentiated from other classes, it is important to examine the consciousness of members of this class of their class position, lifestyles, marriage partner preferences, class mobility/preservation strategies, political attitudes, and so on. Their strategies, activities and lifestyles reflect their attitudes and indicate their subjective efforts to become a class different from others. These issues will be discussed in detail in the next four chapters. As shown in this and in subsequent chapters, the new Malay middle class is still very much in the process of formation.

'First-generation' hypothesis

In this chapter, the 'objective' making of the new middle class will be discussed in terms of the 'first-generation' middle-class hypothesis, the affluence of the new middle class, and their work culture. In developed industrial societies, such as Britain or the United States, the new middle class has already been in existence for several generations (for studies of this phenomenon, see, among others, Mills 1975; Abercrombie and Urry 1984; Butler and Savage 1995).[1] However, in newly independent and industrializing societies, such as those in East and Southeast Asia, the appearance of the new middle class is a fairly recent phenomenon, perhaps only one generation old. In the light of this historical fact, scholars studying the East Asian new middle classes have proposed what is called the 'first-generation' hypothesis to explain the recent emergence and attitudes of the new middle classes in the first-tier NICs – that is, Taiwan, South Korea, Hong Kong and Singapore (Hsiao and So 1999;

Hsiao 1999). This hypothesis suggests that the parents of this new middle class were usually from lower-class backgrounds. These scholars argue that this class only developed during the 1960s and 1970s, at time when these economies began to undergo a process of rapid industrialization. They draw attention to the fact that many members of the new middle class were born after the Second World War, tended to come from worker and peasant family backgrounds, and experienced poverty and hardship during their childhood. Because of this, commentators contend that despite having lived in a 'multi-class family' setting, the 'first-generation' East Asian new middle class has an ambiguous class identity and ambivalent attitudes towards other classes – often exhibiting a sense of injustice, feeling close to the working class, and often standing on the side of the workers in capital-labour conflict (So and Hsiao 1994: 2; Hsiao 1999).

As shown in Chapter 3, not only did Malaysia industrialize later than the first-tier NICs, but its industrial progress has also been much lower than the four 'Tiger Economies' mentioned above. It is therefore useful to examine the 'first-generation' hypothesis in the Malaysian context to see whether it also applies to the Malaysian, including the new Malay, middle class. To address this question, we proceed by comparing the respondents' class positions with those of their parents to see whether they can be classified as a 'first-generation' new middle class. At the same time, we also examine their geographical origins to see how long they have been urbanites, and also their educational levels to assess the differences in 'cultural capital' between them and their parents.

In our sample,[2] all of the respondents were members of the new Malay middle class in the three urban centres. Classifying them by occupation, about two-thirds of the respondents were managers and administrators, while the remaining third were professionals, such as lawyers, accountants, doctors, lecturers, and so on. The proportion of managers and administrators was highest in the Klang Valley sample (83.3 per cent), followed by Kota Bharu (61.2 per cent), and Kuala Terengganu (49.0 per cent) (Table 4.2). By sector, 29.6 per cent worked with the government, with the rest (70.4 per cent) being in the private sector, some of these being owner-managers. The proportion working in the private sector was highest in the Klang Valley (98.1 per cent), a much higher figure than that for either Kuala Terengganu (54.2 per cent) or Kota Bharu (52.5 per cent).

Based on the respondents' ages (Table 4.1), it can be inferred that the oldest respondents (those aged 51 and above) were born during the Second World War, or immediately after, and received their secondary and tertiary education in the 1950s and 1960s. The middle-aged

Table 4.2   Current and first occupation of respondents

Occupation	Klang Valley (n = 108)		Kota Bharu (n = 80)		Kuala Terengganu (n = 96)		All respondents (N = 284)	
	1	*2*	*1*	*2*	*1*	*2*	*1*	*2*
Managers and administrators	83.3	21.9	61.2	21.3	49.0	13.5	65.5 (n = 186)	18.5
Professionals	16.7	32.9	38.8	39.9	51.0	46.9	34.5 (n = 98)	40.6
Clerical	—	15.1	—	6.3	—	10.4	—	10.4
Services	—	23.3	—	15.0	—	17.7	—	18.5
Production	—	6.8	—	17.5	—	9.4	—	11.2
Agricultural	—	—	—	—	—	2.1	—	0.8
Total	100.0	100.0	100.0	100.0	100.0	100.0	100.0	100.0

Notes:
1 = Current occupation.
2 = First occupation after leaving school, college or university.
Source: Survey data 1996 and 1997.

respondents (aged 41–50) were born during the 1950s, had their secondary schooling during the 1960s and tertiary education in the 1970s, and were thus the first batch of NEP beneficiaries. The mid-career group (aged 31–40), who constituted the largest age cohort, were born in the 1960s, had their schooling in the 1970s, and tertiary education in the 1980s; while the youngest cohort (those aged 30 and below) were born in the 1970s, and therefore completed their tertiary education in the early 1990s. It is clear, therefore, that while the first two age cohorts witnessed poverty and may even have experienced it themselves, the latter two, especially the last group, grew up in a transformed middle-income Malaysia.

Table 4.3 records the class positions of the respondents' fathers. It can be seen from the data that many respondents had fathers who were from the peasant and labouring classes (34.9 per cent farmers, 8.0 per cent labourers), with another 39.4 per cent from the old middle class (self-employed) and lower middle class (non-graduate schoolteachers and clerical workers). However, a small proportion of their fathers (17.6 per cent) were members of the new middle class (managers, administrators and lecturers).

Table 4.3   Class positions of fathers of respondents

Fathers' class position	Klang Valley (n = 180)	Kota Bharu (n = 80)	Kuala Terengganu (n = 96)	All respondents (N = 284)
New middle class	20.5	21.3	12.5	17.6
Old and marginal middle class	46.6	37.5	35.4	39.4
Farmers	20.5	32.5	47.9	34.9
Labourers	12.3	8.8	4.2	8.0
Total	100.0	100.0	100.0	100.0

Source: Survey data 1996 and 1997.

These findings suggest that the overwhelming majority of respondents (82.4 per cent) were the children of farmers or labourers, or of lower-grade careers such as clerks, non-graduate schoolteachers and small proprietors. As expected, the proportion of children of farmers and labourers was highest in Kuala Terengganu (50.1 per cent), followed by Kota Bharu (41.3 per cent), while it was lowest (32.8 per cent) in the Klang Valley. On the other hand, the proportion of children of clerks, schoolteachers and small proprietors was largest in the Klang Valley (46.6 per cent), followed by Kota Bharu (37.5 per cent), and lowest in Kuala Terengganu (35.4 per cent). These children were the first-generation to have come out of the lower-class backgrounds after having become managers, professionals and administrators. In family terms, their experience as part of the new middle class was totally new. Only a small minority (17.6 per cent) were themselves children of the new middle class. The finding from Table 4.3, therefore, strongly supports the 'first-generation' hypothesis established in studies of the East Asian new middle class.

If we examine the occupations of the mothers of our respondents, a very high percentage (78.3 per cent) were full-time housewives. Another 10.4 per cent worked as farmers and labourers, 7.2 per cent as clerks, schoolteachers and small proprietors, and only 4.0 per cent were higher-level white-collar employees (or new middle class). This means that not only four-fifths of the respondents were first-generation middle class, but also that an almost equal number had parents who came from single-income households. Many of those whose parents were from double-income households had mothers who were farmers and labourers. This confirms the finding that the majority of respondents of the new Malay middle class originated from humble class backgrounds.

It is instructive to recall the situation of the new Malay middle class a generation earlier (in the 1960s and 1970s) in Malaysia. Unlike today, when the new Malay middle class consists of a large proportion of professionals and managers in the corporate sector together with those in the government, a generation or so earlier, the new Malay middle class comprised mainly of government administrators. In his study of 105 Malay civil servants in Petaling Jaya and Kuala Lumpur conducted in the early 1970s, Nordin (1976: chapter 5) found that the ratio of the first-generation to the second-generation Malay middle class was approximately 9:1. Less than half of the fathers of the Malay administrators he studied came from the peasant and labouring classes, and almost another half from the old and marginal middle classes, while only a very small number came from the new middle class.

In Nordin's study, the proportion of the first-generation new middle class in the 1970s was very large (almost 90 per cent), while the second-generation new middle class was a small minority (10.5 per cent). In our sample, the proportion of the first-generation new Malay middle class was smaller (80 per cent), giving a ratio of first- to second-generation 3new middle class of 4:1, but the first-generation new middle class still remained an overwhelming majority.

In both Nordin's work and this study, a second-generation new Malay middle class had already emerged, although its size is still relatively small. In Nordin's study, some one-tenth of the respondents were second-generation new middle class whose fathers were professionals (judges, editors, accountants, surveyors) and administrators; practically all of them worked within the government. This situation is quite different to that found in the 1990s. In our sample, the second-generation new Malay middle class in the Klang Valley was much larger (one-fifth), consisting mainly of those in their early thirties and below, working as managers and professionals in the private sector. Their fathers were not only government administrators, but also managers and lecturers, who had started their careers in the 1960s and early 1970s. Since their fathers were members of the new middle class with high incomes, it is not surprising that they were able to reproduce their class positions for their children, by providing them with university education, and other opportunities, made possible by Malaysia's rapid economic growth in the late 1980s and early 1990s. However, since the second-generation new middle-class cohort is very small, the first-generation hypothesis still applies today for most of the new Malay middle-class respondents in the Klang Valley, and even more so for those in the two provincial towns.

Many of our new middle-class respondents have been urbanites for quite a while, and are relatively highly educated. In terms of geographical origins, a larger proportion (57.4 per cent) of the Klang Valley new Malay middle-class respondents were born in urban areas. Those born in rural areas were mostly in their forties and above, while those born in urban areas were mostly young and mid-career professionals who were second- or even third-generation urbanites. In Kota Bharu, the proportion born in urban areas was smaller than in the Klang Valley, but they still constituted a majority of all respondents. The picture is different in Kuala Terengganu, where the majority were born in rural areas. On the whole, a substantial proportion of the new Malay middle class in the three urban centres, but especially in Kuala Terengganu and Kota Bharu, had relatively recent urban experiences. Having an urban background could be an advantage, especially when it comes to gaining access to opportunities for higher education. Nevertheless, other factors need to be taken into account for entry into the new middle class.

Since many of the respondents' parents, especially those in Kuala Terengganu and Kota Bharu, were from the lower classes, their economic positions were too weak to enable them to provide tertiary educational opportunities on their own for their children. This became more difficult because they generally had large families, with 75 per cent having five or more children. While the percentage of such large families was 64.8 per cent among respondents in the Klang Valley, in the two provincial towns, it was much higher – 76.2 per cent in Kota Bharu, and 85.4 per cent in Kuala Terengganu. In fact, in Kuala Terengganu, those with six or more siblings constituted two-thirds of respondents, in Kota Bharu it was almost three-fifths, while in the Klang Valley it was almost half.

As expected, the overwhelming majority of all respondents had experienced a period of tertiary education (Table 4.4). The proportion of university graduates among them is also high (51.4 per cent), with 22.5 per cent being college graduates. It can therefore be concluded that the majority of these new Malay middle-class respondents were highly educated, with an overwhelming majority having gone to college or university, while others (about 26.0 per cent) – mainly those in the older age groups – were high school graduates who had risen through experience and hard work. About four-fifths of those with university education studied locally, while the remaining one-fifth studied abroad.

In fact, when the educational level is examined by age group (Table 4.5), a larger proportion of younger respondents had much higher educational

Table 4.4   Educational levels of respondents

Level of education	Klang Valley (n = 108)	Kota Bharu (n = 80)	Kuala Terengganu (n = 96)	All respondents (I = 284)
Secondary school	5.6	3.8	8.3	6.0 (n =17)
Post-secondary*	13.0	25.0	24.0	20.1 (n = 57)
College	50.9	52.5	26.0	22.5 (n = 64)
University (first degree)	24.1	16.3	38.5	47.2 (n = 134)
University (postgraduate degree)	6.5	2.5	3.1	4.2 (n = 12)
Total	100.0	100.0	100.0	100.0

Source: Survey data 1996 and 1997.
* High school graduates.

levels than their older counterparts. For example, among the 30 and below age cohort, 85.5 per cent were university or college graduates, compared to 75 per cent among the 31–40 age group, 62.6 per cent among the 41–50 age group, and 49.9 per cent among the oldest respondents (aged 51 and above). By region, new Malay middle-class respondents in the Klang Valley had the highest educational levels, with 81.5 per cent of the sample being university or college graduates, followed by Kota Bharu

Table 4.5   Educational levels of respondents by age group

Respondents' age (Years)	Secondary school	Post-secondary	College	University (first degree)	University (postgraduate degree)	Total (n = 284)
30 and below	—	14.4	28.9	54.2	2.4	100.0 (29.2)
31–40	5.8	19.2	23.3	50.0	1.7	100.0 (42.2)
41–50	7.5	29.9	16.4	34.3	11.9	100.0 (23.6)
51 and above	28.6	21.4	7.1	42.8	—	100.0 (4.9)

Note: Figures in brackets refer to percentages of respondents by age group.
Source: Survey data 1996 and 1997.

Table 4.6   Level of education of respondents' fathers

Level of education	Klang Valley (n = 108)	Kota Bharu (n = 80)	Kuala Terengganu (n = 96)	All respondents (N = 284)
No schooling	6.8	32.5	38.5	27.3
Primary school	43.8	36.3	47.9	43.0
Secondary school	24.7	12.5	11.5	15.7
Post-secondary	19.1	8.8	2.1	9.2
College	2.7	5.0	—	2.4
First degree	2.7	5.0	—	2.4
Total	100.0	100.0	100.0	100.0

Source: Survey data 1996 and 1997.

(71.3 per cent), and Kuala Terengganu (67.6 per cent). However, what is rather unexpected is that the proportion of university graduates was highest in Kuala Terengganu (41.6 per cent), compared to 30.6 per cent in the Klang Valley and 18.8 per cent in Kota Bharu, although the proportion of respondents from large families was also highest there.

As shown in Chapter 3, higher education was one of the principal channels of social mobility, this being especially pronounced in the case of entry into the new Malay middle class. Under the NEP, scholarships, bursaries, and educational loans provided by various state agencies had been instrumental in providing opportunities for the new Malay middle class to obtain tertiary education. In our sample, over 80 per cent of the respondents received some form of educational grant – scholarship, bursary, or loan – from one state agency or another to pursue higher education, while those who did not make it to college or university were also in receipt of minor scholarships or other forms of financial assistance while pursuing their secondary education. Without such assistance, higher education, especially abroad, would have been out of reach for most of them. In this sense, the new Malay middle class was very much state-created.

When the educational levels of respondents and their parents are taken into account, we find a stark difference between the two generations. As shown in Table 4.6, of the respondents' fathers, those with college or university education consisted of only 4.8 per cent, and those who graduated from high school[3] made up 9.2 per cent, while another 15.7 per cent had secondary education. However, a substantial proportion (27.3 per cent) had no formal schooling, and 43.0 per cent had only experienced primary education. This means that 70.3 per cent of the respondents' fathers had had little or no education at all. This figure was highest among the fathers of the oldest respondents, and lowest among the fathers of respondents in the youngest age group.

As expected, the educational levels of respondents' mothers were far lower on the whole, with 87.2 per cent having had little or no education. This was because before the country's independence, Malaysian women generally had few educational opportunities, especially in higher education. However, a small proportion of the respondents' mothers had been in secondary and tertiary education – 8.4 per cent had secondary education, 4.4 per cent graduated from high school, and 2 per cent were college graduates, although none had gone to university.

The data allow us to draw the conclusion that not only do most members of the new Malay middle class come from humble class backgrounds and large families, but also that their parents had experienced little or no education. In fact, the overwhelming majority (95.2 per cent) were 'first-generation' college or university graduates, meaning that very few of their parents (fathers and, more so, mothers) had ever gone to college or university. The fathers' educational levels were lowest for respondents in Kuala Terengganu, among whom none had achieved a college or university education. Although the largest proportion were first-generation college/university graduates, the proportion of first-generation urbanites was much smaller (50 per cent) since a large number of their parents were themselves urbanites. These figures suggest that urbanization affected the Malays well before the advent of tertiary education and export-led industrialization. As shown in Chapter 3, both tertiary education and export-oriented industrialization (which created openings for many new middle-class jobs, especially in the private sector) were post-1970 phenomena. Before 1969, Malaysia had only one university – the University of Malaya – and a few colleges. Thus, it is not surprising that among the respondents' fathers, very few ever attended university or college. However, if we take high school and college/university graduates together, we find the figure to be much higher (14 per cent), which closely corresponds with the figure of 17.6 per cent among the respondents' fathers who themselves were members of the new Malay middle class.

The above data suggests that what differentiated the new Malay middle class from their parents was their accumulation of far greater cultural capital in the form of higher education. However, it should be noted that members of the new middle class, including the new Malay middle class, not only possessed far more cultural capital in the form of tertiary education compared to their parents, but were also the most educated class in Malaysian society. While among the new Malay middle class respondents, 73.9 per cent had tertiary education, among other classes, it varied from none among the working class, to almost 50 per cent among members of the capitalist class. As shown in another study in the Klang Valley by the author (Abdul Rahman 1998), those with tertiary education made up 48 per cent among the capitalist class respondents, 6.4 per cent among those in the old middle class, and 11.3 per cent among the marginal middle class, while none were found among the working class. In fact, among workers, the majority only had lower secondary education or lower.

However, while educational opportunity had been provided by the state, class and family educational backgrounds could also have played an important role in enhancing the educational attainment of the respondents in this study. First, in terms of their class background, although 42.9 per cent of the Malay new middle-class respondents came from peasant and labouring classes, the majority (57.1 per cent) originated from non-peasant or non-labourer backgrounds. In fact, 17.6 per cent came from new middle-class families, and another 39.4 per cent from the old and marginal middle classes. Coming from the non-labouring and non-farming classes, the majority of the respondents' fathers had an advantage over other parents, because they had some financial means, over and above state financial assistance, to invest in their children's education. Those from the peasant and labouring classes could only secure education through state assistance. In this respect, family class background was an asset for the majority of them in terms of providing better life-chances for their off-spring.

Second, in terms of family educational background, especially the parents' educational level, many in the new Malay middle class had the advantage of having parents (invariably fathers) who had some education, although, of course, the levels were much lower than among the respondents themselves. As shown above, about 30 per cent of the respondents' fathers had secondary education or higher. Thus, in terms of cultural capital, about one-third of the respondents had the advantage of their parents' education, which could have motivated them to proceed further in their studies. By region, it was found that respondents in the Klang Valley had an advantage over their counterparts in the two provincial towns in terms of their fathers' educational backgrounds.

However, more than two-thirds of the respondents' fathers had had little or no education, which is clearly a high percentage. This means that for the majority of the respondents, secondary and tertiary education was a new experience for their families. That being the case, they had to struggle hard to pursue secondary and tertiary education without the advantage of their parents' cultural capital.

It should be stated that the 'first-generation' middle-class hypothesis does not apply to the new *Malay* middle class alone. In the study by the author on the new *Malaysian* middle class in the Klang Valley cited above (Abdul Rahman 1998),[4] it was found that 80 per cent of the 259 members of the new Malaysian middle-class respondents (108 Malay, 110 Chinese and 41 Indian) were first-generation, who had experienced rapid upward social mobility. They mainly came from humble class backgrounds, with about 42 per cent of their fathers being farmers and labourers, 14 per cent from the old middle class, 22 per cent from the marginal middle class, and only some 2 per cent from the capitalist class. Based on these two studies, it is clear that the new middle class, comprised of professionals and managers, is a *new* class historically among all *Malaysians*, although, perhaps, especially among *Malays*.

The new Malay middle class and affluence

It has been argued that members of the new middle class are an affluent group, with high incomes and a high propensity to consume (Robison and Goodman 1996; Hsiao 1993; So and Hsiao 1994; Hsiao 1999). They not only occupy higher-level white-collar jobs, but also enjoy relatively high pay, thus making them a relatively affluent class.

However, affluence is a difficult concept to operationalize. First, fixing a cut-off point of 'affluence' is arbitrary. While a monthly income of RM2000 and above was considered 'high' in the 1970s[5] when the mean monthly household income was only RM505 in 1976, the mean monthly household income had increased to RM2007 in 1995 (Malaysia 1996: 94); thus, the affluent RM2000 figure for the 1970s only approximates the monthly average today, and can no longer be considered high. Thus, for the purposes of this study, monthly earnings of RM4000 to RM5999 are taken to be 'high' income, with RM6000 or more classed as 'very high'. On the lower scale, incomes between RM2000 and RM3999 were considered 'middle' income, between RM2000 and RM1000 as 'low', while less than RM1000 was classed as 'very low'.

However, there is also another problem to be taken into account. In large cities such as Kuala Lumpur or Johor Bahru, where the cost of living is high, earnings would need to be higher in order to maintain the same standard of living as in the regions. Although this does not apply to goods whose prices do not significantly vary by region (especially consumer durables, such as cars, televisions, and other household appliances), prices for certain types of food and other items – in particular, property vary sharply. For example, depending on the location, a single-storey bungalow in Kuala Lumpur or Petaling Jaya, may cost between RM300 000 and RM1 000 000, while in Kota Bharu or Kuala Terengganu, the price is one-third of this or less. Thus, if respondents in the two provincial towns can own a single-storey bungalow – a property assumed to be affordable only to high-income earners – it does not follow that their incomes are higher than those living in double-storey terraced houses in the Klang Valley.

Despite these caveats, we have to contend with some statistical data on incomes. Table 4.7 provides information on individual and joint incomes of respondents. It can be seen that almost two-fifths of the respondents were those with low individual incomes – that is, earning below RM2000 per month. However, most of these respondents were young professionals who had only just started their careers, and would increase their incomes as they advanced their careers. Over one-third of the respondents fell within the middle-income category of RM2000 to RM3999 per month; another 10.9 per cent in the high-income category of RM4000 and RM5999, while less than one-fifth (16.5 per cent), mainly those in their forties and above, earned very high incomes of

Table 4.7   Individual and joint incomes of respondents

Incomes (RM)	Klang Valley (*n* = 108)		Kota Bharu (*n* = 80)		Kuala Terengganu (*n* = 96)		All respondents* (*N* = 284)	
<2000	17.6	13.9	48.8	17.5	50.0	30.2	37.3 (*n* = 106)	20.4 (*n* = 58)
2000–3999	30.6	33.0	45.0	48.8	32.3	43.8	35.2 (*n* = 100)	43.0 (*n* = 122)
4000–5999	14.8	7.8	3.8	31.3	12.5	13.5	10.9 (*n* = 31)	14.4 (*n* = 41)
6000–7999	9.3	6.5	1.3	1.3	—	5.2	3.9 (n = 11)	4.6 (*n* = 13)
8000–9999	11.1	14.8	—	—	2.1	3.1	4.9 (*n* = 14)	6.7 (*n* =19)
>10 000	16.7	24.1	1.3	1.3	3.1	4.2	7.7 (*n* = 22)	10.9 (*n* = 31)
Total	100.0		100.0		100.0		100.0	

Source: Survey data 1996 and 1997.
* Including married and unmarried respondents.

RM6000 or more a month. In fact, 7.7 per cent received the extremely high monthly income of RM10 000 or more.

When their joint incomes are considered, those in the low-income category below RM2000 decreased substantially from almost two-fifths to one-fifth, the middle-income category (RM2000–3999) increased to more than two-fifths (43 per cent), and the high-income category (RM4000 and above) also increased to more than a quarter (26.6 per cent). In addition, those in the top-income category of RM10 000 and above increased from 7.7 per cent to 10.9 per cent. By region, those from the Klang Valley were high-income earners, with 48.2 per cent earning RM4000 and above, and 38.9 per cent earning RM8000 or more. By contrast, respondents in the two provincial towns had much smaller proportions of high income-earners – in Kota Bharu, only 33.9 per cent had joint incomes of RM4000 or more, while in Kuala Terengganu, the percentage was much lower (26.0 per cent). This finding shows that a substantial proportion of new Malay middle-class respondents, especially concentrated in the Klang Valley, were affluent, while others had the potential to become affluent.

In addition to high incomes, new Malay middle-class respondents also enjoyed various perks. As shown in Table 4.8, 14.8 per cent were provided with official cars (including 5.2 per cent with drivers), 62.6 per cent received annual bonuses, while 8.4 per cent were provided with houses.

Table 4.8   Benefits provided by respondents' employers

Benefits	Klang Valley (*n* = 108)	Kota Bharu (*n* = 80)	Kuala Terengganu (*n* = 96)	All respondents (*N* = 284)
Car	1.4	2.5	2.1	2.0
House	—	—	1.0	0.4
Driver	1.4	3.8	3.1	2.8
Bonus	46.6	55.0	45.8	49.0
Car & driver	2.7	—	2.1	1.6
Car & bonus	11.0	2.5	4.2	5.6
House & driver	1.4	—	—	0.4
House & bonus	—	2.5	4.2	2.4
Car, house & bonus	6.4	6.3	3.1	5.2
Car, house, driver & bonus	—	—	1.0	0.8
None	27.4	27.5	32.3	29.3
Total	100.0	100.0	100.0	100.0

Source: Survey data 1996 and 1997.

The proportion provided with drivers was 5.5 per cent in the Klang Valley, 3.8 per cent in Kota Bharu, and 6.2 per cent in Kuala Terengganu. Respondents could enjoy these perks because the organizations they worked for were fairly large. While 45.4 per cent of their organizations had less than 50 employees, the rest had 50 or more, with 47.5 per cent having more than 100 employees. In fact, among this last group, over a quarter worked for very big organizations, with 1000 employees or more.

Work culture and *Melayu Baru*

Wage rates in employment are fixed by employers, whether this is the government or the private sector. However, the high and middle incomes obtained by many new Malay middle-class respondents in this study were partly attributable to their qualifications, skills, experience, and occupational status in the organizational hierarchy. As shown in Table 4.2, above in terms of professional experience, not all respondents became managerial or professional workers immediately after completing their education. For example, while about three-fifths immediately started their career as managerial or professionals workers, and over the years, experienced career mobility in the same professional category, the remaining two-fifths took a different route, beginning near the bottom of their organizations as clerical, service, production and agricultural workers. (Those with secondary education mostly started this way.) However, they worked their way up, and changed jobs several times before becoming managers or professionals. Among respondents, while 48.9 per cent had not changed jobs, more than half had changed their jobs at least once, including 31.7 per cent who had changed twice or more (Table 4.9). This finding shows that over the last two decades, a substantial proportion of the respondents had been fairly mobile in order to advance themselves. By comparison, a larger proportion of the Klang Valley respondents had changed jobs more often than in either Kota Bharu or Kuala Terengganu. Despite their present positions, a significant number also planned to change jobs in the near future, while over one-quarter were still hesitating, although the majority felt quite comfortable with their present position and did not contemplate any change. This suggests that many respondents were ambitious, especially the young and mid-career professionals and managers, including a few in senior management who planned to leave their present jobs and start their own businesses.[6]

Ambitions aside, what they achieved is also very much related to their attitudes and commitments to work. Many respondents, especially those from the Klang Valley, reported that they often worked more than eight

Table 4.9 Occupational mobility of respondents

	Klang Valley (*n* = 108)	*Kota Bharu* (*n* = 80)	*Kuala Terengganu* (*n* = 96)	*All respondents* (*N* = 284)
Do you plan to change your job in near future?				
• Yes	16.7	17.5	16.7	16.9
• May be	38.0	20.0	19.8	26.8
• No	45.4	62.5	63.5	56.3
Number of times of job change				
• None	45.4	56.2	46.8	48.9
• Once	13.9	16.3	28.1	19.4
• Twice	24.1	12.5	11.5	16.5
• Three times	13.0	11.3	6.3	10.2
• Four times	0.9	1.3	3.1	1.8
• Five or more	2.8	2.5	4.2	3.2

Source: Survey data 1996 and 1997.

hours a day. This is so because 98 per cent of respondents there were from the private sector, whose work hours often extended beyond work hours in the government sector.

In terms of the work ethic, about three-quarters of the respondents rated themselves as hard-working or very hard-working, a substantial minority saw themselves as moderately hard-working, and only a few regarded themselves as slow or uncommitted to their work. This finding corresponds with other indicators of the work ethic. In fact, half of the respondents considered themselves to be workaholic, especially those working in the private sector. Many of them took back urgent office work to complete at home. The fact that over one-third very often did not take all their annual leave while another 37 per cent sometimes did not do so suggests the strong commitment to work among the majority of respondents. Many of those who did not use up their annual leave, attributed it to their busy work schedule. Overall, it can be concluded that respondents were generally hard-working, and motivated to perform well in their jobs. All these suggest that there has been a transformation in their work culture and ethics, indicating that they had accepted the work regime of a rapidly industrializing society.

Malay work culture has been a subject of debate for quite some time (Mahathir Mohamad 1970; Senu Abdul Rahman 1971; Tham Soong Chee 1977), the latest being the call to Malays by Prime Minister Mahathir Mohamad in 1991 to change their work culture by becoming *Melayu Baru* (the New Malay) (see Chapter 9 for a detailed discussion of this issue). In practice, as indicated in the study above, many Malay managers and professionals have already developed such a work culture, although they might not describe themselves using the term *Melayu Baru*. The qualitative data obtained by the author through interviews with a number of corporate figures who had groomed many Malay managers and profes-sionals, or who had working experience with them confirm this. Tun Ismail Mohamed Ali, the former Governor of Bank Negara Malaysia (Malaysian Central Bank) for 18 years until 1978, and subsequently Chairman of the Board of Directors of Permodalan Nasional Berhad (PNB) and later Advisor to the board until his death in 1998, had been entrusted by the Malaysian government with numerous tasks of developing and enhancing Malay entrepreneurship, management skills and professionalism. In an interview conducted with the author in January 1996,[7] he admitted to a feeling of pride that as a result of the NEP, Malaysia has seen the emergence of many competent, industrious and talented Malay professionals and managers at the helm not only of Bumiputera companies but also of several locally-based foreign companies. To him, Malaysia's development success was due, in no small way, to the leadership and management skills of these managers and professionals. Another important corporate figure, Tan Sri Geh Ik Cheong[8] who has had considerable experience of working with Malay managers and professionals, held the same view. In his opinion, Malay managers and professionals were just as good, if not better, than many Chinese managers and professionals. As he put it:

> To me, many Bumiputera whom I know are excellent, and some of them are even better than non-Bumiputera. To me, Malay participation [at managerial levels] has developed to a satisfactory level. There is an evidence of this – not only the Bumiputera are able to perform well inside the country, but many have also gone abroad to compete. I think the perception of the Malay *kampung* boy as not being able to learn, perform and assimilate [new work values] has gone by. I think once he is educated, the Malay is as good as anyone else. That is why I am not a great believer in Dr. Mahathir's book, *The Malay Dilemma*. It is all a question of opportunity. It is the type of education you have.[9]

The emergence of this new work culture is also acknowledged by Malay managers themselves. Tan Sri Khalid Ibrahim,[10] a successful Malay manager, who, as the Group Chief Executive Officer in charge of the PNB management under Tun Ismail for many years, felt that from his experience in PNB and many other companies, Malay managers and professionals have proven their mettle.

Conclusions

This chapter has argued that the new Malay middle class in Malaysia is a new class historically, which has emerged and expanded through the rapid process of transformation over more than three decades and is still in the process of formation. Just as in East Asia, the new Malay middle class is a 'first-generation' middle class which has experienced intergenerational mobility. As managers, professionals and administrators, the member of this class work in relatively large organizations, are industrious, have developed a new work culture, and have earned the trust and confidence of others in their ability. In their work, they also receive relatively high incomes and experience newly found affluence. With affluence, they want to secure the better things in life for their families, such as material comfort to develop lifestyles of their own, and to provide opportunities for their children to attain higher education. However, do such activities transform them from a 'class in itself' into a 'class for itself', clearly differentiated from other classes, especially the lower classes? This can be examined by looking into the relations between new Malay middle-class respondents and their families of origin, lifestyles, relationships with the communities they live in, and their roles in politics, democratization, and the growth of civil society. All these questions will be addressed in Chapters 5, 6, 7 and 8.

5
The New Malay Middle-Class Family

This chapter considers several interrelated questions about the impact of modernization, industrialization and urbanization on the new Malay middle-class family. First, what is the pattern of marriage and parenthood among the new Malay middle class? Second, is the Malay middle-class family becoming more egalitarian, with power shared between husbands and wives? Third, is the new Malay middle-class family preoccupied with class reproduction? Fourth, is the fact that the new Malay middle-class family is becoming increasingly nuclear leading to its isolation and the breakdown of extended kin networks? These four questions are discussed in the light of our empirical study conducted among the new Malay middle class in the Klang Valley and in the two provincial towns of Kota Bharu and Kuala Terengganu. In the course of the discussion, comparisons will be drawn, wherever possible, with other studies of both the new middle class and the working class.

Marriage and parenthood among the new Malay middle class

Marriage patterns

It will be suggested in this section that modernization and new middle-class lifestyles have not led to the widespread rejection of marriage, and that parenthood continues to be highly valued in the private lives of modern middle-class Malays in both the metropolitan city and in the provincial towns. This can be seen, among other things, from an examination of the percentage of married respondents, their age at first marriage and choice of spouse as well as the number of children they have or would like to have.

In the sample, the percentage of respondents who had been married at one time or another was high. Of the 284 respondents in the study, 231 (81.3 per

Table 5.1   Respondents' marital status

Marital status	Klang Valley (n = 108)	Kota Bharu (n = 80)	Kuala Terengganu (n = 96)	All respondents (N = 284)
Married	74.1	87.5	84.4	81.3 (n = 231)
Widowed	2.8	—	1.0	1.0 (n = 3)
Divorced	0.9	—	—	0.4 (n = 1)
Single	22.2	12.5	14.6	17.3 (n = 49)

Source: Survey data 1996 and 1997.

cent) were married, 1.0 per cent were widowed, 0.4 per cent were divorced, and 17.3 per cent were still single (Table 5.1). As expected, the percentage of respondents who was, were, or had been, married highest in Kota Bharu (87.5 per cent) and Kuala Terengganu (84.4 per cent), and although lower by comparison, was still high in the Klang Valley (74.1 per cent).

The universal trend in the increase in age at first marriage in Malaysia noted by other scholars (for example, Jones 1994)[1] is also found in this study. The mean age at first marriage of the respondents was 25.9 years old, with the highest being among respondents in the Klang Valley (26.7), followed by Kuala Terengganu (26.0 per cent) and Kota Bharu (25.6) (Table 5.2). The mean age for Malay men was higher, that is, 26.8 years while for women, it was almost two years lower, that is, 24.9 years. The mean age at first marriage of our respondents was two years higher than that of the Malay administrative middle class in Kuala Lumpur and Petaling Jaya as recorded by Nordin (1976: 242) two decades earlier. In the latter study, the mean age at first marriage of all male respondents was 24.1. Our study, nevertheless, corresponds with a recent study by Fatimah Abdullah (1994) of the Malay middle-class family in a housing estate in Kuala Lumpur which found mean ages at first marriage to be 27 and 23.2 years respectively for male and females.

However, there is a clear difference between the mean age at first marriage of the contemporary new Malay middle class and of Malay workers, as well as of the new Chinese and the Indian middle classes. A recent study of a group of Malay workers in the Klang Valley shows that their mean age at first marriage was much lower – that is, 24.3 – while it was 27.3 and 27.9 respectively among new Chinese and Indian middle-class respondents (Abdul Rahman 1998).[2]

Table 5.2   Respondents' age at first marriage

Age at first marriage (years)	Klang Valley (n = 83)*	Kota Bharu (n = 70)*	Kuala Terengganu (n = 82)*	All respondents (N = 235)*
Below 20	1.2	4.3	2.4	2.6
21–25	42.2	51.4	35.4	42.6
26–30	45.8	35.7	52.4	45.1
31–35	7.2	7.1	8.5	7.6
36 and above	3.6	1.4	1.2	2.1
Total	100.0	100.0	100.0	100.0
Mean age at first marriage				
• Male	—	—	—	26.8
• Female	—	—	—	24.9
• All	26.7	25.6	26.0	26.1

Source: Survey data 1996 and 1997.
*Respondents who had been married at some time in their lives.

Another tendency found in our study is the phenomenon of late marriages among a section of new Malay middle-class respondents. As shown in Table 5.2, while 45.2 per cent were already married at 25 years of age or younger, another 45.1 per cent married between the ages of 26 and 30, and about 10 per cent married after reaching the age of 30. The proportion marrying after 30 was highest in the Klang Valley (10.8 per cent), followed by Kuala Terengganu (9.7 per cent) and Kota Bharu (8.5 per cent). This tendency can be corroborated further when we examine the age of 49 respondents – 28 male and 21 female – who were still single at the time of the study. Of this figure, 36.7 per cent were aged 25 and below, 42.9 per cent were in the 26–30 age group, while the remaining 20.4 per cent were 31 or above. By sex, there was a higher proportion of older unmarried female than unmarried male respondents – 89.3 per cent of unmarried males were 30 and below, compared to only 66.6 per cent of unmarried females in our survey; only 10.7 per cent of unmarried males were in the older age group of 31 and above, compared to 33.4 per cent of unmarried females, giving a ratio of 1:2.3. Among unmarried female respondents, a small proportion (4.8 per cent) was still single in their forties.

It becomes clear from further analysis, however, that late marriages, do not mean rejection of marriage, but only marriage delayed.[3] Although our study did not closely examine the reasons for delaying marriage, our interviews suggest that among men, it was a matter of establishing themselves in their careers before making a commitment to marriage. There is a difference for women because they have usually been more passive in choosing spouses and settling down. When it comes to marriage and divorce in Malay culture, Malays invoke *jodoh,* meaning 'fated match', or the lack of it. Thus, when they are not yet married after a certain age, they always attribute it to *tiada jodoh* (no appropriate match) and not to some other reason, such as, not wanting to settle down.

As Muslims, many Malays regard marriage as a sacred social institution to enter into once one comes of age. Nevertheless, this does not mean that divorces are uncommon. Of all our respondents, about 10 per cent had experienced divorce in their marital lives. The figure for divorce was highest in Kota Bharu (11.4 per cent), followed by the Klang Valley (9.6 per cent) and Kuala Terengganu (8.5 per cent). However, the overwhelming majority of respondents had remained in marriage, and all but one of those who had divorced had remarried.

Marriage among new Malay middle-class respondents tends to be homogamous – that is, they tend to marry within the same class. However, although intra-class marriages are quite common, men tend to marry lower, while women marry higher. As shown in Table 5.3, among male respondents, 47.8 per cent of their spouses were housewives, 29.1 per cent were in new middle-class occupations as professionals and managers, and another 23.1 per cent were in the marginal middle class, consisting of lower white-collar employees. The opposite picture, however, prevailed among female respondents. The majority (60.6 per cent) of their husbands were from the new middle class of professionals and managers whose job statuses were higher than theirs. However, 28.8 per cent had married downwards, to members of the marginal middle class.

Table 5.3   Class position of spouses of respondents by sex of respondents

	Class position of spouses				
Respondents' class position	*New middle class*	*Marginal middle class*	*Housewives*	*Retired*	*Total (N = 235)**
Male New Middle Class	29.1	23.1	47.8	—	100.0 *(n = 169)*
Female New Middle Class	60.6	28.8	—	10.6	100.0 *(n = 66)*

Source: Survey data 1996 and 1997.
* Married respondents only

There is a clear difference between the educational levels of the spouses of male and female respondents. While men tended to marry those with lower educational achievements, women tended to marry those at a higher or a similar education al level. Overall, among all male respondents, 68.6 per cent had tertiary education, while among their spouses, the proportion with tertiary education was much lower (35.1 per cent). Among female new middle-class respondents, the opposite is true – that is, their husbands were at the same or a higher educational level. Among men, the higher their qualification, the greater the mismatch between their educational levels and those of their spouses. For example, among 30 male respondents with a first degree, only 35.9 per cent had the same qualifications, while almost two-thirds had college education or less. Among the eight male respondents with postgraduate degrees, only one of their spouses had the same level of qualification, while the remaining seven only had college or secondary school qualifications. Among the 53 male respondents with lower or upper secondary education, the majority of their spouses had the same qualifications. In short, among men, although some married those with the same qualifications, the majority tended to marry lower.

The picture is quite different among female new middle-class respondents. Among the 30 who were college graduates, 50 per cent of their husbands were also college graduates, while another 31.2 per cent had graduated from universities. Among the 16 with first degrees, 80 per cent of their husbands also had the same qualifications, but the remaining 20 per cent were high school or college graduates. All those with postgraduate degrees also had husbands with the same qualifications. These facts suggest that the majority of female new Malay middle-class respondents married men with the same or higher educational qualifications, and only a small proportion married downwards.

Family size

The age of a woman at the first time of marriage affects fertility and hence the number of children. However, as shown in Table 5.4, while 8.9 per cent of married respondents at the time of the study had no children, 29.4 per cent had one to two, 34.4 per cent had three to four, and another 26 per cent had five or more children. In fact, the percentage with four children or more, was much higher, at 43.4 per cent. The overall mean number of children per family at the time of study was 3.2, with the highest figure being recorded in Kota Bharu (3.5), followed by Kuala Terengganu (3.3) and the Klang Valley (3.1).

Table 5.4 Respondents' current and preferred number of children*

Number of children per family	Klang Valley (n = 83)		Kota Bharu (n = 70)		Kuala Terengganu (n = 82)		All Respondents (N = 235)	
	1	*2*	*1*	*2*	*1*	*2*	*1*	*2*
None	6.0	—	7.1	—	13.4	—	8.9	—
One	15.7	1.3	17.2	—	12.2	—	14.0	0.4 (n = 1)
Two	19.3	13.8	10.2	1.4	15.8	3.7	15.4	6.5 (n = 15)
Three	15.7	20.0	22.85	14.3	10.9	13.6	17.4	16.0 (n = 37)
Four	25.3	27.5	7.1	14.3	18.3	16.0	17.4	19.5 (n = 45)
Five and above	18.0	37.5	35.6	70.0	29.4	66.7	26.0	57.6 (n = 133)
Total	100.0	100.0	100.0	100.0	100.0	100.0	100.0	100.0
Mean	3.1	4.2	3.5	5.2	3.3	5.1	3.2	4.9

Source: Survey data 1996 and 1997.
* Including ever married, divorced or widowed.
Notes: 1. Current number of children.
       2. Preferred number of children.

There is a strong possibility that the number of children would have increased since the study because, at the time of the survey, most respondents and their spouses were not only still of reproductive age, but also expressed preference for large families. The overall mean for the total preferred number of children was 4.9, with the highest number again being in Kota Bharu (5.2), followed by Kuala Terengganu (5.1), and the Klang Valley (4.2) (Table 5.4). Of all married respondents, 57.4 per cent wanted large families of five or more children. This was especially the case in Kota Bharu, where 70 per cent wanted five or more children, while in Kuala Terengganu, the percentage was still high (66.7 per cent). Only in the Klang Valley, do we have a much lower, but still a substantial proportion of 37.5 per cent who preferred five or more children.

It is interesting to compare family size among the new Malay middle class over the last three decades to see whether it has tended towards becoming smaller, bigger or remaining the same. In the early 1970s, Nordin's study (1976: 168, 176) of 105 Malay administrative middle-class respondents in Kuala Lumpur and Petaling Jaya found that the number of children that respondents had was slightly smaller than the number in our sample, while the respondents' ages were slightly older by comparison.[4] For example, the average number of children per family in Nordin's sample was 2.85, compared to 3.1 in our Klang Valley sample or an average figure of 3.2 in the three urban centres in our study. In terms of percentage distribution, those with five or more children were only 14.3 per cent in Nordin's sample, compared to almost double the figure (26 per cent) in our overall sample, while those with three or four children made up 36.2 per cent of his sample, only slightly higher than the 34.8 per cent recorded in our sample. Taking all respondents with three or more children per family, the figure was much higher in our sample (60.8 per cent), compared to 50.2 per cent in Nordin's sample. It is true that metropolitan middle-class families, such as those in the Klang Valley, tend to have smaller family sizes than their counterparts in provincial towns. Nevertheless, even if we compare the Klang Valley sample in our study with Nordin's, our respondents still had a bigger family size, with 59 per cent having three or more children, compared to 50.2 per cent in Nordin's study. Even the preferred mean number of children among respondents in Nordin's study was only 3.1, compared to 4.2 in our Klang Valley sample.

These findings correspond to those in Fatimah's study of 200 new Malay middle-class families conducted in the early 1990s in Taman Tun Dr. Ismail, Kuala Lumpur (Fatimah Abdullah 1994). In her study, the mean number of children per family was 2.7. By percentage distribution, 10.7 per cent had large families with five or more children, 45.4 per cent had 3 to 4 children, 36.2 per cent had 1 to 2 children, while 7.7 per cent had none. These figures suggest that a majority (56.1 per cent) had three or more children (Fatimah Abdullah 1994: 130),[5] which was still bigger than in Nordin's sample.

Of course, the samples in all three studies were too 'purposive' to enable us to draw any broad conclusions regarding general trends in marriage and parenthood among the new Malay middle class. Nevertheless, the three studies do suggest that members of the new Malay middle class today tend to prefer large families, and that their average family sizes have not been decreasing, despite the process of modernization.[6] Two major developments could be adduced as reasons for this apparent paradox. While there was a strong emphasis on family planning and birth control in the 1960s and 1970s (as one example of this, the National Family Planning Board was set up in 1966), there was a policy reversal in 1984, when Prime Minister Mahathir Mohamad introduced the population target of 70 million to be achieved by the year 2100 (Azizah Kassim 1984; Abdul Majid Mat Salleh 1989).

At the same time, the period since the 1970s also witnessed the growing influence of the *dakwah* (Islamic revivalist) movement among Malays and Muslims (Chandra Muzaffar 1987; Zainah Anwar 1987; Hussin Mutalib 1990). Regarding children as gifts of God, it is not uncommon today to find members of the Islamic Youth Movement (ABIM) or other Muslim new Malay middle-class groups having large families. There seems to be a positive correlation between religiosity and large family size. The author's personal observations among the religiously-oriented new Malay middle-class friends and acquaintances in the Klang Valley and elsewhere indicate that they have, or plan to have, large families. This is confirmed in this study which shows the mean number of children preferred by respondents who were members of religious movements as being 4.3 – that is, higher than among non-members, which was 4.1. In addition, the preferred mean number of children among the most religiously-inclined respondents was 4.6, compared to 3.7 among the more secular respondents. In fact, when we examine the distribution of respondents who preferred five children or more, it is clear that the more fervently religious topped the list. Thus, it may be concluded that both the 70 million policy propounded by Mahathir and more so the *dakwah* movement have reinforced the traditional Malay preference for large families despite the rapid modernization of Malaysian society over the last three decades.

Power-sharing between new Malay middle-class couples

It has been argued that, following the process of urbanization, industrialization and modernization the middle-class family tends towards a greater equalization of power between husband and wife, with both becoming partners in a more egalitarian or symmetrical relationship (Willmott 1969; Young and Willmott 1973; Edgell 1980; Bell 1968).[7] To what extent was this true among our new Malay middle-class respondents? Are new Malay middle class women merely duty-bound wives at the command of their husbands, or are they partners?

The answer to these questions may be gleaned from our survey data as well as from our interviews. It is found that the most common practice among our respondents has been for both husbands and wives to discuss and make decisions together about various issues, showing a certain degree of partnership and egalitarianism between the partners. For example, when it comes to buying houses and expensive household items, as well as deciding on the children's education, about four-fifths of respondents said they made decisions together (in some cases, they involved their children as well). However, when buying daily necessities, wives usually had a greater say than their husbands.

Nevertheless, despite joint decision-making in most cases, it is still the tendency among Malay families for husbands to have a greater say, especially when it comes to major decisions such as buying the family house and expensive household items. For example, when buying the family house, while 75.8 per cent of the respondents reported that both husbands and wives made decisions together, another 20.3 per cent reported that it was the husbands who made such decisions; in the case of buying expensive household items, while 77.4 per cent made decisions together, in another 16 per cent of cases the decisions only involved the husbands. The tendency to male dominance in decision-making was more pronounced among Klang Valley respondents than among those in either Kota Bharu or Kuala Terengganu. This may be due to the fact that many spouses of Klang Valley male respondents were full-time house-wives who were financially dependent on their husbands, whereas East Coast women, especially those in Kota Bharu, had traditionally been more independent. Nevertheless, it does not mean that wives had no say in such cases. As cautioned by Banks (1983) in his ethnographic study of Malay kinship over a decade ago,

> one should not underplay the great freedom and power of women in Malay society, particularly among the rural poor and among educated urbanites. Women will have an important say in all of the major decisions that their husbands make, and through their passive role, they will have the prerogative of criticizing bad decisions once they have been made, although they should never do so in public. (Banks 1983: 96)

Our findings above, along with Banks' observation, suggest that while there is male dominance to some extent, there is some degree of balance of power within marriage in the Malay middle-class family. Although in the main, wives have to defer to their husbands' wishes in major decisions, their views do have to be heeded. This study, however, is not able to probe deeper into power relationships within families, which would require a more detailed ethnographic approach than that adopted here.

Class reproduction among the new Malay middle class

One major concern of the middle-class family is class reproduction. Will the younger generation be able to reproduce their parents' class position? Will they go up or go down? As shown in earlier chapters, in Malaysia, educational success is perceived as the key avenue for social mobility. Given the 'credential explosion' in Malaysia in the last decade or so, with intense competition among young students to enter tertiary education, new Malay middle-class respondents manifested a 'fear of falling' with regard to their children's future. They were aware that the ability of their children to reproduce their class position was not assured, and thus put tremendous pressure on them to excel in their studies.

As Malaysia gradually moved up the technological ladder, education in science- and technology-related subjects has been accorded greater emphasis in the school curriculum. Among the subjects emphasized are English and Mathematics (and also Computer Studies) in which students were expected to do well so that they could pursue tertiary-level courses considered to be in great demand in the market. To score good results in public examinations, many parents feel their children cannot merely rely on formal teaching and coaching from their schoolteachers. Thus, private tuition has become a flourishing industry, thriving on the insecurity of parents, especially those from the new middle class.

Our respondents took particular interest in their children's education in the hope that they would do well. In our study, it was found that two-thirds of new Malay middle-class parents with school-going children sent the latter for English and Mathematics tuition, while another 58.1 per cent sent their children for computer lessons (Table 5.5). The reliance on private tuition in these three subjects was highest in the Klang Valley sample, involving more than three-quarters of respondents, compared to much lower percentages in the Kota Bharu and Kuala Terengganu samples.

Besides tuition in curricular subjects, it has also become a trend among middle-class parents, especially those in metropolitan cities, to send their children for art lessons (such as music, dancing or painting) because of the belief that such lessons would not only inculcate finer qualities in them but also to enhance their social status. This trend is particularly pronounced in the Klang Valley, where 60.7 per cent of our respondents with children attending school sent their children for art lessons. By contrast, in the two provincial towns, however, this trend had not really caught on: In Kota Bharu, only 25 per cent of the parents sent their children for art lessons, while in Kuala Terengganu, the percentage was higher (36.7 per cent).

Table 5.5   Tuition and other outside school lessons/activities for children of new Malay middle-class and working-class respondents

Tuition/ activities	Malay middle-class respondents				Malay workers in Klang Valley
	Klang Valley	*Kota Bharu*	*Kuala Terengganu*	*All Malay middle class respondents*	
	*(n = 61)**	*(n = 48)**	*(n = 44)**	*(N = 158)**	*(N = 57)**
English tuition					
• Yes	75.4	64.6	56.3	66.2	40.8
• No	24.6	35.4	43.8	33.8	59.2
Mathematics tuition					
• Yes	78.7	58.3	59.6	66.7	40.8
• No	21.3	41.7	40.4	33.3	59.2
Computer lessons					
• Yes	75.4	48.9	40.4	58.1	40.8
• No	24.6	51.1	59.6	41.9	59.2
Art lessons					
• Yes	60.7	25.0	36.7	42.4	22.4
• No	39.3	75.0	63.3	57.6	77.6
Religious instruction					
• Instruction by religious teacher	98.4	70.8	81.6	84.8	57.1
• Instruction by parents	1.6	29.2	18.4	15.2	42.9
Join Summer Camp					
• Yes	32.8	15.2	14.9	22.1	—
• No	67.2	84.8	85.1	77.9	100.0

Source: Survey data 1996 and 1997.
*Respondents with *school-going* children attending school.

Malay parents, especially those in big cities, are very anxious about the religious and moral upbringing of their children. Among Malays, the traditional practice has been for every child to be taught the basic tenets of Islam and to become a practising Muslim by the time he or she reaches puberty. In the past, the children's religious and moral upbringing was considered to be the responsibility of parents, while religious teachers in the community played a very important role in teaching children how to read the Quran. Today, much of this role has been transferred to other institutions such as schools, religious instructors and motivation 'experts'.

While Islamic Studies has already been made compulsory for Muslim students in government schools,[8] many Malay parents still do not have confidence that the level of religious instruction in the school curriculum is sufficiently effective to instill moral and religious values in their children. This issue has been thrown into sharp focus in recent years, following pronouncements by ministers and other public figures about moral problems among youth that have triggered moral panic in the country.[9]

This concern with what was perceived as a 'moral crisis' was clearly reflected among our respondents in the three urban centres. Many new Malay middle class parents in our study responded to these challenges by sending their children to attend religious instruction outside school hours, and by sending them to 'summer camps', organized by self-proclaimed motivation 'experts' over and above the Islamic Studies already taught in schools. While a few parents, especially those in Kota Bharu and Kuala Terengganu, took it upon themselves to guide their children as far as religion was concerned, the overwhelming majority relied on *ustaz* or *ustazah* (religious teachers) for various types of religious instruction, such as Quran reading, as well as reciting and performing prayers. This heavy reliance on outside institutions was most pronounced among Klang Valley middle-class respondents, whereby 98.4 per cent sent their children for religious instruction, while 32.8 per cent also sent them for short motivation courses held at the weekends or during school holidays. However, in Kota Bharu and Kuala Terengganu, although many parents sent their children for religious instruction, none sent them to attend motivation courses (Table 5.5). This is understandable because very few 'summer camps' are organized in the two provincial towns and, furthermore, the parents' perception of the 'moral crisis' is that it is largely a problem of big cities such as Kuala Lumpur and Petaling Jaya.

The extent of interest shown in their children's education by many new Malay middle-class parents which leads them to send them to additional and tuition classes in order that they will excel in their studies illustrates their high expectations of their children. Such high expectations can also be seen in their preferences for their children's future careers. Compared to Malay working-class parents, new Malay middle-class parents tended to be clearer about the career choices for their children. This is evidenced by the fact that only about a quarter of new Malay middle-class respondents in this study would leave such decisions to their children, compared to more than two-fifths of Malay working-class parents. This tendency reflects greater middle-class concerns for class reproduction, while working-class respondents were more likely to leave their children to

Table 5.6   Parents' preference for son's career*

	Klang Valley (n = 62)		Kota Bharu (n = 66)		Kuala Terengganu (n = 69)		All respondents (n = 197)	
	1	*2*	*1*	*2*	*1*	*2*	*1*	*2*
Medicine	19.4	3.3	18.2	6.2	36.2	7.4	24.9	5.7
Engineering	32.3	11.7	16.7	7.7	17.4	16.2	21.8	11.9
Information Technology	14.5	26.7	1.5	9.2	11.6	8.8	9.1	14.5
Accountancy	9.7	23.3	10.6	10.8	1.4	7.4	7.1	13.5
Education	—	5.0	7.6	3.1	—	5.9	2.5	4.7
Business	19.4	23.3	6.1	10.8	5.8	20.6	10.2	18.1
Let children decide	4.8	6.7	39.4	52.3	27.5	33.9	24.4	31.6
Total	100.0	100.0	100.0	100.0	100.0	100.0	100.0	100.0

Source: Survey data 1996 and 1997.
* Respondents with male school-going children only
Notes: 1 = First choice.
        2 = Second choice.

make such choices since they themselves were not highly educated. Nevertheless, many Malay working-class respondents also had high expectations of their children, reflected in the fact that two-fifths sent their children for tuition in English, Mathematics and Computer Studies (Table 5.5).

Table 5.6 shows parents' career preferences for their male children, many of them preferring their sons to be doctors (24.9 per cent), engineers (21.8 per cent), businessmen (10.2 per cent), or to pursue a career in information technology (9.1 per cent), while an extremely small proportion (2.5 per cent) would want their children to be lecturers or teachers. Even as a second choice, teaching still attracted only a very small number (4.7 per cent). When preference for occupational sector is examined, the government sector has become a sector of last resort in both first and second choices, attracting less than 20 per cent of the respondents. For example, while in Kota Bharu and Kuala Terengganu, about a quarter to a fifth of the new Malay middle-class respondents preferred their children to work with the government, in the Klang Valley, the proportion was only 4.7 per cent. The majority of parents in the metropolitan city wanted their children to set up their own businesses, or to join the private sector. Preference for work in the private sector or for setting up their own businesses and being independent of the state was very strong in each of the three urban centres.

Table 5.7   Parents' preference for daughter's career*

	Klang Valley (n = 60)		Kota Bharu (n = 67)		Kuala Terengganu (n = 67)		All respondents (N = 194)	
	1	*2*	*1*	*2*	*1*	*2*	*1*	*2*
Medicine	24.6	7.7	14.9	1.6	26.9	7.7	22.0	5.5
Engineering	1.8	1.9	1.5	—	—	3.1	1.0	1.6
Information Technology	8.8	11.5	7.5	3.1	4.5	9.2	6.8	7.7
Accountancy	24.6	32.7	6.0	12.5	6.0	7.7	11.5	16.6
Education	21.1	23.1	26.9	25.0	25.4	20.0	24.6	22.6
Business	12.3	15.4	4.5	4.7	3.0	10.8	6.3	9.9
Let children decide	7.0	7.7	38.8	53.2	34.4	41.5	27.7	35.9
Total	100.0	100.0	100.0	100.0	100.0	100.0	100.0	100.0

Source: Survey data 1996 and 1997.
* Respondents with female school-going children only.
Notes: 1 = First choice.
2 = Second choice.

There are, however, some differences among new Malay middle-class respondents with regard to career preferences for their daughters. While 22 per cent expressed a preference for their daughters to become doctors, just as for their sons, only one per cent wanted them to be engineers (Table 5.7). However, a substantial number of parents regarded education and accountancy as suitable for girls. For example, 24.6 per cent of parents preferred their daughters to be lecturers or teachers, and another 11.5 per cent to be accountants, while only 6.3 per cent were prepared to allow them to become businesswomen. In terms of occupational sector, the tendency of moving out of the government was also strong (only 36.1 per cent preferred the government sector) although for sons, the tendency was stronger. The majority of parents preferred their female children to work with the private sector or to set up their own businesses.

In contrast to new Malay middle-class parents, about two-fifths of Malay working-class respondents would rather let their children choose their own careers (Table 5.8). However, among those working-class parents who indicated career preferences for their children, there were also gender differences. Many working-class respondents (33.3 per cent) expressed a preference for their daughters to be teachers, while for sons, the corresponding percentage was very low (3.6 per cent), since they preferred the latter to be engineers (16.4 per cent) or doctors (10.9 per

Table 5.8   Malay workers in the Klang Valley: parents' preference for children's careers (first choice only)

	Son (*n* = 55)*	Daughter (*n* = 57)**
(a) Career In		
• Medicine	10.9	5.3
• Engineering	16.4	3.5
• Information Technology	5.5	3.5
• Accountancy	7.3	8.8
• Education	3.6	33.3
• Business	7.3	5.3
• Let children decide	49.0	40.3
(b) Occupational sector		
• Government sector	27.3	42.1
• Private sector	58.2	47.4
• Set up own business	14.5	10.5

Source: Survey data 1997.
* Those with male children only.
** Those with female children only.

cent). By sector too, only a small proportion (27.3 per cent) preferred their male children to work for the government, whereas for female children, the percentage was much bigger (42.1 per cent). Nevertheless, for both male and female children, the majority of Malay working-class parents preferred their children to work with the private sector or to be self-employed.

The above data suggest that a transformation of values regarding career preferences among Malays has taken place over the last three decades. While in the 1960s, careers as government administrators and politicians were considered the 'in thing' among Malays (Alatas 1972: chapter 5), today, doctors, engineers, managers and other professionals working in the private sector or for themselves have come to be regarded as prestigious and preferable. This is true among both the new Malay middle class and the Malay working class. The value transformations among Malays, however, could already be detected since the 1970s, probably from the implementation of the NEP in 1971. In Nordin's study (1976: 270), while one-third of his Malay administrative middle-class respondents left it to their children to decide their careers, 61 per cent wanted their children to become professionals (such as doctors, engineers, architects, accountants and lawyers), including a small proportion (7.6 per cent) who wanted them to go into business. However, even though the 1970s was a decade during which such values germinated, the 1990s have seen the consolidation of these values across Malay society.

Nuclear family and relationships with extended kin

Have the emergence of the nuclear family and the attendant concern of the new Malay middle class for their children affected their relations with their extended kin? This chapter questions the notion that the emergence of the conjugal nuclear family leads to its isolation and the breakdown of extended kin relations. It is argued here that although nuclearization is the dominant trend and the nuclear family[10] is the dominant family form among the new Malay middle class, members of the new middle class nevertheless maintain close links with their extended kin, as extended family relations are being reconstituted and reaffirmed continuously, transforming them into what Litwak (1960a, 1960b) termed a 'modified extended family'.[11]

Based on official census reports, it is clear that there has been a general trend towards family nuclearization in the last few decades accompanying the processes of urbanization and industrialization in Malaysia. Taking Malaysia as a whole, it is found that the proportion of people living in nuclear families has risen from 55 per cent in 1980 60 per cent in 1991 (Department of Statistics 1995a: 160), while extended families declined from 28 per cent to 26 per cent over the same period. In our study, the percentage of nuclear families was not unexpectedly much higher than the national figure, with 78 per cent being nuclear, while extended families, classified as those with one or both parents staying with the respondents, made up only 22 per cent. The proportion of extended families was lowest in the Klang Valley (16.5 per cent), and highest in Kuala Terengganu (27.4 per cent) (Table 5.9).

Among respondents' parents who were still alive, only a small proportion (22.2 per cent) stayed with the respondents, while a substantial proportion (40.4 per cent) stayed with respondents' siblings, and 37.4 per cent stayed on their own (with their spouses), mostly in their original home towns or villages. Nevertheless, the respondents maintained links with their parents through regular financial support for and visits to their parents during *Hari Raya* (the Muslim *id* celebration at the end of the fasting month of Ramadan) and on other occasions. As shown in Table 5.10, over 90 per cent of the respondents gave financial support to their parents, either monthly or every few months, with the majority (63.8 per cent) giving between RM100 and RM300 a month. The majority

Table 5.9   Place of stay of respondents' parents*

	Klang Valley	Kota Bharu	Kuala Terengganu	All respondents
	(*n* = 91)	(*n* = 66)	(*n* = 73)	(*N* = 230)
Stay with respondents**	16.5	24.2	27.4	22.2
Stay alone (husband and wife)	36.3	43.9	32.9	37.4
Stay with single sons	8.8	4.5	4.1	6.1
Stay with single daughters	7.7	4.5	5.5	6.1
Stay with married sons	6.6	3.0	1.4	3.9
Stay with married daughters	5.5	3.0	8.2	5.6
Rotate among children	18.7	16.7	20.5	18.7
Total	100.0	100.0	100.0	100.0

Source: Survey data 1996.
*Respondents whose parents (one or both) were still alive.
**This figure is taken to show the proportion of extended families among Malay middle-class respondents.

of respondents stated that their relationships with both their parents, and especially with their mothers, were very good.

Their relationships with elderly parents and relatives were continuously reconstituted and reaffirmed through the practice of *balik kampung* (literally meaning returning to the home village) during the *Hari Raya* festival. Every year, at the end of Ramadan, Malays who had migrated to towns and cities would return home in large numbers. In our study, 89.8 per cent of respondents *balik kampung* – that is, visited their kith and kin regularly during *Hari Raya* (Table 5.11). Such trips – always looked forward to by respondents and more so by their children – not only contain strong emotional content and nostalgia, but are also seen by Malays as an effective way of reaffirming their roots and identity. (See also Chapter 7 which discusses the *Hari Raya* 'open house'.)

Besides the annual *balik kampung* for *Hari Raya*, the majority of new Malay middle-class respondents also kept in touch with close relatives on a regular basis. As shown in Table 5.12, well over 95 per cent of the respondents who still had close relatives in their original birthplace maintained links with them either by telephone, visits or other means. Almost three-quarters contacted them regularly, while more than one-fifth did so once or twice a year. At the same time, they also kept in touch with close relatives who lived in the same city or town as them, as well as those in other states. The majority of them (81.7 per cent) kept renewing such contacts regularly. There is no significant difference between the

Table 5.10 Respondents' relationship with and financial support for parents

	Klang Valley	Kota Bharu	Kuala Terengganu	All respondents
	(*n* = 108)	(*n* = 80)	(*n* = 96)	(*N* = 284)*
Relationship with:				
FATHER				
Very good	56.2	70.0	57.3	61.0
Good	32.9	11.3	29.2	24.5
Average	10.9	18.7	13.5	14.4
MOTHER				
Very good	63.0	82.5	64.6	69.9
Good	28.8	8.8	24.0	20.5
Average	8.2	8.7	11.4	9.6
Do you give money to your parents?				
No	8.3	15.0	7.3	9.8 (*n* = 28)
Yes, every month	66.7	70.0	80.2	72.2 (*n* = 205)
Yes, several times a year	25.0	15.0	12.5	18.0 (*n* = 51)
Amount per month				
RM100 & below	21.9	27.5	1.2	27.3
RM101–RM200	45.2	58.7	43.7	49.0
RM201–RM300	13.7	10.0	19.8	14.8
RM301–RM400	9.6	—	2.1	3.6
RM401–RM500	5.5	—	2.1	2.4
RM501–RM600	4.1	3.8	1.0	2.8
Total	100.0	100.0	100.0	100.0

Source: Survey data 1996.
* Including those whose parents had passed away.

practice among new Malay middle-class respondents in the Klang Valley and those in the two provincial towns.

The practices and attitudes of the new Malay middle-class respondents in the three urban centres studied suggest that extended kin networks – although disrupted by urbanization and migration – are being reconstituted and reaffirmed through family gatherings during *balik kampung* for *Hari Raya* and other occasions, financial support for elderly parents as well as regular contacts with close relatives in their original birthplace or in other places. In this respect, the new Malay middle-class family,

Table 5.11   Respondents' activities during *Hari Raya**

Activities	Klang Valley (*n* = 108)	Kota Bharu (*n* = 80)	Kuala Terengganu (*n* = 96)	All respondents (*N* = 284)
*Balik kampung***	25.0	18.8	26.0	23.6 (*n* = 67)
Balik kampung and holiday with family	7.4	2.5	7.3	6.0 (*n* = 17)
Balik kampung and hold open house	30.6	42.5	34.4	35.2 (*n* = 100)
Balik kampung, holiday and hold open house	28.7	23.8	21.9	25.0 (*n* = 71)
Holiday with family	0.9	2.5	—	1.0 (*n* = 3)
Hold open house	1.9	7.5	9.4	6.0 (*n* = 17)
Holiday with family and hold open house	5.6	2.5	1.0	3.2 (*n* = 9)
Total	100.0	100.0	100.0	100.0

Source: Survey data 1996 and 1997.
* Muslim *Id* celebration held after end of fasting month of Ramadan.

Table 5.12   Respondents' relationshp with close relatives

	Klang Valley	Kota Bharu	Kuala Terengganu	All respondents
Do you keep in touch with close relatives from your place of origin?	(*n* =103)	(*n* = 35)	(*n* = 45)	(*N* = 183)*
• Never	1.0	5.7	2.2	2.2
• Once or twice a year	72.8	77.1	71.1	73.2
• Often	23.3	17.1	26.7	22.9
• No close relatives anymore	2.9	—	—	1.6
Do you keep in touch with close relatives in your present place of residence and in other places?	(*n* =108)	(*n* = 80)	(*n* = 96)	(*N* = 284)
• Never	3.7	1.3	2.1	2.5
• Once or twice a year	10.2	12.5	7.3	9.8
• Often	80.6	83.8	81.3	81.7
• No close relatives here or other places	5.6	2.5	9.4	6.0
Total	100.0	100.0	100.0	100.0

Source: Survey data 1996 and 1997.
* Respondents who migrated to present urban centres only.

Table 5.13   Respondents' attitudes regarding ideal living arrangements for elderly parents

	Klang Valley (n = 108)	Kota Bharu (n = 80)	Kuala Terengganu (n = 96)	All respondents (N = 284)
Stay with married sons	6.5	6.3	9.4	7.4 (n = 21)
Stay with married daughters	13.0	15.0	6.3	11.3 (n = 32)
Rotating among married sons	4.6	2.5	1.0	2.8 (n = 8)
Rotating among married daughters	2.8	1.3	2.1	2.1 (n = 6)
Rotating among children	18.6	28.8	36.5	27.4 (n = 78)
Stay on their own but near children	29.6	23.8	26.0	26.8 (n = 76)
Let parents decide	13.9	15.0	9.4	12.7 (n = 36)
Old people's home	0.9	1.3	—	0.7 (n = 2)
Others	10.2	6.3	9.4	8.8 (n = 25)
Total	100.0	100.0	100.0	100.0

Source: Survey data 1996 and 1997.

although nuclear in form, is not isolated or alienated. While members of the original family 'break out' through migration, this does not necessarily lead to the breakdown of family relations. The practices among the new Malay middle-class respondents and their kin suggest that kin relations are an important source of companionship and support (emotional, financial, and so on) in the heart of the modern city.

This proposition may be validated when we examine the family values of respondents. As shown in Table 5.13, the family values of respondents were still strong, which helped to nurture and strengthen the practices discussed above. When asked for their views regarding ideal living arrangements for elderly parents, more than half felt that they should stay with their children, slightly more than one-quarter felt that they should stay own their own but near their children, and 12.7 per cent would leave it to their parents to decide. Only two respondents (0.7 per cent) felt that they should stay in an old people's home.

Strong family values were also reflected in the new Malay middle-class respondents' attitudes regarding their responsibility towards elderly

Table 5.14   Respondents' perceptions regarding the family

	Klang Valley (*n* = 108)	Kota Bharu (*n* = 80)	Kuala Terengganu (*n* = 96)	All respondents (*N* = 284)
Do you agree that it is the responsibility of children to look after their elderly parents?				
• Strongly agree	63.0	72.5	66.7	66.9
• Agree	23.1	16.3	28.1	22.9
• Not sure	9.3	6.3	1.0	5.6
• Disagree	2.8	5.0	3.1	3.5
• Strongly disagree	1.9	—	1.0	1.1
Do you agree that husband and wife relationship is more important than relationship with elderly parents?				
• Strongly agree	4.6	8.8	3.1	5.3
• Agree	18.5	20.0	17.7	18.7
• Not sure	21.3	11.3	18.8	17.6
• Disagree	48.1	52.5	52.1	50.7
• Strongly disagree	7.4	10.8	8.3	7.7
Do you agree that work is more important than family?				
• Strongly agree	—	2.5	2.1	1.4
• Agree	6.5	6.3	3.1	5.3
• Not sure	16.7	11.3	9.4	12.7
• Disagree	61.1	63.7	62.5	62.3
• Strongly disagree	15.7	16.3	22.9	18.3
Do you agree that family members are the best persons to turn to when one is in financial difficulty?				
• Strongly agree	23.1	36.3	30.2	29.2
• Agree	25.0	35.0	44.8	34.5
• Not sure	24.1	16.3	12.5	18.0
• Disagree	25.0	12.5	11.4	16.9
• Strongly disagree	2.8	—	1.0	1.4
Total	100.0	100.0	100.0	100.0

Source: Survey data 1996.

parents. In this study, 90 per cent of respondents agreed that it was the responsibility of children to look after elderly parents, while only 4.6 per cent disagreed (Table 5.14). Many also did not regard the husband–wife relationship as antithetical to relationships with parents. While 24 per cent agreed that the husband–wife relationship was more important than relationships with parents, 58.4 per cent disagreed, and another 17.6 per cent were unsure.

Most respondents felt that the family is a very important institution as a support system, and should not be sidelined by career commitments. For example, when asked whether they considered work to be more important than family, only 6.7 per cent agreed, while the overwhelming majority (80.6 per cent) disagreed, and 12.7 per cent were undecided. In times of difficulties, including financial difficulty, almost two-thirds of respondents felt that family members were the best people to rely on, 18 per cent were unsure, and only 18.3 per cent disagreed with the idea (Table 5.14).

Conclusions

This chapter has shown that the new Malay middle-class family is predominantly a nuclear family with a strong emphasis on the marriage relationship. The marriage pattern is primarily homogamous, although men tend to marry lower, and women higher. Despite the age at first marriage being higher than the average among all Malay workers, or the Malay middle class in the 1970s, our respondents had relatively larger family sizes, and preferred to have more children. Although there is male dominance in some families, especially in the Klang Valley, when it comes to major decisions, there is generally a tendency towards equalization in power-sharing within marriage, suggesting the growing independence of new Malay middle-class women. While new Malay middle-class respondents were concerned for their children's future, they were not isolated from their families of origin. Their extended kin networks were reconstituted and reaffirmed continuously in various ways, thus holding kin relations together despite the experiences of industrialization, urbanization and modernization. These continuing relationships with their extended kin could, in part, be due to the fact that our respondents were mainly from the first-generation middle class. The findings presented in this chapter cast serious doubt on the notion of the isolation of the conjugal nuclear family and the breakdown with other kin. Rather, they support Litwak's thesis that the modern urban middle- class family exists within a modified extended family framework adapted to urban conditions.

6

New Malay Middle-Class Lifestyles and Culture

This chapter examines several interrelated issues pertaining to the new Malay middle-class lifestyles and culture, such as living conditions, asset ownership, consumption patterns, and leisure activities. At the same time, it also discusses an important issue in class analysis – that is, the self-evaluation by members of the new Malay middle class of their own class positions – to see if their subjective evaluations match our objective definition of the new middle-class. This chapter aims to show that the new Malay middle class lifestyles and cultural preferences are not homogenous; and that while the more affluent sections of the new Malay middle class have developed distinct high-status lifestyles and cultural preferences, many still have lifestyles and cultural preferences that do not differentiate them as a social category distinct from the lower classes.

Asset ownership as lifestyles indicator

Ownership of various assets such as houses, cars and expensive household gadgets, and various types of financial assets are important indicators of one's wealth and living standards and also one's lifestyle and social standing. It is expected that being relatively more affluent, the new middle class has greater access to better-quality housing and other assets than the working class.

Housing

Housing is a basic necessity for human beings since it provides them with ontological security – that is, security of living and existence. While a few may own houses through inheritance, the overwhelming majority have to acquire them through their own efforts. Being scarce and costly, especially in the Malaysian urban areas today, house ownership is

Table 6.1   Housing status of respondents

Housing status	Klang Valley (n = 108)	Kota Bharu (n = 80)	Kuala Terengganu (n = 96)	All new Malay middle-class respondents (N = 284)	Malay workers in Klang Valley (N = 133)
Own houses	67.6	60.0	59.4	62.7 (n = 178)	38.9 (n = 52)
• Own two or more houses	36.1	12.5	21.9	24.6 (n = 70)	3.8 (n = 5)
Rented houses	26.9	27.5	17.7	23.9 (n = 68)	36.8 (n = 49)
Houses provided by employer	1.9	2.5	9.4	4.6 (n = 13)	22.7 (n= 30)
Parents' house	3.7	10.0	13.5	8.8 (n = 25)	1.6 (n = 2)
Total	100.0	100.0	100.0	100.0	100.0

Source: Survey data 1996 and 1997.

dependent upon price and also geographical location since property prices vary from area to area. Financial institutions provide loans, enabling prospective buyers to purchase houses, but such loans are limited by the ability of borrowers to repay them.

This study found unequal distribution of house ownership among members of the new Malay middle class themselves, as well as between the new Malay middle class and the working class. As shown in Table 6.1, more than three-fifths of new Malay middle-class respondents owned houses, with house ownership being highest among respondents in the Klang Valley. Wealth differences can also be seen among the new Malay middle-class respondents in the three urban centres. Among all house owners, a quarter owned two or more houses, the highest proportion in this category being in the Klang Valley, partly because a larger proportion of the Klang Valley new middle-class respondents – being high-income earners – were wealthier (see Chapter 4). Those with two or more houses could receive additional incomes in the form of rents.

However, more than one-third did not own houses at the time of the study. They mostly lived in rented houses, while a few – mainly younger and also unmarried respondents – lived with their parents or close relatives, or in houses provided by their employees. Compared to those living in the Klang Valley (many of whom originally migrated from

Table 6.2   Types of living quarters of respondents

Type of house	Klang Valley (n = 108)	Kota Bharu (n = 80)	Kuala Terengganu (n = 96)	All new Malay middle-class respondents (N = 284)	Malay workers in Klang Valley (N = 133)
Single-unit bungalow	17.6	42.5	22.9	26.4	9.9*
Semi-detached double-storey bungalow	12.0	3.8	8.3	8.1	
Semi-detached single-storey bungalow	—	3.8	3.1	2.1	
Condominium	5.6	—	—	2.1	—
Double-storey terraced house	41.7	12.5	7.3	21.8	8.4
Single-storey terraced house	10.2	6.3	13.5	10.2	29.1
Apartment/Flat	8.4	1.3	3.1	4.6	41.2**
Other types	4.6	30.1	41.6	24.3*	8.4***
Total	100.0	100.0	100.0	100.0	100.0

Source: Survey data 1996 and 1997.
*Including single-unit semi-concrete wooden houses (known in Malay as *rumah kampung*, found mainly in Kota Bharu and Kuala Terengganu) and residential units above shop-lots (mainly in the Klang Valley).
**Including hostels and low-cost houses.
***Including wooden houses in squatter areas.

outside the area), those living with their parents could be found in greater proportions among respondents in Kuala Terengganu and Kota Bharu.

Living space is a major problem in big cities like Kuala Lumpur and its surrounding suburbs, and this also has a significant impact on the lives of the new Malay middle class. This partly explains why there is a difference between the living quarters of Klang Valley new middle-class respondents and those in Kota Bharu and Kuala Terengganu. As shown in Table 6.2, while less than one-third of new Malay middle-class respondents in the Klang Valley lived in more spacious single units or semi-detached bungalows, a much larger proportion lived in similar houses in the two provincial towns. Among Klang Valley Malay new middle-class respondents, the majority lived in double- or single-storey terraced house' while a few lived in condominiums.

An important point to note is that, compared to the Klang Valley, terraced housing and high-rise living is a relatively new and less widespread phenomenon in both Kota Bharu and Kuala Trengganu: there are few housing estates in either town. Consequently, such types of housing are not that widespread among new Malay middle-class respondents there. In Kota Bharu, for example, only one-fifth of our respondents lived in terraced houses or apartments, while in Kuala Terengganu, the figure was less than a quarter. Apart from many respondents living in single-unit or semi-detached bungalows, a sub-stantial number lived in semi-concrete single-unit wooden houses (known locally as *rumah kampung* or 'village-houses') – 30.1 per cent in Kota Bharu and 41.6 per cent in Kuala Terengganu. This suggests that respondents in the two provincial towns enjoyed more spacious living environments than their counterparts in the Klang Valley. This is related to the greater availability of land and less costly housing in the former as well as to the way of life of their people, who had been more accustomed to living in single units with some land space around their houses, rather than living in terraced or high-rise houses, as commonly found in the Klang Valley.

As expected, there were clear differences between our new Malay middle-class respondents and the Klang Valley Malay workers in terms of the level of house ownership and housing conditions (Tables 6.1 and 6.2). The majority of the workers had to rent houses or flats, or lived in hostel accommodation provided by their employers, while less than two-fifths were house owners. The most common types of housing for Malay workers were low-cost flats or apartments as well as low-cost houses, although some lived in single-storey terraced houses. A very small proportion lived in rented single units or semi-detached bungalows, or in double-storey terraced houses. In fact, a small number had to live in wooden houses in squatter areas.

Other assets

Apart from house ownership, the ownership of other assets – such as vehicles (various types of cars and motorcycles), household entertainment gadgets (television, video and hi-fi sets), personal computers and Internet facilities, mobile phones and financial assets such as shares and insurance all reflect the modern lifestyles of the new middle class. While house ownership was not universal among the new Malay middle-class respondents, car ownership was more widespread. In our sample, over

Table 6.3   Ownership of assets by respondents: comparison between new Malay middle class and working class

	Klang Valley (*n* = 108)	Kota Bharu (*n* = 80)	Kuala Terengganu (*n* = 96)	All new Malay middle-class respondents (*N* = 284)	Malay workers in Klang Valley (*N* = 133)
Vehicles					
Cars					
One car	37.0	52.4	40.7	42.6	42.0
Two cars	38.0	30.0	43.8	37.7	—
Three cars	13.0	5.0	7.3	8.8	—
Four cars or more	3.0	2.5	1.0	2.1	—
Motorcycles only	9.0	10.2	7.2	8.8	36.6
No vehicles	—	—	—	—	21.4
Television set	100.0	100.0	100.0	100.0	78.6
Video set	67.6	60.0	54.1	61.3	35.9
Hi-fi set	53.7	41.3	34.4	43.7	30.0
Personal computer	67.6	36.5	42.5	50.0	16.0
• Already using internet	*16.7*	*10.4*	*8.75*	*12.3*	*16.8*
• Going to use internet	*73.2*	*41.7*	*66.3*	*60.6*	*54.2*
Mobile phone	63.0	40.6	46.3	50.7	14.5
Antiques, paintings, etc.	12.0	5.2	6.3	8.1	3.1

Source: Survey data 1996 and 1997.

90 per cent had one or more cars, while only a very small proportion had motorcycles (Table 6.3). Cars and motorcycles are essential means for physical mobility, for work, leisure, and other social activities. Unlike houses, which are normally purchased much later in one's career, owning cars (or at least a motorcycle) is considered essential once a person has secured a job.

Status differentiation among the new Malay middle class can be seen both in the number and types of cars in their possession. In the Klang Valley, the ownership of two or more cars is quite common among the new middle class, with more than half of our respondents falling into that category. As expected, it is quite different in the two provincial towns where the majority had only one car, or, at most, two.

There were clear differences in the types of cars owned by the new Malay middle-class respondents. Among those in the Klang Valley, the proportions using ordinary cars and those using luxury cars were about the same (Table 6.4). Luxury cars seemed to be the preference of top-level executives and senior managers. Over 90 per cent of the luxury cars were imported' mostly from Europe (such as Mercedes, Volvos and BMWs), while a smaller number came from Japan (such as Honda and Toyota Camry).[1] As would be expected, the picture is quite different in the two provincial towns, where most respondents used ordinary cars, the overwhelming choice being the locally produced Proton which were more affordable.

Besides cars and motorcycles, most respondents also possessed modern household gadgets such as colour televisions, videos and hi-fi sets for family entertainment. Practically all of our respondents had television sets, while more than three-fifths had videos, and more than two-fifths had hi-fi sets. However, tastes for the finer aspects of culture such as art was still confined to a very small minority. For example, antiques and wall paintings were still rather scarce among the new Malay middle class, with only a small proportion having them, mostly among new Malay middle-class respondents in the Klang Valley. What are most often seen in the living rooms of new Malay middle-class homes are Islamic calligraphy, pictures of the Ka'abah in the Mecca Mosque, pictures taken with dignitaries, and sometimes a few pictures from the family album.

Many members of the new middle class also possess the latest information technology gadgets. Personal computers (PCs) have become increasingly widespread in new Malay middle-class homes, with many having access to the Internet. At the time of the survey in 1996–97, one-half of the respondents had PCs – the highest proportion being in the Klang Valley with more than two-thirds, followed by Kuala Terengganu (42.5 per cent), and Kota Bharu (36.5 per cent). A small proportion of respondents (12.3 per cent) used the Internet, while another 60.6 per cent intended to use it soon, suggesting that computer ownership and Internet usage would increase rapidly among new middle-class respondents. (In fact, with the government nationwide campaign of 'one household one computer', computer ownership among all classes, especially the middle class, would have increased considerably today.) Mobile phones were also common by this time, with half of all respondents owning them, the highest concentration being among new Malay middle-class respondents in the Klang Valley.

Table 6.4 Ownership of ordinary and luxury cars (local and imported) among new Malay middle-class respondents in the Klang Valley and in two provincial towns

	Malaysian*		Japanese		European		M'cycles		Total
	Ordinary	Luxury	Ordinary	Luxury	Ordinary	Luxury	Ordinary	Superbikes	
Klang Valley Top-level executives/ senior managers	41.7	1.9	4.6	17.7	3.7	28.7	—	—	108 (100.0)
	25.0	3.8	3.8	17.3	1.9	48.1	—	—	52 (100.0)
Middle managers Professionals								5.3	38 (100.0)
	55.3	—	5.3	15.8	5.3	13.2		—	18
	61.1	—	5.6	22.2	5.6	5.6			(100.0)
Kota Bharu	49.4	—	27.9	6.3	5.1	3.8	7.7	—	80 (100.0)
Kuala Terengganu	38.9	2.2	22.2	8.9	4.4	6.8	15.5	1.1	96 (100.0)

Source: Survey data 1996 and 1997.

*Refer to Proton cars produced through a joint venture between the Malaysian-owned Perusahaan Otomobil Nasional Berhad (Proton) and the Japanese Mitsubishi.

Note:

Figures on car ownership show that at least one of the cars in the respondents' possession are of the type stated.

However, car ownership and the ownership of other assets is not solely confined to the new middle class. Members of the working class also aspire to better living standards. As shown in Table 6.3, among Malay workers in the Klang Valley, 42 per cent had cars while another 37 per cent owned motorcycles. Such means of transport are very essential in the city. Most workers also had TV sets, about one-third had videos and hi-fi sets, while a much smaller proportion owned PCs and mobile phones. However, ownership of these assets was mainly confined to a small proportion, mostly the better-paid workers.

Though members of the new middle class appear affluent and are able to flaunt their various material possessions, they acquire them not so much through wealth inheritance, but through their access to well-developed loan and hire-purchase systems. Being mostly from the 'first-generation' new middle class, consisting of salaried professionals, administrators and managers, these findings are to be expected. The existence of well-developed financial institutions as loan providers makes it possible for them to take loans for expensive items such as houses and cars, but it also exposes them to debts, some of which are huge in comparison to their incomes. At the time of the study, almost two-thirds of our new Malay middle-class respondents had one or two loans, with the lowest amount being RM10 000 and the highest over RM200 000 (Table 6.5). Most of them took out loans between RM10 000 and RM100 000. The purposes of obtaining the loans were mostly to buy cars and houses, while a few used them to dabble in the stock market or to start businesses.

At the time of the study, slightly more than one-third had not taken out any loans or had already paid up their loans, and thus were not exposed to interest rate volatility, which could make their financial positions vulnerable. However, two-thirds of the respondents were still in debt since they had yet to settle their outstanding loans plus interest. A small proportion of respondents were quite heavily indebted to banks and finance companies, to the tune of more than RM100 000 – an amount which would usually take them more than ten years to settle. Those owing between RM50 001 and RM100 000 numbered 15.7 per cent, while those with outstanding debts between RM10 000 and RM50 000 accounted for a third, while only 8 per cent had debts of less than RM10 000.

The above findings suggest that the majority of our new middle-class respondents were not really on a secure financial footing and were, therefore, vulnerable to crisis situations. As happened in the 1997–98 financial and economic crisis, many of them were hard hit because of the sharp increase in the interest rates from about 8 per cent before the crisis to as high as 16 per cent at its height in early 1998. Some had their cars or

Table 6.5   Amount of loans obtained and outstanding loans to be settled by new Malay middle-class respondents

Amount	Klang Valley (*n* = 108)		Kota Bharu (*n* = 80)		Kuala Terengganu (*n* = 96)		All respondents (*N* = 284)	
	1	*2*	*1*	*2*	*1*	*2*	*1*	*2*
Below RM10 000	8.2	2.7	3.8	10.0	—	10.4	7.2	8.0
RM10 000–50 000	31.5	39.7	32.5	38.7	24.0	24.0	28.9	33.3
RM50 001–100 000	8.2	15.1	6.3	12.5	25.0	8.7	14.1	15.7
RM100 001–150 000	11.0	8.2	5.0	2.5	4.2	4.2	6.4	4.8
RM150 001–200 000	6.8	2.7	6.3	1.3	3.1	3.1	5.2	2.4
RM200 001–250 000	—	—	—	—	3.1	1.0	1.6	0.4
RM250 001–300 000	1.4	—	1.3	1.3	2.1	1.0	1.6	0.8
RM300 001 & above	1.4	—	—	—	2.1	1.0	0.8	0.4
Did not take loan	31.5	31.5	33.8	22.8	36.5	36.5	34.1	34.1
Total	100.0	100.0	100.0	100.0	100.0	100.0	100.0	100.0

Source: Survey data 1996 and 1997.
Notes:
1 = Amount of loan obtained.
2 = Amount of outstanding loan to be settled.

houses repossessed by banks or finance companies for their failure to service their loans (see Abdul Rahman 2001).

Financial assets

In terms of financial assets, members of the new Malay middle class take the issue of personal savings seriously, not only because they have excess income over consumption, but because they see their savings as part of contingency in times of crisis, as something to fall back upon in their old age, and also something to be used to fund their children's education. All of the respondents in our study had regular savings, but the amount varied significantly, with two-thirds saving below RM500 a month. Nevertheless, almost one-fifth comprised of wealthier middle-class fractions could save over RM2000 monthly.

Besides saving in banks, new Malay middle-class respondents also saved in the form of stocks and shares, unit trusts and insurance policies. Nevertheless, despite the relatively developed stock market in Malaysia, respondents generally adopted conservative attitudes and avoided risk-taking. Overall, only about one-third of new Malay middle-class respondents invested in the stock market, while around two-thirds preferred the more secure state-guaranteed Amanah Saham Bumiputra (ASB) and Amanah Saham Nasional (ASN) unit trust schemes managed by Permodalan Nasional Berhad (PNB). Besides shares, almost half of the respondents purchased insurance policies. However, there is some difference between the new middle-class Malays in the Klang Valley and their counterparts in provincial towns in terms of the savings practices. While many of those in the Klang Valley bought stock market shares and insurance policies, very much smaller proportions did so among respondents in Kota Bharu and Kuala Terengganu. It is not that the two provincial towns had no online connections with the Kuala Lumpur Stock Exchange (in fact, facilities for share transactions were available in both places). Rather, the culture of risk-taking has not yet really developed among the new middle-class Malays, especially in the east coast states.

Consumption levels

Household and personal spending

It has been shown by several researchers (for example, Robison and Goodman 1996) that one of the indulgences of the new middle class is their high consumption levels. An examination of the array of durable consumption goods – from houses to cars and household gadgets – consumed by respondents in our study as discussed above suggests that this observation is also true among a section of the new Malay middle class. However, among a significant proportion of new Malay middle-class respondents (especially those in the two provincial towns), their consumption was less extravagant or conspicuous, showing internal differentiation among the new middle class.

Table 6.6 compares the monthly household and personal expenses of new Malay middle-class respondents in both the metropolitan area and provincial towns. Overall, the majority of respondents (61.5 per cent) monthly spent RM500 or less for household expenses (here, it refers only to food and related items), although a small proportion spent more than RM1000 a month. By comparison, respondents in the Klang Valley, partly due to the higher costs of living, spent more as shown by the fact that 45.2 per cent spent more, than RM500 a month, including 11 per cent who spent more than RM1000 on household expenses. In Kota Bharu and Kuala Trengganu, where the cost of living is much lower, the respondents' household expenses were much less – only slightly more than a third in

Table 6.6 Monthly household and personal expenses of respondents

Monthly expenses	Klang Valley (n = 108)		Kota Bharu (n = 80)		Kuala Terengganu (n = 96)		All new Malay middle-class respondents (N = 284)	
	1	*2*	*1*	*2*	*1*	*2*	*1*	*2*
RM100–500	54.8	40.7	62.5	42.5	65.3	47.9	61.5	43.7
RM501–1000	34.2	26.8	35.0	42.5	29.2	32.3	32.5	33.1
RM1001–1500	11.0	5.6	2.5	10.0	5.2	10.4	6.0	8.4
RM1501–2000	—	14.8	—	2.5	—	7.3	—	8.8
RM2001+	—	12.0	—	2.6	—	2.0	—	6.0
TOTAL	100.0	100.0	100.0	100.0	100.0	100.0	100.0	100.0
Credit cards								
• Ordinary	51.9		26.0		42.5		40.5	
• Gold	48.2		6.3		17.5		25.4	

Source: Survey data 1996 and 1997.
1 = Household expenses.
2 = Personal expenses.

both places spent more than RM500 a month, while those spending more than RM1000 made up less than 5 per cent.

However, there is a clear difference between the household expenses and the personal expenses of new Malay middle-class respondents. For example, while overall, only 6 per cent of respondents spent more than RM1000 a month on household expenses, almost a quarter spent more in personal expenses. Their personal expenses, which included expenses for petrol, food, refreshments, tobacco, recreation and entertainment, reading materials, and other incidentals, also varied between different fractions of the new middle class. While over two-fifths spent a relatively modest sum of RM500 or less a month, another one-third spent between RM501 and RM1000. However, almost a quarter can be considered as big spenders, spending more than RM1000 a month, and this figure includes 6 per cent who spent over RM2000. The big spenders were mainly found among new Malay new middle-class respondents in the Klang Valley, among whom about one-third spent over RM1000 monthly in personal expenses, while in Kota Bharu and Kuala Terengganu, the corresponding figures were very much smaller, at 15.1 per cent and 19.7 per cent respectively.

These expenses, especially personal spending, were facilitated by the use of credit facilities provided by banks. Among all new Malay middle-class respondents, about two-thirds had credit cards. Credit card holders were also unevenly distributed among respondents, indicating income differentials, with the highest proportion being in the Klang Valley, where all respondents possessed them, but in Kota Bharu and Kuala Terengganu, the figures were respectively a third and three-fifths. As expected, the proportion of those with gold credit cards, was also highest in the Klang Valley where almost half of them possessed gold credit cards compared to only 6.3 per cent in Kota Bharu and 17.5 per cent in Kuala Terengganu.

Shopping preferences

In terms of shopping preferences for their personal items as well as food for their households, new Malay middle-class respondents looked for both quality and reasonable prices. They did their shopping for personal items (for example, clothes, shoes and toiletries) mostly at supermarkets or shopping complexes, and many would also go to other outlets offering 'cheap' sales. Nevertheless, about a quarter, to be found mostly among the Klang Valley new Malay middle-class respondents, purchased designer clothes from boutiques on a fairly regular basis.

As for food items, the majority of new Malay middle-class respondents patronized wet markets and supermarkets, depending on the items they required. For fresh vegetables, fish, meat, and sundries, they would go to wet markets rather than supermarkets because it was more economical in the former, though for other items, such as rice, sugar, fruits, and so on, the preference was for supermarkets. However, the degree of reliance on wet markets and supermarkets varied between the new Malay middle-class respondents in the Klang Valley and in the two provincial towns. While about half of the new Malay middle-class respondents in the Klang Valley patronized supermarkets for food items, very much smaller proportions among their counterparts in the two provincial towns would do so. The preference for wet markets for the supply of provisions was very strong among those in the provincial towns.

Besides wet markets, other informal sector markets such as night markets and farmers' markets (*pasar tani*) also exist and are supported strongly by the new Malay middle class. Night markets offer a limited assortment of goods (for example, clothes, kitchen utensils, food, and vegetables) at relatively cheaper prices. These markets were introduced in the early 1980s (initially in the Klang Valley, and later in other towns) to enable busy urbanites, who work during the day, to purchase vegetables, groceries and other items at their convenience. These markets are often located at strategic locations in selected residential areas in both middle-class and working-class areas.

On the other hand, farmers' market are more specific, selling cheaper agricultural products, especially *kampung* vegetables. Farmers' markets were introduced at about the same time as night markets. The aim was to provide outlets to farmers to market their agricultural produce directly in urban centres without having to go through the middlemen. However, though various types of agricultural produce sold at farmers' markets are popular among Malays, these markets are fewer in number, and they are normally held once a week in the morning (often on weekdays), making them less accessible to potential customers. This partially explains why a smaller proportion of new Malay middle-class respondents patronized them – compared to supermarkets or wet markets, which are easily accessible.

The shopping preferences of new Malay-middle class respondents and Klang Valley Malay workers were, unsurprisingly, somewhat different. While many would also patronize the same shopping complexes or supermarkets to purchase personal items, cheaper prices were the main concerns of most of the Malay workers. A few, especially the more fashion-conscious, would undoubtedly patronize boutiques, despite their higher prices. However, the consumer market also provided an alternative for them. Business in branded imitation goods is a thriving enterprise, especially in big cities such as Kuala Lumpur, and this provided an opportunity for many among young Malay workers to purchase those items they otherwise would never have dreamt of acquiring in the formal market.

Unlike many new Malay middle-class respondents, in our sample Klang Valley Malay workers mostly relied on wet markets and night markets to purchase their regular food supplies. For those who lived near farmers' markets, the latter were also a popular spot for Malay workers. Only a small proportion among them purchased their food provisions at supermarkets.

To some customers, including both new Malay middle-class and working-class respondents, there is another attraction of wet markets, night markets and farmers' markets. Unlike supermarkets or sundry shops which sell at fixed prices, customers at these markets can bargain with sellers for price discounts for some of their goods. To some customers, this is important since they thus enjoy not only relatively cheaper products, but also a greater feeling of consumer satisfaction.

Leisure activities

Leisure activities are becoming increasingly important in modern society, especially among the new middle class. With a large proportion of their time spent at work, individuals naturally look forward to their free time for the opportunities it offers to wind down and relax after their daily work hours, as well as during weekends and public holidays. They also take personal leave (including annual leave) to go on vacation. Since members of the new middle class have greater purchasing power, their propensity to spend their free hours on leisure activities is relatively stronger than among the working class. This section first examines how our new Malay middle-class respondents spend their free time together with their families and children in activities such as watching television, eating out, and going on holidays and travelling together. (In the discussion, all respondents are considered together, irrespective of their marital status, since those who were single mostly lived with their parents or relatives and participated together in these activities.) Second, it also examines what respondents do on their own for leisure, such as golfing as well as socializing at karaoke bars and coffee house lounges.

Television viewing

Television viewing is a favourite pastime within modern homes. Although some television programmes may not be watched together, since parents may have different tastes from their children, this activity is classified as a family activity since parents are assumed to be together with their family members at home during these hours. As shown in Table 6.7, the majority (almost 60 per cent) of all our new Malay middle-class respondents spent on average between one and two hours a day watching television, with the rest spending three hours or more. However, there is some regional variation in television viewing among the respondents, with those in provincial towns spending more time watching television programmes than their Klang Valley counterparts. Besides having to spend more time at work (since the majority of the Klang Valley sample work in the private sector) and being often caught up in traffic jams to and from work, it is to be expected that the Klang Valley respondents would spend less time watching television. At the same time, other forms of entertainment and recreation were also readily available in the metropolitan city.

The most common television programmes watched by the respondents were news and talk shows, as well as entertainment programmes such as drama, films, sitcoms, and music and songs. The most popular programme is the news, which over 90 per cent watched daily. Besides

Table 6.7 Time spent viewing television among respondents

Average no. of hours daily watching TV	Klang Valley (n = 108)	Kota Bharu (n = 80)	Kuala Terengganu (n = 96)	All new Malay middle-class respondents (N = 284)	Malay workers in Klang Valley (N = 133)
One hour	31.5	21.3	18.8	24.3	21.8
Two	29.6	37.5	38.5	34.8	32.3
Three	25.0	30.0	25.0	26.4	26.3
Four & above	13.9	11.2	17.7	14.4	19.5
Total	100.0	100.0	100.0	100.0	100.0

Source: Survey data 1996 and 1997.

news items, new Malay middle-class respondents also watched local weekly talk shows such as *Minda, Wawancara, Forum Perdana Hal Ehwal Islam* and *Global*. *Minda, Wawancara* and *Forum Perdana Hal Ehwal Islam* are weekly talk shows in Malay broadcast the state-owned Radio and Television Malaysia (RTM) Channel One – the first two deal with current national economic, political and social issues, while the third is about Islam. The latter is aired every Thursday night after the Muslim *Isya'* prayers,[2] which is considered an appropriate time to welcome Friday, the most favoured day among Muslims. *Global* on the other hand, is a weekly talk show in English aired over RTM Channel Two, which features discussions on numerous topics such as globalization, environment, population, women's rights, consumer affairs, and so on. Among the four talk shows, the one on Islam was the most popular among new Malay middle-class respondents, with two-thirds watching it regularly.

There is a marked difference in preferences for such programmes between new Malay middle-class respondents in the Klang Valley and their counterparts in the two provincial towns. By comparison, higher proportions of the latter preferred local talk shows in Malay on religious issues, while for programmes in English (mostly on current affairs), the regular viewers were mostly those from the Klang Valley. Being more religiously-inclined, it is to be expected that higher proportions of respondents in Kota Bharu and Kuala Terengganu – about three-quarters in each town – were regular viewers of programmes about Islam. In the Klang Valley, the proportion watching religious programmes – although lower than in the two provincial towns – was still quite high, reaching well over 50 per cent. Viewers of programmes in English, such as news and commentaries on Cable News Network (CNN) and *Money Matters* (a weekly late-night talk show aired over Sistem Television Malaysia or TV3, a private TV station, featuring business and stock market news and commentaries) were expectedly smaller in number, confined mostly to Klang Valley respondents.

Though many new Malay middle-class respondents depended on certain television programmes for entertainment, they were not overly dependent upon them. For example, only 45.4 per cent (mostly those in the Klang Valley) regularly watched television drama series or films, but most of them only watched these programmes once in a while and some did not watch them at all. The proportion who regularly watched local sitcoms such as *Pi Mai Tang Tu* was much lower (33.3 per cent), while Malay music shows such as the weekly *Hiburan Minggu Ini* (Entertainment This Week) attracted the least number of regular viewers (less than 10 per cent). This finding suggests that they were critical of such programmes. In fact, when asked the kind of programmes they would like to see less of on television, the majority felt that television stations should cut down on entertainment programmes, and should instead broadcast more educational and religious programmes and documentaries.

While the time spent watching television daily did not differ significantly between our new Malay middle-class and Klang Valley working-class respondents (Table 6.6), their preferences for non-entertainment and entertainment programmes discussed above differed significantly. As expected, there was much less interest among Malay workers in watching non-entertainment programmes, for most of them preferred light entertainment. For example, while only 72.2 per cent among them watched news broadcasts regularly (compared to over 90 per cent among middle- class respondents), much smaller proportions (mostly below 10 per cent) were regular viewers of other programmes such as *Global, Minda, Wawancara, Money Matters* or *CNN news*. Besides news broadcasts, only programmes on Islam attracted more regular viewers (about 50 per cent) among Malay workers, but even here the proportion was still very much lower than among new Malay middle-class respondents.

Eating out

Among our new Malay middle-class respondents, eating out was another favourite pastime, partly because people wanted a change of culinary taste and also to lighten the domestic burden of wives. This is especially so since over two-thirds of our respondents were those with dual career

Table 6.8 Practices of eating out with family members by new Malay middle-class and Malay working-class respondents

Eating outlets	Klang Valley (*n* = 108)	Kota Bharu (*n* = 80)	Kuala Terengganu (*n* = 96)	All new Malay middle-class respondents (*N* = 284)	Malay workers in Klang Valley (*N* = 133)
Hotel					
• Very often	10.2	6.3	5.2	7.4	1.5
• Often	16.7	13.8	16.7	15.8	1.5
• Sometimes	46.3	17.5	20.8	29.6	9.8
• Very rarely	26.8	56.2	57.3	45.4	87.2
Restaurant					
• Very often	28.2	23.8	26.1	26.4	24.1
• often	38.1	35.0	40.6	37.3	17.3
• Sometimes	25.0	22.5	14.6	20.8	23.3
• Very rarely	10.2	18.8	18.8	15.5	35.3
Stall					
• Very often	27.7	22.5	24.0	24.9	42.1
• Often	27.8	25.0	41.7	31.7	15.0
• Sometimes	25.9	12.5	7.3	15.8	7.5
• Very rarely	18.5	40.0	27.1	27.5	35.3
'Fast food' restaurant					
• Very often	30.5	17.5	15.7	21.8	12.8
• Often	25.9	32.5	37.5	31.7	24.8
• Sometimes	26.9	17.5	17.7	21.1	24.8
• Very rarely	16.7	32.5	29.2	25.4	37.6

Source: Survey data 1996 and 1997.
Notes:
Very often = Two to three times a week.
Often = Once a week.
Sometimes = Once a month.
Very rarely = Once or twice a year.

families, with only 14.1 per cent employing live-in maids. Their favourite eating places included budget restaurants, hawker stalls (or food courts), fast food restaurants and hotels (Table 6.8). Of these four, budget restaurants were the most popular, with almost two-thirds frequenting them regularly (understood as at least once a week). The next most popular eating outlet were hawker stalls, followed by fast food restaurants.

Hotels, being more expensive, were less popular among the majority of respondents. About one-fifth – mostly those in the higher-income brackets – frequently dined at hotels with their family members – once a week on average, especially during weekends. The regular hotelgoers were mainly found among Klang Valley respondents, followed by those in Kuala Terengganu and Kota Bharu.

Among Klang Valley Malay workers, eating out was also popular. However, most would normally patronize hawker stalls and, to a certain extent, budget restaurants and fast food restaurants. As expected, there were very few regular hotelgoers among Malay workers.

Holidays and travel

Holidays and travel are a middle-class activity. While eating out activities may not clearly differentiate members of the new Malay middle class from Malay workers, holidays and travel, especially to other countries, show up the differences more clearly. The overwhelming majority (92.3 per cent) of our new Malay middle-class respondents indicated that they liked to take holidays and travel somewhere – either inside the country or abroad – when they had the opportunity (Table 6.9). By comparison, preference for such activity was most clearly expressed by Klang Valley respondents, followed by those in Kuala Terengganu and Kota Bharu.

Such preferences were translated into actual activity, although the majority of travel was inside the country. In this study, we took the period of two years prior to the survey as our cut-off point.[3] Among the new Malay middle-class respondents, more than four-fifths had taken vacations and travelled inside the country in the two years prior to the study. The most popular holiday destinations were seaside resorts (such as Port Dickson and Malacca), island resorts (such as Pulau Langkawi, Pulau Tioman and Pulau Redang), and mountain resorts (such as Genting Higlands and Cameron Highlands).

Besides domestic travel, our respondents also liked to travel abroad. In the two-year period prior to the study, about half of them spent their holidays abroad with their families. However, their foreign destinations were mostly neighbouring Asian countries such as Indonesia, Thailand, Hong Kong, China, and Japan, although quite a number went to Europe and the United States. Most of those who travelled abroad had been only once in the two-year period of our study, with a number going twice or more during those two years. Among those who travelled abroad for vacations, almost four-fifth took the opportunity to do their shopping there.

Table 6.9   Holidays and travel among new Malay middle-class and Malay working-class respondents

	Klang Valley (n = 108)	*Kota Bharu (n = 80)*	*Kuala Terengganu (n = 96)*	*All new Malay middle-class respondents (N = 284)*	*Malay workers in Klang Valley (N = 133)*
Do you like to travel for holidays?					
• Yes	95.4	88.7	91.7	92.3	87.2
• No	4.6	11.3	8.3	7.7	12.8
Did you travel for holiday inside the country in the last two years?					
• Yes	89.8	82.5	85.4	86.3	27.8
• No	10.2	17.5	14.6	13.7	72.2
Did you travel abroad for holiday in the last two years?					
• Yes	57.4	50.0	35.4	47.9	23.3
• No	42.6	50.0	64.6	52.1	76.7
How many times did you travel abroad in the last two years?					
• None	42.6	50.0	64.6	52.1	76.7
• Once	34.3	44.2	33.4	36.6	23.3
• Twice	15.0	3.6	1.0	7.0	—
• Three and more	8.1	2.2	1.0	4.3	—
Do you shop while travelling abroad? (referring only to those who traveled abroad)					
• Yes	84.9	73.6	71.8	77.2	23.3
• No	15.1	26.4	28.2	22.8	76.7

Source: Survey data 1996 and 1997.

Again, in terms of travel within Malaysia, it was the new Malay middle-class respondents in the Klang Valley who travelled most, compared to their counterparts in Kota Bharu and Kuala Terengganu, although the difference in this case was rather small. For example, 89.8 per cent of the former went on local holidays, compared to 82.5 per cent from Kota Bharu and 85.4 per cent from Kuala Terengganu. In considering foreign travel,[4] the difference was sharper. While 57.4 per cent of the Klang Valley respondents went abroad for holidays, among those in Kota Bharu and Kuala Terengganu, the proportions were much lower – that is, 50 per cent and 35.4 per cent respectively. In this regard, the Klang Valley new Malay middle-class respondents were more cosmopolitan and widely travelled, while those in the two provincial towns were more insular.

Among Malay workers, the overwhelming majority (87.2 per cent) also liked to take holidays and travel (Table 6.9). However, for financial and other reasons, only slightly more than one-quarter had managed to go on domestic travel to any of the popular holiday destinations. The proportion who went abroad for holidays was much smaller, making up only 23.3 per cent. Finally, in the case of the Malaysian working class, their destinations were mainly neighbouring countries such as Thailand, Indonesia, Singapore and the Philippines.

Golfing and other recreational activities

While shopping, eating out and travel by our new Malay middle-class respondents discussed above were family activities, golfing and certain other recreational activities only involved respondents. Golfing is still a highly exclusive activity, involving only very small proportions of the more affluent new Malay middle-class. In this study, only 10.5 per cent of our respondents were members of golf clubs and played golf on a regular basis (Table 6.10). Those who were not yet members, but intended to join at some time in the future made up another 7.3 per cent. The overwhelming majority (87.5 per cent) were neither members nor did they intend to become members. In golfing as well as travel, the cosmopolitan Klang Valley new Malay middle-class respondents were more active than those in the two provincial towns. For example, among Klang Valley respondents, one-fifth were already golfers and another 15.7 per cent wanted to follow suit, thus increasing the proportion to more than a third. In Kota Bharu, only 3.8 per cent were golfers and 10 per cent wanted to sign up for membership later. In Kuala Terengganu, the proportion of golfers was slightly higher than in Kota Bharu, but it was still very small (5.2 per cent), and those intending to become new golf club members were also few (7.3 per cent).

Table 6.10   Membership of golf clubs and other recreational activities among respondents

	Klang Valley (*n* = 108)	Kota Bharu (*n* = 80)	Kuala Terengganu (*n* = 96)	All new Malay middle-class respondents (*N* = 284)	Malay workers in Klang Valley (*N* = 133)
Are you a golf club member?					
• Yes	20.4	3.8	5.2	10.5	Nil
• Not yet, but intend to be member	15.7	10.0	7.3	11.3	Nil
• No	63.9	86.3	87.5	78.2	100.0
Do you frequent coffee houses?					
• Often	8.3	5.0	7.3	7.0	Nil
• Sometimes	38.9	25.0	21.9	29.2	Nil
• Never	52.8	70.0	70.8	63.7	100.0
Do you frequent karaoke pubs?					
• Often	17.6	2.5	2.1	8.1	Nil
• Sometimes	42.6	11.3	13.5	23.9	5.0
• Never	39.8	86.3	84.3	67.9	95.0

Source: Survey data 1996 and 1997.

These findings correspond with those from some other studies (for example, Norani Othman et al. 1996; Tan Poo Chang et al. 1996; Rahimah Aziz et al. 1998) which show that golfing in Malaysia is confined to a small minority, even among the new middle class of various ethnic groups. However, the situation was very different among the Malay administrative middle class in Nordin's study in the early 1970s (Nordin 1976: 283). In Nordin's sample, three-fifths were golf club members.[5]

Patronizing coffee houses and karaoke pubs – as a form of recreation and socializing – are also favourite pastimes among a small section of the new Malay middle class, especially in the Klang Valley. Overall, only 7 per cent of our respondents were regular patrons of coffee houses, and 8.1 per cent regularly patronized karaoke bars (Table 6.10). The proportions, however, would increase to 36.2 per cent and 32 per cent respectively if we include the more infrequent patrons of these places. By comparison, larger proportions of Klang Valley respondents participated in these activities compared to their counterparts in Kota Bharu and Kuala Terengganu. For example, while 47.2 per cent of the former were regular and not-so-regular patrons of coffee houses, the corresponding proportions were 30 per cent and 28.9 per cent respectively in Kota Bharu and Kuala Terengganu. Karaoke bars were more popular with Klang Valley respondents, with slightly over three-fifths patronizing them either regularly or occasionally. However, in the two provincial towns, they were less popular than coffee houses. In Kota Bharu, for example, the proportion socializing at karaoke bars was only 13.8 per cent (including 2.5 per cent of regular patrons), while in Kuala Terengganu, the corresponding figure was 15.6 per cent (including 2.1 per cent who classified themselves as regular patrons).

As indicated above, golfing and socializing at coffee houses and karaoke bars were overwhelmingly middle-class activities, confined mostly to a small section of the new Malay middle class, and being most common among those in the Klang Valley. Such activities were not found among Malay workers, except for a few who patronized karaoke bars once in a while.

Reading habits and cultural preferences

One of the concerns with the growth of the new middle class is whether it can serve as a modernizing force, standing at the intellectual and cultural frontiers of society. Being the most educated class, members of the new middle class are expected to have developed preferences for intellectual or cultural pursuits such as reading and other forms of high culture.

As discussed earlier, television talk shows that generally have an intellectual and educational bent (such as *Global*, *Minda* and *Wawancara*) attracted a small minority of all new Malay middle-class respondents, although news and current affairs attracted an overwhelming majority. Such preferences can also be corroborated by an examination of their reading habits. In this study (see Table 6.11), it was found that practically all respondents took an interest in news and current affairs by reading newspapers on a regular basis, with over two-thirds buying two newspapers or more daily. Besides newspapers, they also read magazines and periodicals for news and current affairs, although the proportion of regular readers was much lower than for newspapers.

In terms of reading materials on news and current affairs, respondents in the Klang Valley were well ahead of their counterparts in the two

Table 6.11 Reading of newspapers and magazines among respondents (%)

	New Malay middle class in Klang Valley (n = 108)	New Malay middle class in Kota Bharu (n = 80)	New Malay middle class in Kuala Terengganu (n = 96)	All new Malay middle-class respondents (N = 284)	Malay workers in Klang Valley (N = 133)
News & current affairs					
Do you read daily papers regularly?					
No	1.8	3.7	2.1	2.0	6.8
Yes	98.2	96.3	97.9	98.0	93.2
No. of newspapers read					
None	1.8	3.7	2.1	2.0	6.8
One	17.6	47.5	30.2	30.3	66.7
Two	41.7	40.0	58.3	46.8	27.1
Three or more	39.0	8.8	9.4	20.9	—
Time spent reading newspapers daily					
None	1.8	3.7	2.1	2.5	6.8
One hour or less	62.0	67.5	65.6	64.8	80.4
Two hours or more	36.2	28.8	32.3	32.7	12.8
Do you read Malay magazines/ periodicals?					
No	51.9	33.8	37.5	41.9	60.9
Once in a while	25.0	22.5	20.8	22.9	27.1
Often	23.1	43.7	41.7	35.2	12.0
Do you read English magazines/ periodicals?					
No	13.9	50.0	44.8	34.5	87.2
Once in a while	21.3	16.2	21.9	20.1	6.0
Often	64.8	33.7	33.3	45.4	6.8

Table 6.11   Reading of newspapers and magazines among respondents (%)
(*continued*)

Entertainment materials Do you read entertainment magazines?					
No	33.3	30.1	21.9	28.5	25.6
Once in a while	55.6	51.2	60.4	56.0	57.1
Often	11.1	18.7	17.7	15.5	17.3
Materials on religion Do you read magazines on religion?					
No	33.3	26.3	12.5	24.3	35.3
Once in a while	46.3	25.0	44.8	39.8	40.6
Often	20.4	48.8	42.7	35.9	24.1

Source: Survey data 1996 and 1997.

provincial towns. For example, 80.7 per cent read two or more newspapers on average (in both Malay and English) daily, and about two-thirds regularly read magazines and periodicals in English – the most popular being *Asiaweek* and *Far Eastern Economic Review*, although a small number also read *Time*, *Newsweek* and the *Economist*. New Malay middle-class respondents in the Klang Valley preferred materials in English, as evidenced by the fact that only 23.1 per cent read Malay magazines and periodicals regularly, compared to almost three times that figure who read English materials. Among respondents in Kota Bharu and Kuala Terengganu, their language preferences were for magazines and periodicals in Malay (such as the monthly *Dewan Masyarakat* and *Dewan Budaya* and the weekly *Massa*) as evidenced by the fact that more than two-fifths read Malay magazines and periodicals regularly, compared to less than half reading in English.

While interest in entertainment magazines was not strong among all respondents, there was a far greater preference for materials on religion, especially among respondents in Kota Bharu and Kuala Terengganu; about half of respondents in the former and over two-fifths in the latter regularly read such magazines, compared to only one-fifth among those in the Klang Valley.

Table 6.12   Languages used by new Malay middle-class and Malay working-class respondents in daily communications

	Klang Valley (*n* = 108)	*Kota Bharu* (*n* = 80)	*Kuala Terengganu* (*n* = 96)	*All new Malay middle-class respondents* (*N* = 284)	*Malay workers in Klang Valley* (*N* = 133)
Malay only	1.9	26.3	26.0	16.9	48.9
English only	1.9	—	1.0	1.1	—
Malay and English	88.0	63.8	69.8	75.0	43.6
Malay, English and local dialect	8.3	8.8	3.1	6.7	7.5
Do you use English more than Malay in your daily communications?					
Yes	69.4	17.5	17.7	10.5	—
No	30.6	82.5	82.3	89.5	—

Source: Survey data 1996 and 1997.

Though newspaper and magazine reading was popular among respondents, books and novels were much less popular. While about three-fifths read books and over a third read novels, the number who did not read them was relatively large. Furthermore, those who did read books and novels only read a limited number. In fact, over 70 per cent admitted that their reading habit was only 'moderately strong', 21.5 per cent described theirs as 'weak', and only 7.4 per cent regarded themselves as 'avid readers'. Among all respondents, more than one-third did not have personal book collections or home libraries, while the majority who had home libraries possessed relatively small collections of less than 100 titles.

Although Malay is the national and official language of Malaysia, members of the new Malay middle class use both English and Malay in their daily communications (Table 6.12). However, Malay middle-class respondents in the Klang Valley were more anglicized. In fact, the majority (69.4 per cent) used English frequently in their daily communications, compared to only 30.6 per cent who frequently used Malay.[6] Among respondents in Kota Bharu and Kuala Terengganu, the opposite prevailed as over four-fifths in both towns frequently used more Malay

Table 6.13   Self-evaluation by new Malay middle-class and Malay working-class respondents of their class position

Self-evaluation of class position	Klang Valley (n = 108)	Kota Bharu (n = 80)	Kuala Terengganu (n = 96)	All new Malay middle-class respondents (N = 284)	Malay workers in Klang Valley (N = 133)
Upper class	—	1.3	—	0.4	—
Upper middle class	8.2	1.3	5.2	4.8	3.0
Middle middle class	56.2	53.8	36.5	48.0	27.8
Lower middle class	30.1	37.5	50.0	40.2	44.4
Lower class	2.7	1.3	6.3	3.6	20.3
Do not belong to any class	2.8	5.1	2.0	2.8	4.5
Total	100.0	100.0	100.0	100.0	100.0

Source: Survey data 1996 and 1997.

than English, showing clearly the language 'divide' between the metropolitan Malay middle class and their provincial counterparts.

Self-evaluation of class position

Given the heterogeneous lifestyles of different sections of the new Malay middle class, it would be interesting to examine how members of the new Malay middle class perceived their own class positions. As shown in Table 6.13, they perceived themselves as being stratified into five groups. About half of the respondents perceived themselves as being from the 'middle' middle class, but a very small minority (5.2 per cent) – comprised of high-income earners – identified themselves as 'upper class' or 'upper middle class'. However, a substantial proportion (40.2 per cent) of respondents, especially those in Kota Bharu and Kuala Terengganu, perceived themselves as belonging to the 'lower middle class', and about 4 per cent (mostly those from Kuala Terengganu) perceived themselves as belonging to the 'lower class'. However, eight respondents, or 2 per cent, regarded themselves as not belonging to any class because according to them, as Muslims, 'everybody was equal before God'.

Among Malay workers, the majority perceived themselves as belonging to the 'lower middle class' (41.4 per cent) or the 'lower class' (20.3 per cent), while another 4.6 per cent claimed that they 'did not belong to any particular class'. This finding suggests that only a small proportion (less than 10 per cent) of the new Malay middle-class respondents (mostly those from the Klang Valley and Kuala Terengganu) who identified themselves as 'upper class' and 'upper middle class', consciously saw themselves as clearly differentiated from other middle-class fractions and from the working class. Some 3 per cent of the more affluent Malay workers regarded themselves as 'upper middle class'.

Conclusions

As indicated in Chapter 4, of special interest to scholars of the new middle class is the question of 'middle-classing and lifestyling' – that is, to what extent have new middle-class lifestyles transformed them from 'a class in itself' to 'a class for itself', with distinct class attributes, such as status symbols, status consciousness, and class solidarity, which differentiate them from other classes – in particular, the lower classes (Yang 1999; Chang 1994; Gerke 1995; Robison and Goodman 1996). In this chapter, however, it has been shown that, in the main, two general differentiating tendencies were found to be operating among the new Malay middle class. On the one hand, there is the homogenizing process among the more affluent sections – the 'new rich' – consisting mainly of western-educated and widely travelled high-income managers and professionals, whose values and lifestyles were very much cosmopolitan in nature. This group of cosmopolitan urbanites – which constituted only a small fraction of the new middle class – objectively and subjectively differentiated themselves from other middle-class fractions, and especially from the lower classes. On the other hand, despite being more affluent, better educated, urbanized and modernized than their parents or their country cousins, broad sections of the new Malay middle class indulged in relatively modest lifestyles, as measured terms of living conditions, consumption, travel and recreation. Their modest lifestyles also correspond with their self-evaluation of their own class positions. While a small proportion of the 'new rich' has distinct lifestyles and cultural preferences and is more cosmopolitan in orientation, the majority of the new Malay middle-class respondents does not appear to constitute a 'class for itself', with distinct social status attributes and consciousness. In this sense, they are very much 'folk urbanites' – an issue discussed in Chapter 7.

7
The New Malay Middle Class and Community

Introduction

The term 'community' implies having something in common. However, community – a social phenomenon found in every society, even during modern times – is often associated in people's minds with rural environments, and is thought to be something unfamiliar in urban and, especially, metropolitan settings. Since the nineteenth century, one central concern in social theory has been that the processes of urbanization and industrialization would result in the demise of community. The 'loss of community' thesis was first advanced by the German sociologist Tönnies (1957) in his work entitled *Gemeinschaft und Gesellschaft* (first published in 1887), in which he showed the change from the personal, the emotional and the traditional in the *Gemeinschaft* to the impersonal, the rational and the contractual of the *Gesellschaft*. While agreeing that both *Gemeinschaft*-like and *Gesellschaft*-like relationships could be found in rural and urban settings, he argued that there was a greater tendency towards *Gemeinschaft*-like relationships in rural areas. This idea was developed by a number of later scholars, the most well known being George Simmel and Louis Wirth (discussed in Lee and Newby 1994). Following Tönnies and Simmel, Wirth suggested that as people move from the countryside to the city, so they leave behind a 'rural way of life' and take on the values and behaviour of 'urbanism as a way of life' (Wirth 1938; discussed in Lee and Newby 1994: 47).

However, while a number of contemporary works support the above view, there are several studies in major industrial societies such as Britain, the United States and Japan which suggest that community-like social groups sometimes survive or grow in urban conurbations in the midst of cities. The well-known communities studied have included Bethnal

Green, a metropolitan borough in the East End of London (Townsend 1957; Young and Wilmott 1957; Willmott and Young 1960; Frankenburg 1969), and the West End neighbourhood in Boston's inner city in the United States (Gans 1962).

In Japan, under the influence of works pioneered by Yanagita Kunio (1875–1962), and later developed by Kamishima Jiro, Kosaku (1992: 98–103) argues that when Japanese villagers migrated to the city, they brought with them village-style social organizations and belief systems, and formed 'secondary villages' or 'quasi-villages' within cities; thus, even after the disintegration of 'natural villages', traditional patterns of order persisted in these urban quasi-villages. Kosaku notes that in Japan, the company is frequently regarded as the epitome of the quasi-village, and the social principles of the traditional village community are considered to have reproduced themselves in informal groupings developed among company employees. Kosaku's thesis – which he calls the 'reproductionist' (or 'extensionist') theory of modern society – depicts modern industrial society as a coherent and uniform whole, and views the village community as the prototype of modern Japanese society. In short, contra Wirth and others, Kosaku sees modern city living in Japan as an extension or a reproduction of the Japanese traditional village settings, implying continuities rather than ruptures in the processes of urbanization and industrialization.

My study adopts a slightly different position. While acknowledging that the opposing arguments of 'ruptures and change' on the one hand, and 'continuity, reproduction and extension' on the other have their merits, this study proposes that in multi-ethnic and multicultural Malaysia, the dynamics of modern social class formations and urban living are more complex, producing a myriad of cultural forms including a complex array of adaptations, innovations, and changes.[1] The greater the complexity of society, such as found in the multi-ethnic and multicultural metropolitan area of Kuala Lumpur and Petaling Jaya, the greater the tendency of members of the new Malay middle class to exhibit cultural varieties and nuances, compared to their counterparts in the less urbanized and more homogenous Kota Bharu and Kuala Terengganu.

As shown in earlier chapters, members of the new Malay middle class – in adapting to the new environment – attempt to reconstitute and reaffirm those family and kinship ties which have been altered by the processes of rapid social change, and try to ensure that their family exists within a 'modified extended family' framework adapted to urban conditions. In Chapter 6, we showed that new Malay middle-class lifestyles were not homogenous; though the more affluent middle-class fraction adopts high-status lifestyles and become cosmopolitan urbanites, others lead relatively modest lifestyles not dramatically different from the lower classes. In this chapter, we examine further the social culture[2] of the new Malay middle class by examining the processes in which new middle-class Malays attempt to establish communities within new urban environments, and the relationship between these processes with their religious commitment and activities. It shows that the *surau* (a Muslim prayer-house smaller than the mosque) is pivotal in community-building among the new Malay middle class, and although Malay urban communities are built by relying on certain cultural resources acquired by Malays when they grew up in their *kampung*,[3] they also contain new, innovative elements created under changed material conditions. This chapter examines in particular the phenomenon of 'folk urbanites' – that is, urban-dwellers whose lifestyles are relatively modest, with relatively strong family and community orientation, rather than being cosmopolitan, individualistic and isolated from kin and community. Contrary to cosmopolitan urbanites who adopt cosmopolitan urban living, 'folk urbanites' – though living in modern urban settings – tend to operate within the domain of Malay cultural values and religious practices, and, by utilizing the cultural resources mentioned above, attempt to construct '*kampung*-like' communities in the city or town, based on their nostalgic images of the Malay traditional village.[4] However, it is argued here that although it may give a semblance of maintaining tradition, their cultural attachment to the 'pastness' is essentially modern. In this regard, I share Clive Kessler's (1992: 133–57) view that what appears to be 'tradition' in modern urban society is not simply 'residual' but something 'essentially new, modern, contemporary – a recent construct'.[5]

It must be made clear that the term 'community' is not synonymous with neighbourhood. The neighbourhood is a fixed and bounded locality, but community, consisting of a network of relationships, is more of a local social system – that is, as a set of social relationships which take place wholly, or mostly, within a locality. But there is another dimension to the meaning of community as a type of social relationship providing a sense of identity between individuals – something like the 'spirit of community', or 'communion' (see Lee and Newby 1994: ch. 4), engendering a sense of belonging among its members. Thus, in this study, when we refer to the new Malay middle-class community in the urban milieu, we mean not only the social relationships established by members of the new Malay middle class in the physical locality in which they live, but also the extensive networks of relationships they maintain with their kin and friends in the same city, in the home village or birthplace, and elsewhere.[6]

As shown by other scholars, in such communities, interactions can be kin- or ethnic-based; economic; political; ritual or religious, or recreational (Frankenburg 1969: 249), though in our study, most of the interactions referred to are kin and ethnic, political, recreational, as well as ritual or religious.

Urban residential areas and presence of communities

In Britain, it has been noted that town planners and housing authorities generally see the housing estates they build as more than just aggregations of dwellings; rather, they see them as neighbourhoods which will evolve into communities, and their expectation is that residents should not only live side by side, but come to be 'good neighbours and friends'. Such planning and ideology seeks to impose an idealized version of village life on the town dweller in housing estates (Frankenburg 1969: 197). In Malaysia, two contrasting trends have emerged. While similar planning and ideology prevail, stressing the importance of community, a trend towards appropriating global icons preferred by the new rich, including the cosmopolitan urbanites, is also to be found, especially in metropolitan cities. The first trend is often expressed in the form of names prefixed to housing estates – for example, prefixing the word *desa* or *kampung* (both words meaning 'village') to housing areas such as Desa Sri Petaling in Kuala Lumpur and Kampung Tunku in Petaling Jaya, or the word *taman* (meaning 'garden') to places like Taman Tun Dr. Ismail, Taman Aman, Taman Danau Desa and Taman Bukit Kajang. These are attempts to project an identity for the area, not only as green and beautiful, but more importantly, as constituting a peaceful community suitable for family living. More up-market developers, however, stress class more than community, by appropriating anglicized names such as Country Heights, Damansara Heights and Ukay Heights, the global cultural icons projecting exclusive high-class profiles to create a niche market for property in the area. While the practice of choosing names for residential areas in the metropolitan Klang Valley – all the above-named places are found there – reflects both the tendency of cultural homogenization among the new rich (that is, identification with the cultural tastes of the western rich) and particularization (in other words, stressing local communities) among other middle-class fractions, the practice in Kota Bharu and Kuala Terengganu consistently stresses community, rather than class. The words *desa, kampung* and *taman* are common names for housing estates in these two provincial towns, while anglicized names denoting westernized upper-class tastes are rarely used there (except for names of certain mansions belonging to the wealthy elite).[7] However, besides these practices, in keeping with the NEP, Malaysian town planners and housing authorities also consciously work to ensure a more multi-ethnic composition of housing estates by stipulating that at least 30 per cent of houses in any new housing area be allocated to Bumiputera buyers.

How were these residential areas or housing estates perceived by our new Malay middle-class respondents? Were they seen as mere aggregations of urban dwellings, or as communities?

The idea of the Malays having cultural attachment to their traditions can be found in the minds of respondents and is reflected in their words and actions. As shown in Table 7.1, many respondents perceived urban residential areas that Malays move into or grow up in as having a number of important characteristics which make them similar to rural villages. If these characteristics did not yet exist in the area they moved in, they would attempt to construct them. This is suggested in our sample in which more than three-quarters of new Malay middle-class respondents felt that Malays usually attempt to set up *kampung*-like communities wherever they go. This was true of respondents from the middle class in the three areas studied, especially in Kota Bharu and Kuala Terengganu, and also true of working-class respondents in the Klang Valley.[8] While 73.1 per cent of new Malay middle-class respondents in the Klang Valley agreed that Malays attempt to construct *kampung*-like communities in urban areas, a much higher proportion of their counterparts in Kota Bharu and Kuala Terengganu – 86.3 per cent and 75.0 per cent – felt the same. Even among Klang Valley Malay workers, a large proportion (around three-quarters) also held the same view as that of respondents from the new Malay middle class.

Consistent with the perception among the majority of respondents that there was such attachment to older traditions among urban Malays, 78.1 per cent felt that their residential areas had characteristics *semacam kampung tetapi bukan kampung*, meaning that their residential areas had some *kampung*-like characteristics but were not *kampung* (villages) in the traditional sense. By comparison, the proportion who perceived that their residential area had *kampung*-like characteristics was highest in Kota Bharu (90 per cent), followed by Kuala Terengganu (86.6 per cent). Although the proportion was much lower in the metropolitan Klang Valley, it was still quite high considering that more than three-fifths of the respondents agreed that their residential area possessed such characteristics. This finding suggests that most residential areas in the two provincial towns in which the new Malay middle-class respondents lived were perceived, not as mere aggregations of dwellings, but as communities in

Table 7.1 Respondents' perceptions of their residential area

	Klang Valley (n = 108)	Kota Bharu (n = 80)	Kuala Trengganu (n = 96)	All Malay middle-class respondents (N = 284)	Malay workers in Klang Valley (N = 133)
Do you agree that Malays attempt to set up communities in urban areas with characteristics similar to a *kampung*?					
• No	26.9	13.7	25.0	22.5	25.0
• Agree	61.1	55.0	51.0	56.0	43.0
• Strongly agree	12.0	31.3	24.0	21.5	31.3
Do you agree that your residential area has characteristics similar to a *kampung*?					
• No	38.0	10.0	13.5	21.8	23.8
• Agree	47.2	45.0	32.3	41.5	40.8
• Strongly agree	14.8	45.0	54.2	36.6	35.4

Source: Survey data 1996 and 1997.

which various interactions take place. In the metropolitan Klang Valley, community life was also perceived to be present in the residential areas, though it is considered relatively weaker.[9]

However, perceptions concerning urban Malays were not homogenous especially among the new Malay middle-class respondents in the Klang Valley. Over a quarter of the latter, consisting mostly of the cosmopolitan Malay middle-class urbanites, felt that there was no such attachment to tradition, meaning that Malays do not attempt to construct such characteristics in their social relations and practices when they move into urban areas. They felt that there was change or even a rupture from tradition, resulting in a cultural uprooting, among Malays who moved to urban areas. They argued that *kampung*-like communities could not exist when people were too busy attending to their jobs, had little time for their neighbours (and even their families), and when they mainly cared for themselves. What is quite unexpected is that in small towns such as Kuala Terengganu, which is predominantly Malay, a quarter of respondents felt the same way as some of their Klang Valley counterparts – that is, they felt that Malays did not attempt to set up *kampung*-like communities in urban areas.

To establish the criteria for the presence of communities with *kampung*-like characteristics in urban Malay middle-class areas, the study first asked respondents to indicate the presence in their residential area of seven items considered to be indicators of such community; then, we asked respondents if they agreed that any residential area with these criteria could be considered a community with characteristics similar to a *kampung* (Table 7.2). The items considered as indicators of community are: the presence of *surau*-based activities; the extent to which neighbours know each other and the flows of gifts among neighbours; the practice of *gotong royong* or mutual help among neighbours, especially for certain *rite de passage* activities (for example, during the preparation of their children's wedding feasts and while welcoming guests); group socialization of children in basic religious education, for example, Quran reading; and residents' concern for neighbours who face family tragedies (for example, death of a member of the family) by visiting them as well as attending *kenduri/tahlil* (feasts that come together with thanksgiving religious rituals) in their houses.

All respondents were asked each of these items in order to measure the presence of these activities in their neighbourhoods and then they were asked to state whether a neighbourhood with these characteristics could be considered a community with *kampung*-like characteristics. From the respondents' replies, the overwhelming majority (four-fifths) agreed that if all or most of the criteria listed by the study were met by residents in a particular residential area, then in their opinion the area was a community with *kampung*-like characteristics.

What are the dynamics of community life among Malays? Malays, who have been Muslims for more than 600 years, regard the prayer-house – the *surau* or the mosque – as an important religious-cum-social institution which brings believers together and forms the basis of community interactions. Such an institution – a common feature of traditional Malay villages – is reproduced everywhere Malays go,[10] including in urban areas. Compared to rural areas, the *surau* as a social institution in the changed material conditions of new urban settings, where neighbours are often strangers, becomes all the more important. *Surau*-based religious and social activities help Malay urbanites to get to know each other and to interact more frequently as neighbours. This can be regarded as a cultural innovation in a new environment based on their traditional cultural resources.

New Malay middle-class respondents generally had positive images of their residential area as far as neighbourliness was concerned. For example, as shown in Table 7.2, over 90 per cent of new Malay middle-class respondents regarded their respective housing area as having congregation prayers and other *surau*/mosque-based activities, with the highest proportions being among respondents in Kota Bharu and Kuala Terengganu, followed by the Klang Valley. Besides *surau*-based activities, 85.8 per cent of respondents acknowledged that their residential area also had places where their children could attend Quran reading lessons, something every Muslim child is expected to do. In terms of respondents' interactions as neighbours, over 90 per cent said their neighbours knew one another. This knowledge was cemented with expressions of neighbourliness, such as exchanging food gifts, or participating in *gotong royong* activities when their help was required. This happened, for example, when neighbours held wedding feasts for their children in the compound for which neighbours' help was sought not only to play host to wedding guests, but also to allow part of the neighbours' compounds and even their houses to be used for purposes of preparation. (This was necessary especially for those who lived in linked houses, but those in single-unit bungalows or other single-unit houses would require less use of their neighbours' compounds, but still they required their physical assistance).[11] Also, when misfortune befell any neighbour (such as the death of a family member), more than four-fifths of respondents said that other residents would pay condolence visits to share the sorrow of the neighbour; over 90 per cent also said that

Table 7.2 Respondents' assessment of *kampung*-like community activities in their residential area

	Klang Valley (*n* = 108)	Kota Bharu (*n* = 80)	Kuala Terengganu (*n* = 96)	All Malay middle-class respondents (*N* = 284)	Malay workers in Klang Valley (*N* = 133)
Are there *surau*/mosque-based activities in the neighbourhood?					
• No activities	9.3	2.5	6.2	6.3	5.4
• I don't know	2.8	3.8	—	2.1	1.5
• Yes, to a certain extent	10.2	21.3	6.3	12.0	17.7
• Yes	77.8	72.5	87.5	79.6	75.4
Do neighbours know each other?					
• No, they don't	6.5	3.8	1.0	3.9	2.3
• I don't know if they do	4.6	3.8	5.2	4.6	6.2
• Neighbours know each other to a certain extent	45.4	27.5	25.0	33.4	31.5
• Yes, neighbours know each other	43.5	65.0	68.8	58.1	60.0
Is it common for neighbours to exchange food?					
• No	23.1	3.8	9.4	14.4	15.4
• I don't know	10.2	6.2	5.2	7.4	13.8
• Yes, to a certain extent	35.2	45.0	37.5	38.7	28.5
• Yes	31.5	40.0	47.9	39.4	42.3
Do neighbours participate in *gotong royong* (mutual help) when they prepare rites of passage activities such as wedding feasts for their children?					
• No	8.3	3.8	3.1	5.3	12.3
• I don't know	13.9	5.0	3.1	7.7	6.9
• Yes, to a certain extent	13.0	18.8	11.5	14.1	19.2
• Yes	64.8	72.5	82.3	72.9	61.5

Table 7.2 Respondents' assessment of *kampung*-like community activities in their residential area (*continued*)

	Klang Valley (n = 108)	Kota Bharu (n = 80)	Kuala Terengganu (n = 96)	All Malay middle-class respondents (N = 284)	Malay workers in Klang Valley (N = 133)
Are there places for children to attend Quran reading lessons?					
• No	9.3	5.0	5.2	6.7	4.6
• I don't know	11.1	3.8	6.2	7.4	15.4
• Yes, to a certain extent	6.5	13.8	10.4	9.8	11.5
• Yes	73.1	77.5	78.1	76.0	68.5
Do neighbours pay condolence visits to families who suffer bereavement with the death of family members?					
• No	8.3	3.8	3.1	5.3	6.2
• I don't know	13.9	5.0	3.1	6.2	4.6
• Yes, to a certain extent	13.0	18.8	11.5	10.4	23.8
• Yes, they always do	64.8	72.5	82.3	78.1	65.4
Do residents attend *tahlil/kenduri* (feasts held with religious rituals) at neighbours' houses?					
• Yes					
• No	9.3	2.5	3.1	5.3	6.9
• I don't know	5.6	2.5	3.1	3.9	15.4
• Yes, to a certain extent	25.0	16.3	16.7	19.7	20.0
• Yes	60.2	78.8	77.1	71.1	57.7
Do you agree that any residential area can be considered a *kampung*-like community if all or most of the above activities exist there?					
• I don't agree	24.1	12.5	22.9	20.4	22.4
• Yes, I agree	75.9	87.5	77.1	79.6	79.6

Source: Survey data 1996 and 1997

neighbours were often invited to attend thanksgiving feasts such as *tahlil* or other *kenduri* held by other neighbours. As expected, the most positive assessment of the presence of these community activities came from respondents in Kota Bharu and Kuala Terengganu, but many in the Klang Valley also felt the same. This finding of respondents' positive assessment of their community corresponds with their overall perception that their residential area had many important *kampung*-like characteristics.

Besides the respondents' assessment of the presence of these activities in their neighbourhood, they were also asked the extent to which they themselves participated in these activities. Though the majority of respondents said that their residential area had *surau*-based activities, those who regularly prayed at the *surau* made up only slightly more than one-third, while the majority were not-so-regular, and about 10 per cent admitted that they did not attend congregational prayers at the *surau*. The proportion of respondents who knew their neighbours was high – more than a third claimed to know many neighbours, with a proportion saying that they knew many of them well. (Some, especially among regular *surau*-goers, said they knew more than 50 neighbours well.) About one-third also participated regularly in *gotong royong* such as wedding preparations when their neighbour's children were getting married. Unlike in Kota Bharu or Kuala Terengganu, the proportion of Klang Valley middle-class respondents who regularly participated in *gotong royong* was predictably low (17.6 per cent), partly because some of them held their children's wedding ceremonies in hotels and also because of a weaker sense of neighbourliness in the metropolitan area. When it comes to paying condolence visits to grief-stricken neighbours due to the passing away of family members, over 90 per cent of respondents paid such visits. Many also participated in the flow of food gifts between neighbours, and attended *tahlil* or *kenduri* at their neighbours' houses.

However, in all these activities, new Malay middle-class respondents in Kota Bharu and Kuala Terengganu were, by far, well ahead of their Klang Valley counterparts. For example, while more than two-fifths in both Kota Bharu and Kuala Terengganu could be categorized as regular *surau*-goers, the proportion in the Klang Valley that fell under the same category was less than one-fifth. In addition, there was a much higher proportion of respondents in the two provincial towns who knew their neighbours well, participated in *gotong royong* activities, or visited their grief-stricken neighbours. While only about 10 per cent of Klang Valley respondents made it a regular practice to exchange food with their neighbours, about one-third or more did so regularly in Kota Bharu and Kuala Terengganu. This finding corresponds with the earlier finding that the overwhelming majority of respondents in both towns regarded their residential community as having characteristics similar to a *kampung*.

In the communities discussed, vertical impersonal ties to centralized decision-making bodies such as the local authorities as well as the state and central governments existed, especially when it concerned official matters regarding the affairs of citizens as ratepayers, voters, and so on. However, these vertical relationships did not replace horizontal ties – that is, ties with kin, friends, neighbours and community.[12] Both vertical and horizontal ties are strong, while the presence of the former does not replace the latter. Nevertheless, compared to those in Kota Bharu and Kuala Terengganu, horizontal (read: community) ties among a substantial proportion of Klang Valley respondents were weaker.

Ethnic composition of urban communities

From the preceding discussion, we can infer that for many new Malay middle-class respondents, urban residential areas which might be anonymous to them in the beginning, gradually transformed into familiar places through social interactions with neighbours, in particular, through their *surau*-based activities. After a while, new communities were formed and horizontal relationships continued to be reinforced. The question is: what are the contributory factors for the emergence of this phenomenon? One important factor is the ethnic composition of local residents: the higher the proportion of Malays in the area, the greater the probability of it developing into a community, though it need not necessarily be so in all cases. In Kuala Terengganu and Kota Bharu, almost all respondents reported that Malays were the majority in their area. In the Klang Valley, the composition is more varied; about half of the Klang Valley respondents reported that Malays made up the majority in their area, and over one-third said that while their area had many Malays, they did not constitute a majority. This study found a strong correlation between ethnic composition and the existence of community. Table 7.3 shows that residential areas in which Malays constituted the majority were regarded by new Malay middle-class respondents as having community characteristics, while the opposite is true in areas where Malays were a minority. Because of this, it is not surprising that the proportions of respondents who regarded their neighbourhoods as communities were higher in Kota Bharu and Kuala Terengganu, and lower in the Klang Valley.

Another factor that may be relevant is the age of the housing area. Most of the housing areas in Kota Bharu in which respondents lived were

Table 7.3   Correlation between residents' ethnic composition and respondents' perception of residential area as community

Ethnic composition of residential area	Perception of residential area as community			All Malay middle-class respondents (N = 284)
	No	*Yes, to a certain extent*	*Yes*	
Malays a minority	85.0	10.0	5.0	100.0
Many Malays, but not majority	36.2	53.2	10.6	100.0
Majority Malays	14.3	47.6	38.1	100.0

Source: Survey data 1996 and 1997.

relatively old, having been in existence for more than 15 years, while the rest were between 11 and 15 years old. By comparison, the residential areas in which respondents in Kuala Terengganu and the Klang Valley lived were relatively new; only 56 per cent of the residential areas in Kuala Terengganu were more than 10 years old, while in the Klang Valley, housing areas of the same age were much smaller in number. This finding suggests that the longer the residential area had been in existence, the greater the probability of it developing into community, provided that Malays constituted the majority or a large proportion of residents in the area.

Nevertheless, we should not assume that those more ethnically homogenous residential areas that have been established for a longer period of time would automatically develop into communities. As suggested by the data in Table 7.3, 14.3 per cent of respondents in Malay majority areas felt that their residential areas had no characteristics of *kampung*-like communities, while another 47.6 per cent felt that they only had such characteristics to a certain extent. The presence of community activities and relationships depends on what the actors (that is, respondents) themselves do in their everyday social interactions.

Religion and community

Today, all societies in the world are affected in one way or another by the multilayered processes of globalization (Robertson 1992; Beyer 1994; Mittelman 1996). As Beyer (1994: 3) points out, one paradox of globalization is that while the global system undermines inherited, ascribed or constructed cultural and personal identities through homogenization processes, at the same time, it promotes the construction and revitalization of particular identities as ways of gaining control over systemic power. One particular cultural and personal identity discussed in this chapter is religion.

As a number of other developing countries, rapid industrialization and modernization have not diminished people's beliefs in religion and participation in religious movements and activities in Malaysia. The resurgence of religious movements in Malaysia especially the rise of Islam, in the 1970s and 1980s, has been a subject of study for many scholars (Chandra Muzaffar 1987; Zainah Anwar 1987; Ackerman and Lee 1988; Jomo and Ahmad Shabery Cheek 1992; Sharifah Zaleha 1997). In this study, it was found that next to political parties, religious movements seem to attract the highest number of respondents from the new Malay middle class, while membership in other organizations was much lower (see Chapter 8).

While religion is closely associated with politics in Malaysia (a subject that is discussed in Chapter 8), religiosity is also crucial in revitalizing and reinforcing the sense of community and identity discussed above. As shown earlier, the *surau* was a key institution which helped to develop the community, while *surau*-based activities could only be sustained if there were enough regular *surau*-goers, that is, members of the community committed to their religion and who regularly performed collective religious rituals, namely congregational prayers. Table 7.4 shows the respondents' self-assessment of their religiosity, attendance at religious activities as well as their Quran reading practices. The data in the table suggest that new middle-class Malays had become more religious over the years, with some becoming very religious, though most regarded themselves as only 'moderately' religious. This is evidenced by the fact that 95.1 per cent stated that they were 'very religious' or 'quite religious' today compared to 83.5 per cent ten years earlier, while those classified as 'not religious', who made up 16.5 per cent a decade earlier, had now been reduced to less than 5 per cent. The self-assessment of their religiosity corresponds with their performance of various rituals. For example, the majority (61.6 per cent) said that they regularly attended religious activities held in the neighbourhood and outside, while those who seldom or never did so, that is, those considered as 'secular', were a small minority (16.2 per cent). On reading the Quran, 97.9 per cent said they did so, though not necessarily on a regular basis, while only 2.1 per cent said they never took the trouble to read the Holy Book. Almost three-fifths said that they not only read and recited the Quran in Arabic, but also read and studied its translation, suggesting that they not only recited it as part of religious rituals, but also tried to understand its contents through the translated text since most Malays are non-Arabic speakers.

Table 7.4 Respondents' participation in religious activities, Quran reading, and self-assessment of their religiosity

	Klang Valley (*n* = 108)	*Kota Bharu* (*n* = 80)	*Kuala Terengganu* (*n* = 96)	*All Malay middle-class respondents* (*N* = 284)	*Malay workers in Klang Valley* (*N* = 133)
Respondents' self-assessment of their current level of religiosity	8.3	20.0	18.8	15.1	10.5
• Very religious	83.3	77.5	78.1	79.9	77.4
• Quite religious	8.3	2.5	3.1	4.9	12.1
• Not religious					
Respondents' self-assessment of their religiosity 10 years ago					
• Very religious	10.2	7.5	14.6	10.9	7.5
• Quite religious	67.6	78.8	72.9	72.5	72.9
• Not religious	22.2	13.7	16.5	16.5	9.1
Attending religious activities					
• Never	1.9	1.3	—	1.1	4.5
• Seldom	25.9	7.5	9.4	15.1	12.0
• Sometimes	24.1	20.0	21.9	22.2	30.1
• Often	32.4	47.5	44.8	40.8	42.1
• Very often	15.7	23.8	24.0	20.8	11.3
Quran reading					
• Read in Arabic only	50.9	31.2	32.3	39.1	40.8
• Read in Arabic and translation	44.5	68.8	66.7	58.8	55.8
• Never read Quran	4.6	—	1.0	2.1	3.3

Source: Survey data 1996 and 1997.

Although the majority of respondents were very or quite religious, at the time of the study only 50 respondents (17.6 per cent) had performed the *haj* – the fifth pillar of Islam. Of these, six respondents had gone to Mecca twice (three each from the two provincial towns, none from the Klang Valley). Again, the highest proportion of those who had performed the *haj* were from Kota Bharu and Kuala Terengganu. The relatively small number of respondents who had been on the pilgrimage to Mecca should not be interpreted to mean that the *haj* is not popular among Malaysian Muslims. Many of them feel that they should perform the *haj* later in their life, perhaps in their forty or fifty. By this age, they feel that they would not only be financially prepared, but more importantly, they would be prepared spiritually to be the 'guests of Allah' in the Holy Land. In fact, many new middle-class Malays would go on the minor *haj* or *umrah* first before performing the *haj* proper in the month of Dzulhijjah, the last month in the Muslim calendar.

Among Klang Valley Malay workers, the trend of becoming religiously oriented was also clear. For example, there was an increase over the years of those who were fervently religious from 7.5 per cent to 10.5 per cent (Table 7.4). Nevertheless, the opposite tendency towards what is regarded as 'secularization' also existed, as suggested by the increase in the proportion of those with a secular orientation from 9.1 per cent to 12.1 per cent. Overall, it can be concluded that new Malay middle-class respondents were more religiously inclined than Malay workers in the Klang Valley. Their commitment to religious practices and rituals partially explains the existence of community life in Malay middle-class neigh-bourhoods, especially in the provincial towns.[13]

When new middle classes of different ethnic groups are compared, the members of the new Malay and the Indian middle classes are found to be more religiously inclined than the new Chinese middle class. A study of 520 respondents of all ethnic groups in the Klang Valley (Abdul Rahman forthcoming) found that while there were a few freethinkers among new Chinese middle-class respondents, there were none among Malays and Indians. Among Malays, 16 per cent regarded themselves as 'very religious', 73 per cent as 'quite religious', while more secularly-oriented or nominal Muslims constituted a minority (11 per cent). This pattern was also found among Indian respondents, of whom 17.1 per cent regarded themselves as 'very religious', 59.8 per cent as 'quite religious', and 23.1 per cent as secular. Among Chinese (respondents in the sample were mainly Buddhists), the proportion who regarded themselves as 'very religious' was much smaller (9 per cent), with another 33 per cent 'quite religious', while the majority (56 per cent) regarded themselves as non-religious.

The new Malay middle class and inter-ethnic relations

The discussion above shows that ethnic and religious identities are strong and important among the new Malay middle class, and this factor helped them to forge community relationships and awareness. The tendency of the new Malay middle class to construct ethnic- and religious-based communities in towns and cities has several implications. However, does this mean that they only conduct their lives within the confines of their own ethnic boundaries, leading to a lack of contact or interaction with other ethnic groups in their daily lives? Or do they also have social circles beyond their own ethnic groups?

As shown above, in the Klang Valley, and especially in Kuala Lumpur, which has traditionally been identified with the Chinese ethnic group, housing estates today consist of households from at least three major ethnic groups – Malays, Chinese and Indians – though in some areas, a particular ethnic group may be numerically more dominant than others. As part of its national integration policy, the Malaysian government has tried to ensure a more balanced ethnic mix in housing estates. In Kota Bharu and Kuala Terengganu, however, where Malays had traditionally been numerically dominant, there is only a small number of non-Malays. But urban housing areas are also generally mixed, though in some cases, one may only find Malay households there. The reasons for this may not be so straightforward. It may partly be because of land policy (Malay land reserves can only be owned by Malays), but may be more a reflection of the fact that non-Malays are few in number. At the same time, cultural and religious preferences may lead some households to decide to settle down in more ethnically homogenous areas.

However, culturally and socially, Malays are not averse to other ethnic groups. As history has shown, Malays had been very accommodating with foreigners from other lands, who later came and settled in the Malay Peninsula, and even intermarried with some of them (Alisjahbana, Nayagam and Wang Gungwu 1965; Alisjahbana 1983). Despite the colonial 'divide-and-rule' policy and the creation of a Furnivallian 'plural society' (Furnivall 1956),[14] in which different ethnic groups lived in separate compartments and only encountered one another at the marketplace, Malays and non-Malays lived together and gradually came to accept each other. Save for the 13 May ethnic riots in Kuala Lumpur following the 1969 general elections in 1969, no other major incidents of ethnic unrest have occurred since then. The social transformation of the last 30 years has had a significant effect on inter-ethnic relations. While the view that there has increasingly been a de-emphasis on ethnic politics, leading to a shift to the politics of developmentalism (Loh Kok Wah 1997), may be overly optimistic, one cannot deny that inter-ethnic relations have improved tremendously over the years, although squabbles and tensions over specific issues may surface from time to time.

This generally peaceful and friendly macro-level scenario is reflected at the micro-level in some degree of intermingling between respondents of different ethnic groups. In terms of cultural tastes, members of the new Malay middle class are not averse to various cultural items of other ethnic groups. In this study, it was found that new Malay middle-class respondents watched and enjoyed not only Malay programmes to fill their leisure hours, but also Chinese, Indian and western programmes. This is true not only in the Klang Valley, but also in Kota Bharu and Kuala Terengganu. Tamil and Hindi movies, and, lately, Chinese *kong-fu* films – all of which come with Malay subtitles – are popular among Malay viewers. In terms of regular viewers, overall, over one-fifth of new Malay middle-class respondents watched Chinese television programmes regularly, and, quite unexpectedly, a greater proportion watched them in Kuala Terengganu and Kota Bahru compared to the Klang Valley. As for Indian television programmes, again about the same number watched them regularly, with proportions in Kota Bharu and Kuala Terengganu again being higher that in the Klang Valley.

Although one's cultural preferences such as watching Chinese and Indian television programmes by themselves may not tell much about one's everyday relations with other ethnic groups, this finding can be verified by examining other aspects of inter-ethnic relations such as whether new Malay middle-class respondents mix with, and have friends among, the Chinese and Indian communities. The data in Table 7.5 and my personal observations suggest that there were three categories of new middle-class Malays in terms of levels of inter-ethnic relationships. The first is a small group who had close relations with Chinese and Indian friends. They had many friends from other ethnic groups, frequently attended 'open houses' held by them to celebrate either the Chinese New Year or the Indian *Deepavali*, and tried to understand and appreciate the cultures of other ethnic groups. This group of new middle-class Malays can be regarded as more multi-ethnic, 'Malaysian' and cosmopolitan in their attitudes and ways of life. The second group, which was much larger (about half the respondents), had Chinese and/or Indian friends, interacted with them, and sometimes attended the 'open houses' held by the latter. But, their circle of non-Malay friends was smaller and their interactions were much less. The third group, smaller in proportion, did not have friends from other ethnic groups, did not attend the latter's

Table 7.5   Respondents' friends from other ethnic groups

	Klang Valley (*n* = 108)	*Kota Bharu* (*n* = 80)	*Kuala Terengganu* (*n* = 96)	*All respondents* (*N* = 284)
Do you have Chinese friends?				
• No	22.2	28.8	28.1	26.1
• Yes, 10 or less	48.1	52.5	54.2	51.4
• Yes, more than 10	29.6	18.7	17.7	22.5
Do you have Indian friends?				
• No	25.0	48.8	39.6	36.6
• Yes, 10 or less	54.6	36.2	54.2	49.3
• Yes, more than 10	20.4	15.0	6.3	14.1
Do you attend 'open house' held by Chinese and Indian neighbours/friends? If so, how many times in the last one year?				
• I have never attended any	28.7	46.3	57.3	43.3
• Once	39.8	33.7	22.9	32.4
• Twice	16.7	8.8	10.4	12.3
• Three and above	14.8	11.2	9.4	12.0

Source: Survey data 1996 and 1997.

cultural festivals, and did not try to understand or appreciate the meanings of their cultural activities. They can be regarded as conducting their lives mainly within their own ethnic community.

By comparison, a larger proportion from among the Klang Valley new Malay middle-class respondents can be classified as belonging to the first category in that they have closer relationships with other ethnic groups than those in Kota Bharu and Kuala Terengganu, as shown by the data on the number of non-Malay friends and attendance at the latter's 'open houses' (see Table 7.5). However, in the Klang Valley there is also an almost equal number of new Malay middle-class respondents who belonged to the third category – that is, who conducted their lives mainly within their own ethnic group, with no circles of friends outside their ethnic boundary. These findings suggest that one's presence in a multi-ethnic surrounding such as Kuala Lumpur or Petaling Jaya does not automatically induce one to establish meaningful relationships with people from other ethnic groups. On the contrary, it may make one feel a greater need to stay within ethnic boundaries. In Kota Bharu and Kuala

Terengganu, the proportions of respondents who had Chinese and Indian friends were smaller, and the number with no friends from other ethnic groups was higher than in the Klang Valley. However, these findings need to be read carefully. The fact that larger proportions of new Malay middle-class respondents in Kota Bharu and Kuala Terengganu had no Chinese or Indian friends does not necessarily mean that they shunned non-Malays. It may simply reflect the fact that in the two provincial towns, Chinese and, in particular, Indians are only very small minorities. In fact, one may argue that in predominantly Malay areas such as Kota Bharu and Kuala Terengganu where there are less inter-ethnic rivalries, Malays feel more secure and may be more open towards non-Malays, while in the Klang Valley, where such rivalries are more common, attitudes and feelings vary from being open, secure and confident, to being less open, insecure and suspicious of other ethnic groups.[15] This finding is corroborated by another study I conducted in 1999 on the culture and practice of pluralism in Malaysia (Abdul Rahman 2000). This latter study shows the close relationships between Malays and non-Malays in Kota Bharu and how non-Malays have assimilated some aspects of Malay culture, including the use of Malay in their everyday interactions.

One of the activities of members of the new Malay middle class that may involve interactions with other ethnic groups is the Malay *Hari Raya* (the Muslim *id* celebration that comes after the end of the fasting month of Ramadan). At this time Malays, especially those from the new middle class, do two things. First, as already discussed in Chapter 5 on the Malay middle-class family, they *balik kampung* (that is, return to the village or town of their birth) to visit their parents or relatives and reaffirm their kin ties. In our sample, 89.8 per cent of our respondents *balik kampung* for the *Hari Raya* annually, the largest proportion being from the Klang Valley (91.7 per cent), followed by Kuala Terengganu (89.6 per cent) and Kota Bharu (87.6 per cent) (see Table 5.11 in Chapter 5).[16] It is not surprising that the proportion from the Klang Valley was so very high, because most respondents there were migrants from outside the area who may still have parents or relatives in their former home village or town. Second, Malays, especially from the new middle class, hold the *Hari Raya* 'open house', which is normally carried out after their return to their urban homes from their *balik kampung* exodus. The festive mood goes on for the whole month of Syawal (the month following Ramadan) and the 'open house' can be held any time during this one month. The function is meant to entertain nearby relatives, neighbours, friends and office-mates, thus strengthening their community networks. In our sample, 69.2 per cent of our respondents regularly held such *Hari Raya* 'open house' functions (see

Table 5.11 in Chapter 5). Just as a proportion of new Malay middle-class respondents attended 'open houses' of their non-Malay neighbours and friends, a number of neighbours, friends and office-mates from other ethnic groups also attended Malay 'open houses' to celebrate *Hari Raya*. Such occasions are marked by relaxed and free mingling between hosts and guests, as well as generous offers of various Malay culinary delights. Foreigners who visited Malaysia have often remarked that *Hari Raya* 'open house' – though a Malay/Muslim festival – is shared by other ethnic groups and has become 'a time for celebration as a nation'.[17] From the author's observations and experiences in attending many 'open house' functions over the years, this is not an overstatement, but applies particularly to those who have many non-Malay friends.

Conclusions

In his study of the new Malay middle class and culture, Kahn (1994: 39) drew three conclusions. First, though the Malay middle class may be 'firmly urban-based and urban-oriented', they still have 'not yet ... adapted culturally to city life (for) they have not yet produced a characteristically urban culture'; second, they 'feel ill at ease in cities which they perceive as dominated by alien peoples and patterns of life, of Western and/or Chinese origin'; and third, they constitute 'a breeding ground for new forms of anti-Chinese sentiments'.

My study of the three urban centres discussed above suggests a more complex picture. Some members of the new Malay middle class may have become 'firmly urban-based and urban-oriented', reflected in the attitudes and lifestyles of the cosmopolitan urbanites who enjoy city life, and feel secure and confident, rather than ill at ease in the city. The 'folk urbanites', on the other hand, have developed rather different lifestyles, have set up urban communities, based on the *surau* and other activities, through which they establish new networks of friends in their neighbourhood and outside, while, at the same time, reaffirming their kin ties. Their construction of these communities, which have several important *kampung*-like characteristics, is their way of culturally adapting to urban living, and over the years, they have become rooted and begun to 'feel at home' in the urban milieu, which they no longer find hostile or anonymous. Though they *balik kampung* during *Hari Raya*, on their return, they hold 'open houses' for their neighbours, friends and office colleagues, including many non-Malays. When asked by elderly parents or relatives to stay back a bit longer during their *balik kampung* trips, they often reply by saying that they have to return to their urban homes quickly, not only because they have to get back to work, but also because '*kawan-kawan mahu datang ziarah Hari Raya*' (friends want to come and visit for *Hari Raya*). While it is true that ethnic identities and religious sentiments are strong among the new Malay middle class, and may involve anti-Chinese sentiments and suspicions, it is too hasty to draw the conclusion that they constitute 'a breeding ground for new forms of anti-Chinese sentiments'. As shown in this chapter, members of the new Malay middle class may be divided into three groups in terms of levels of relationships with non-Malays that is, (i) those who have close relationships with non-Malays and have developed multi-ethnic perspectives; (ii) those who have some non-Malay friends, but whose contacts and interactions are still limited; and (iii) those who confine themselves within their own ethnic boundary and interact with non-Malays only at the marketplace. Thus, just as the new Malay middle class is not homogenous politically (see Chapter 8), they are also not homogenous socially and culturally, that is, that while some may confine themselves within their own ethnic boundary, others have developed multi-ethnic social circles.

It was also argued in this chapter that although a significant proportion of new Malay middle-class respondents attempted to build *kampung*-like communities, or communities with *kampung*-like characteristics in urban areas, these are not necessarily traditional or extensions of the traditional rural villages. Some characteristics of the rural villages have been dropped, but others, such as *surau*-based activities, *gotong royong*, mutual flows of food and other gifts, and other characteristics, exist. However, these are constructed within a new milieu and modified according to the changed material conditions. Thus, the cultural attachment of the new Malay middle class to their 'traditions' is essentially modern, or contemporary, although it may give a semblance of maintaining strong links with the past.

8
Malay Middle-Class Politics, Democracy and Civil Society

Introduction

The problem of middle-class politics, and the role of the new middle class in championing democracy and civil society, has attracted the attention of many scholars studying the new middle class in the West as well as in Asia (see, for example, Huntington 1991; Hsiao 1993; Vidich 1995; Robison and Goodman 1996; Hsiao and Koo 1997; Cox 1997).[1] The term 'civil society', as used here, refers to the space between the individual and family on the one hand, and the state and market on the other. It is suggested by commentators that this space exerts a certain degree of autonomy, counterbalancing the power of the state and the market. Such space becomes the realm of autonomous group action distinct from both corporate power and the state, and within this space exist 'autonomous groups articulating the views and interests and fears of the less powerful' (Cox 1997: 10). Such groups may consist of 'clubs, religious organizations, business groups, labour unions, human rights groups, and other associations located between the household and the state and organized on the basis of voluntarism and mutuality' (Hefner 2000: 23). In Asia, capitalist development in various countries has generated the class basis for the development of civil society. The middle class and the working class are considered to be the main social forces involved in this emerging civil society, and are expected to play the central role in expanding this social space.

Scholars researching and writing about civil society in Asia draw attention to the growth of what is called the non-profit sector, and the role of the new middle class in leading non-government organizations, or NGOs (Yamamoto 1995; Lee 1995; Corrothers and Suryatna 1995). They argue that the emergence of a sizable urban middle class serves to provide leadership in the non-profit sector, the development of which is critical to the emergence of private non-profit organizations. In Indonesia, for example, 'NGOs have been able to reflect on and articulate more general concerns for the environment, human rights and democratization now emerging most obviously, but by no means exclusively, among the middle class' (Yamamoto 1995: 11). As summed up by Huntington (1991: 67), 'Third wave movement for democratization were not led by landlords, peasants, or (apart from Poland) industrial workers. In virtually every country the most active supporters of democratization came from the urban middle class.'

The preceding arguments assert a kind of 'developmental optimism' that the middle class has an historical role to play in the democratization process and in expanding civil society in Asian countries, as the latter embark along the road of industrialization and modernization.[2] This 'democratization thesis' – which posits the liberal-democratic notion of the middle class as a champion of democracy, an agent for democratic transformation, and an advocate of civil society – is based in part on western experience, and in part on political struggles waged by the organized sections of the middle class in some post-colonial non-western societies. In this chapter, we shall discuss the 'democratization thesis' in the context of Malaysia, by focusing on the role of the new Malay middle class in Malaysian politics, democracy and civil society.

Parliamentary democracy, participation in political parties and the electoral process

In a study of the political role of the new middle class in Malaysia conducted in the late 1980s, Saravanamuttu (1989) argued that the Malaysian middle class was politically conscious, participated in movements championing democracy, and had emerged as a force to be reckoned with in national politics, posing resistance to the institutionalization of state authoritarianism. Saravanamuttu's study supports the 'democratization' thesis in the context of Malaysia. He predicted that the middle class would continue to play this role by attempting to expand the space for civil society despite various setbacks imposed by the authoritarian state. However, his sample of 468 respondents was drawn from the organized members of the middle class, particularly leading elements in various NGOs. In fact, 78 per cent of the respondents were top leaders of these organizations, serving as presidents/chairs, deputy presidents/ chairs, vice-presidents/chairs, and secretaries. It is perhaps not surprising, therefore, that his findings would suggest active the political involvement of the middle class in the espousal of democratic ideals.

However, while the above findings are tenable if we confine ourselves to the organized or leading middle-class elements, a rather less conclusive picture would emerge if we considered a different sample, for example, if they are selected on the basis of their occupational status, as has been the case in this study. Though a proportion of the sample in this study did consist of organized elements, the rest were not. Such a sample gives a different picture of the role of the middle class in politics and democratization.

To gain an idea of the role of the new Malay middle class in politics and how far the new middle class has engaged with issues of public and national interest in the public domain, this study tries to assess both the respondents' views about politics and public affairs and their actual involvement in political parties and public interest associations, including religious organizations. The study differentiates between the level of politicization and actual political involvement – the former referring to political awareness, interest and concern in public and national affairs that respondents show, while the latter refers to membership and actual involvement in organized movements. For analytical convenience, organized movements are categorized as political parties and public interest associations, including religious movements.

However, participation in political parties and voting during elections serve only as indicators of the politicization of the middle class and their involvement in formal democratic processes respectively. Formal democracy allows citizens to join political parties to participate in elections, which have been held on a regular basis; they can also canvass for candidates, and vote in elections to choose representatives to form the government, or to be in the opposition. A high degree of electoral canvassing, or a high level of voter turnout shows that formal democracy exists and that people can exercise some democratic rights, but it does not necessarily point to a growth in civil society. Neither does it show the role that members of the new middle class may play in championing democracy and civil society. In the case of Malaysia, the country has regularly held general elections since 1955, with the latest being held in November 1999. However, it does not follow that civil society has grown alongside the development of parliamentary democracy. In fact, the ideology and political orientation of some parties taking part in the electoral process, especially the victorious ones, may in fact turn out to be an obstacle to the growth and expansion of democracy and civil society. Nevertheless, an analysis of the involvement of the new middle class in political parties and elections should reflect their political mobilization and their party alignment, including their attitude towards the party in power, and whether they are very much bound up with and dependent upon the ruling party and the state, or are quite autonomous of it.

The political system in Malaysia – formally a parliamentary democracy – has been described by some writers as 'neither authoritarian nor democratic' (see, for example, Crouch 1993, 1996). It has the institutional framework of a formal democracy, but tends to be authoritarian in dealing with differences and with opposition. Thus, in studying the role of the new Malay middle class in promoting democracy and civil society in this chapter, it is important not only to study their involvement in political parties and elections, but also to investigate their involvement in certain NGOs which are ostensibly independent of political parties and the state. At the same time, it is also important to analyse their attitudes and positions on major public and national issues, to assess whether they are ideologically inclined towards democracy, or towards authoritarianism. However, since political attitudes and consciousness are difficult to capture in surveys, the author has also relied on ethnographic observations and interviews to complement the survey data in order to gain insights into this issue.

Participation in the electoral process and party alignments

The level of involvement of the new Malay middle class in the electoral process and in political parties is high, in fact far higher than that of the non-Malay, especially the Chinese, middle class. Members of the new Malay middle class have accepted the rules of the game that in a parliamentary democracy, they can exercise their democratic right, not only by becoming members of a political party, but also by going to the ballot box to elect candidates to be their representatives.

As shown in Table 8.1, 43.7 per cent of all new Malay middle-class respondents studied were members of political parties. The figure was highest in the Klang Valley (48.1 per cent), followed by Kuala Terengganu (43.8 per cent), and Kota Bharu (37.5 per cent). They were either in UMNO, the backbone of the BN government which has been ruling the country since 1955, or in PAS, the Islamic party holding power in the Kelantan state since 1959 (except for the period between 1978 and 1990). In fact, PAS has recently extended its power base – it captured the oil-rich state of Terengganu in the November 1999 general election after 35 years of BN rule, and made important inroads into other Malay heartland areas in Peninsular Malaysia, particularly Kedah and Perlis. UMNO and PAS are

Table 8.1   Membership of new Malay middle-class respondents in political parties and participation in the 1995 General Election

	Klang Valley (n = 108)		Kota Bharu (n = 80)		Kuala Terengganu (n = 96)		All respondents (N = 284)	
	Yes	No	Yes	No	Yes	No	Yes	No
Party member	48.1	51.2	37.5	62.5	43.8	56.3	43.7 (n = 124)	56.3 (n =160)
Registered as voter	88.0	12.0	92.5	7.5	92.7	7.3	90.8 (n = 258)	9.2 (n = 26)
Voted in election	83.3	16.7	88.8	11.2	88.6	11.4	85.9 (n = 246)	14.1 (n = 38)
Campaigned for a particular candidate	12.0	88.0	21.3	78.7	21.9	78.1	18.0 (n = 51)	82.0 (n =233)
Donated to a particular party	12.0	88.0	6.3	93.7	15.6	84.4	11.6 (n = 33)	251 (n = 88.4)

Source: Survey data 1996 and 1997.

seen as political organizations representing respectively Malay and Muslim interests. From the survey, it is clear that they are able to mobilize support among substantial sections of the new Malay middle class, in both provincial towns and rural areas, as well as in metropolitan cities.

Contrary to claims often made by UMNO leaders that the new Malay middle class, especially in the larger towns, abstain from voter registration and voting, this study found that voter registration and voting among all respondents in the three urban centres were high. Over 90 per cent of all respondents registered as voters for the 1995 election, with the highest being in Kuala Terengganu and Kota Bharu. Though the figure was slightly lower in the Klang Valley, the proportion of registered voters here was still high (88 per cent). Voter turnout of new Malay middle-class respondents was high at 85.9 per cent, with the highest being in Kota Bharu (88.8 per cent), followed by Kuala Terengganu (88.6 per cent), and the Klang Valley (83.3 per cent).

To assess where voter turnout among new Malay middle-class voters stands in relation to turnout among other voters, let us briefly examine the overall voter turnout for all three urban centres. The 1995 election results released by the Election Commission showed that total voter turnout was 71.1 per cent in the Kota Bharu and 74.1 per cent in the Kuala Terengganu parliamentary constituencies. In the Klang Valley, voter turnout was slightly lower; for example, in the Petaling Jaya Selatan parliamentary constituency (where most of our respondents lived), the turnout was 66.6 per cent (*Utusan Malaysia*, election results special issue, 27 April 1995). From these figures, it is clear that a much higher proportion of the new Malay middle-class sample studied came out to vote than the rest of the electorate in their respective constituencies.

Among new Malay middle-class respondents, a small core has emerged as very active – campaigning for candidates and donating to parties. This is shown by the fact that almost one-fifth of all respondents campaigned for their candidates, and a smaller proportion contributed money to their party election fund (Table 8.1). When we compare the participation of new Malay middle-class respondents in the Klang Valley with their counterparts in the two provincial towns, it was found that those in Kota Bharu and Kuala Terengganu were even more active. They topped the list not only in terms of voter registration and turnout at elections, but also in campaigning for their candidates. In fact, in both Kuala Terengganu and Kota Bharu, more than one-fifth of our respondents actively campaigned for their candidates in the 1995 election, while in the Klang Valley, the percentage was lower.

High involvement in election campaigning among respondents in Kuala Terengganu and Kota Bharu compared to those in the Klang Valley may be attributed to the keen competition between the two dominant Malay-based parties – UMNO and PAS – and also because candidates and respondents in the two urban centres were from the same ethnic group. During the 1995 election, there were 14 parliamentary and 43 state seats contested between PAS and the UMNO-led BN in Kelantan, while in Terengganu, the figures were eight and 32 seats respectively (Gomez 1996: 19). (Though the now-defunct Semangat 46 Party also contested the election, it then aligned itself with PAS through the formation of the Angkatan Perpaduan Ummah, or APU.) All of the parliamentary and state seats in Kota Bharu and Kuala Terengganu, where the study was conducted, were contested by the two parties. In the Kota Bharu parliamentary constituency, the APU candidate garnered 24096 votes, defeating the BN candidate by the considerable figure of 6268 votes. In Kuala Terengganu, PAS gave the BN a good fight, and seized one of the three state seats (*Utusan Malaysia*, election results special issue, 27 April 1995).

The same cannot be said of constituencies in Petaling Jaya or Kuala Lumpur in the Klang Valley. The fight here was not between Malay-based parties, but between the UMNO-led BN and the Chinese-backed Democratic Action Party (DAP), as in the case of Petaling Jaya Selatan,

Table 8.2   Party alignment of new Malay middle-class respondents in the 1995 General Election

	Klang Valley (*n* = 90)*	*Kota Bharu* (*n* = 71)*	*Kuala Terengganu* (*n* = 85)*	*All respondents* (*N* = 246)*
Voted Barisan Nasional	86.7	57.7	60.0	69.1
Voted opposition party	12.2	15.5	23.5	17.1
My vote a secret**	1.1	26.8	16.5	13.8
Total	100.0	100.0	100.0	100.0

Source: Survey data 1996 and 1997.
*The figure only refers to those who voted in the 1995 election.
**This is interpreted to mean voting mostly for the opposition.

where the BN fielded a Chinese candidate from the Malaysian Chinese Association (MCA). While a high percentage of new Malay middle-class respondents in the Klang Valley came out to vote, their involvement was largely confined to supporting their party candidate on voting day – only a very small proportion would take time off to campaign for any candidate, especially if the latter was not a Malay from UMNO.

The party alignment of new Malay middle-class respondents in the Klang Valley and in the two provincial towns is also an important indicator of the different stances adopted by the respondents with regard to the ruling party in the central government, and their preparedness to stand by their party. As shown in Table 8.2, party alignment also differs quite sharply; in fact, the trend of supporting the opposition among the new Malay middle-class respondents in Kota Bharu and Kuala Terengganu was very clear in the 1995 general election, well before the election in 1999 in which the BN was completely routed in both places. In our study, it was found that while the overwhelming majority of the new Malay middle-class respondents in the Klang Valley voted for the BN in the 1995 election, in Kota Bharu and Kuala Terengganu, much smaller proportions voted for the ruling party. This shows that while only a small proportion of the new Malay middle-class respondents voted for the opposition in the Klang Valley, in Kota Bharu and Kuala Terengganu, their proportion was high – over 40 per cent.[3] According to the sample, this means that in contrast to the metropolitan new middle-class Malays, many new Malay

Table 8.3   Party membership and voting of the Klang Valley working class in the 1995 General Election, by ethnic group

	Malays (*n* = 133)		Chinese (*n* = 58)		Indians & others (*n* = 50)		All respondents (*N* = 241)	
	Yes	*No*	*Yes*	*No*	*Yes*	*No*	*Yes*	*No*
Party member	23.5	76.5	20.7	79.3	20.0	80.0	20.1 (*n* = 54)	79.9 (*n* = 187)
Registered as voter	84.1	15.9	70.7	29.3	86.0	14.0	81.3 (*n* = 195)	18.7 (*n* = 45)
Voted in 1995 election	74.2	25.8	65.5	34.5	78.0	22.0	72.9 (*n* = 175)	27.1 (*n* = 65)
Campaigned for a particular candidate	9.8	90.2	3.4	96.6	10.0	90.0	8.3 (*n* = 20)	91.7 (*n* = 220)

Source: Survey data 1997.

middle-class respondents in the two provincial towns were more inclined to vote against the ruling UMNO, and support the opposition PAS even before the 1999 general election.

It is interesting to compare the political behaviour of respondents from the new Malay middle class and the Malay working class. In order to examine their similarities and differences, the same set of questions was administered by the author to a group of 241 workers in the Klang Valley in 1997 (comprised of 133 Malays, 58 Chinese and 50 Indians).[4] The study shows that new Malay middle-class respondents had a far higher level of involvement in political parties than those from the Malay working class. Among the latter, only about one-quarter were party members, 84.1 per cent registered as voters, and 74.2 per cent came out to vote in the 1995 general election (Table 8.3). Each of these figures was much lower than the corresponding figures for the new Malay middle class. In terms of party membership, for example, it was proportionately lower among Malay working-class respondents, with about one-quarter being members, compared to over 40 per cent among the new Malay middle-class respondents. UMNO's alienation from young people, including Malay workers, was already quite clear in this study. At this time, UMNO is increasingly dominated by corporate figures, and is perceived to be a party of the new middle class and the rich (Gomez 1991, 1994), rather than a party of, and for, ordinary people. Many Malay workers in this study stayed away from the party partly because they felt little identification with it (except as Malays), while this was not so for many new Malay middle-class elements. However, in terms of voting choices, the majority voted for the BN in the 1995 election, but more than a quarter voted against it. Compared with the new Malay middle-class respondents in the Klang Valley, a much higher proportion of Malay working-class respondents voted against the BN, showing a certain degree of alienation and disillusionment with the BN (in this case, UMNO) among them. [5]

It is also important to see if there is any difference between the new Malay, Chinese and Indian middle classes with regard to politics. A study of new middle-class politics in the Klang Valley conducted in 1996 (Abdul Rahman 1999), shows that party membership was lowest among the new Chinese middle class (12.7 per cent), and only slightly higher among the new Indian middle class (14.6 per cent). In terms of voter registration and turnout, it was much lower among the new Chinese and Indian middle classes, than among the new Malay middle class. However, when it comes to voting alignment, there was a higher proportion of new Chinese middle-class respondents not supporting the BN in the 1995 election compared to Indian and Malay respondents.[6]

Among Chinese and Indian workers, the author's 1997 study among workers in the Klang Valley also shows that there was a higher percentage of party membership (Chinese 20.7 per cent, Indians 20 per cent), higher voter registration, and voter turnout among Chinese and Indian workers than that found in the new Chinese and Indian middle classes (Table 8.3). It is also important to note that among Chinese workers, support for and opposition to the BN in the 1995 election was almost equally split. Among Indian workers, the proportion supporting the BN was very much higher, accounting for almost three-fifths of the sample. This was consistent with the national trend whereby Indian voters mostly supported the ruling party.

The sample shows that the new Malay middle class – both in the metropolitan capital and in the two provincial towns – took an active part in party as well as electoral politics, much more than the Malay working class. (Since no study was conducted among Malay workers in Kota Bharu and Kuala Terengganu, a similar exercise cannot be carried out for these two towns.) In terms of degree, members of the new Malay middle class in the two provincial towns were more politically organized, and were more politically and ideologically independent of UMNO than their counterparts in the Klang Valley, and because of PAS activities, they were more prepared to go against mainstream politics. The new Malay middle class is also more politically conscious and involved in politics than their Chinese and Indian counterparts – a fact which became increasingly evident in the political crisis following the sacking of former Deputy Prime Minister Anwar Ibrahim in September 1998 (see Chapter 10).

Participation in NGOs

As stated above, the growth of NGOs and citizens' participation in these organizations is an important indicator of the 'opening up' of democratic space for civil society. NGOs feature prominently in the emerging civil society, and their leadership is largely – though not exclusively – drawn from the new middle class. What is significant is that some NGOs are also part of social movements. And, as argued by some writers, the study of social movements can suggest likely future transformations (see, for example, Giddens 1991: 158).

In this study, five types of NGOs have been chosen – namely, consumer, environmental, professional, resident and religious organizations. Though these organizations are often identified as championing the interests of the new middle class, and are largely middle-class-dominated and -led – since members of the new middle class are better educated and believed to have more developed leadership capabilities than members of the working class – they are not exclusively new middle-class in composition (except for professional associations) for they also include members of the working class. Consumer associations and environmental organizations are part of national movements and the issues they fight for involve demands for changes in some aspects of social arrangements.

Table 8.4 shows the respondents' participation in consumer, environmental, professional, resident and religious associations among new Malay middle-class respondents in the Klang Valley, as well as in the provincial towns of Kota Bharu and Kuala Terengganu. Taking all respondents from the three urban centres together, it was found that their involvement and participation in organizations such as religious, resident, and professional organizations was higher than in other organizations. Thus, while in religious organizations (see Chapter 7) as well as resident associations, almost one-third of respondents were involved, and in professional associations about one-fifth, their participation in other organizations, such as consumer associations and environmental organizations, was very much lower.

There is some difference in the level of participation in these organizations between the metropolitan new Malay middle-class and their provincial counterparts. For example, Malay middle class respondents in the Klang Valley were more actively involved in both resident and professional associations than their counterparts in Kota Bharu or

Table 8.4 Participation of new Malay middle-class respondents in consumer, environmental, professional, resident and religious associations

	Klang Valley (n = 1 08)		Kota Bharu (n = 80)		Kuala Terengganu (n = 96)		All respondents (N = 284)	
	Yes	No	Yes	No	Yes	No	Yes	No
Consumer association	10.2	89.8	13.8	86.3	11.5	88.5	11.6 (n = 33)	88.4 (n = 251)
Environmental association	12.0	88.0	3.8	96.3	9.4	90.6	8.8 (n = 25)	91.2 (n = 259)
Professional association	39.8	60.2	11.3	88.8	20.8	79.2	25.4 (n = 72)	74.6 (n = 212)
Resident association	37.0	63.0	27.5	72.5	29.2	70.8	31.7 (n = 90)	68.3 (n = 194)
Religious organization	31.5	68.5	40.0	60.0	27.1	72.9	32.4 (n = 92)	67.6 (n = 192)

Source: Survey data 1996 and1997.

Kuala Terengganu. As regards their participation in consumer associations, there was no significant difference between the three urban centres. However, when it comes to environmental organizations, members of the new Malay middle class in the Klang Valley participated more actively than in the provincial towns, especially in Kota Bharu. As for religious organizations, quite a high percentage of new middle-class respondents in the Klang Valley were involved in them, although the highest involvement was found in Kota Bharu.

These findings suggest that a proportion of the new Malay middle class were being drawn into activities in the public domain, and were getting organized in civil society organizations. This could translate into positive developments enlarging the democratic space necessary for the growth of civil society, provided they attain some degree of autonomy from the state and corporate power. (For some recent writings on civil society in Malaysia, see Nair 1999, Saliha 2000.)

Two things that stand out from the findings above require some explanations. First, there is a greater degree of involvement in religious, resident and professional associations than in consumer and environmental movements among the new Malay middle-class respondents. This is the case partly because religious, resident and professional associations have a much longer history in Malaysia and have been in the collective memory of the public for quite some time. These organizations also cater to the immediate material and spiritual interests of the new middle class. While resident associations cater to the specific and immediate interests of their members in their neighbourhood and professional associations take care of their career interests, religious organizations are other-worldly oriented, and provide members with a sense of identification with a spiritual community and promise personal spiritual salvation.

On the other hand, consumer and environmental concerns are relatively new, having emerged mainly in the 1980s, and they are often perceived as 'western-inspired'. Because of this, consumer and environmental concerns are still seen as rather 'distant', although in actual fact, they affect the everyday lives of individuals, including members of the new middle-class. Many new Malay-middle class respondents tended to stay away from organizations that appear 'distant' from their immediate interest, especially if these organizations take an overtly oppositional political stance. In this case, the causes championed by the two other groups (consumer and environmental movements) – though ostensibly concerning consumer rights and the environment – are often perceived as political and oppositional in nature. At times, these groups appear to be confrontational towards the powers-that-be. Consumer movements and environmental groups in Malaysia (such as the Consumer Association of Penang – CAP; the Federation of Malaysia Consumer Associations – FOMCA; and the Environmental Protection Society of Malaysia – EPSM) have been known to be vocal and critical of Malaysian government policies on consumer affairs[7] and environmental management. This may explain why many Malay middle-class elements, whose political views were more oriented towards maintaining security, stability and growth (see discussion below), may shy away from participation in such NGOs. The fact that certain NGOs have often been attacked by many government leaders, who have accused them of peddling 'western' agendas, has also made the Malay middle class hesitant about joining such NGOs, and even led them to become suspicious of them.[8]

Second, the high proportion of non-involvement in NGOs should not be assumed simply to reflect apathy towards public issues or towards the growth of democracy and civil society. As noted by various scholars, ethnicity has been and is still an important factor in Malaysian politics (Brown 1994; Shamsul 1994; Crouch 1996). This is especially so in the Klang Valley, though in Kota Bharu and Kuala Terengganu it is not an important issue. Several political NGOs, including progressive political parties such as the People's Party of Malaysia (PRM) which fights on a multiracial platform, have often, rightly or wrongly, been identified by some sections as championing 'non-Malay' interests. Politicized new Malay middle-class elements may be active in PAS, or even constitute a democratic faction within UMNO, but they often still perceive things in ethnic terms, and might not be keen in joining or associating with such NGOs other than those championing the interests of Malays and Muslims. Furthermore, there is a small number of new Malay middle-class elements, especially intellectuals, who prefer to take independent stances irrespective of their organizational involvement in political parties such as UMNO or other parties. Some may not even be members of any party or NGO. Yet they air critical views about various important issues, and contribute towards the opening of greater political space nationally. In other words, we have to look not only at political parties and NGOs but also beyond them to capture the democratic space representing civil society.

Views and stances on public and national issues

A separate study by the author on Malaysian middle-class political attitudes among the three major ethnic groups (comprised of 520 respondents) in the Klang Valley conducted in early 1996 (Abdul Rahman 1999) found an underlying contestation and tension between demands for development and social order on the one hand, and demands for democracy, greater space for citizens' views and participation on the other. Members of the new middle class wanted development and social order, but at the same time, they also wanted democracy and more political space. The study concluded that a paradox seems to exist in the attitudes of the middle class regarding democracy and authoritarianism. While the middle class supports democracy, it tolerates and seems not averse to the institutionalization of state authoritarianism. It views the latter, that is, strong and effective government – often a euphemism for authoritarianism, as necessary for national development and economic growth, provided some degree of democracy prevails in society.

For this study of the new Malay middle class, a different, though related set of questions was asked to explore the views and stances of the respondents in the Klang Valley and in the two provincial towns, with regard to certain issues concerning the country's governance in so far as it pertains to wealth distribution, democracy and freedom. Though the emphasis is slightly different, this discussion will be compared with the findings of the earlier Klang Valley study to see if there were certain similarities in the views and stances of the new Malay middle class with those of the new Malaysian middle class captured in that study.

Two main concerns have emerged in development discourses in Malaysia since the 1970s, when the government embarked on the NEP, while enjoying their more than two-thirds majority control of Parliament. The first concerns socio-economic questions of inter-ethnic and class disparity, while the second involves the political questions over the abuse of power and authoritarianism.

The main concern in development planning has not been with growth per se, but rather growth with equitable distribution, namely to address the problem of inter-ethnic disparity, and that of the gap between rich and poor. As shown in earlier chapters, the new Malay middle class is a product of the NEP, and the emergence of this class came about through the government's 'restructuring' and poverty reduction efforts. Thus, it was pertinent to probe into the views of the new Malay middle class on whether they felt the government had succeeded in tackling such disparities.

With regard to wealth distribution among ethnic groups through the implementation of the NEP, respondents appreciated the achievements of the government's policy. While a tiny minority felt the government had a poor record, the majority were pleased in varying degrees with the progress. Their views, however, were more divided over the question of wealth distribution between rich and poor, with less than half agreeing that the government had succeeded in reducing the gap between rich and poor. Many others were somewhat sceptical, while a similar proportion felt the government had failed to reduce the gap – the latter view being strongest among the new Malay middle-class respondents in Kuala Terengganu.[9] The continuing concern among new Malay middle-class respondents over the possible widening of the gap between rich and poor was expressed, especially with regard to the effects of the government's privatization policy. While most agreed that in the long run, privatization would benefit the people, an overwhelming majority worried about its likely adverse effects on social justice and equitable distribution.

The abuse of political power and the rise of authoritarianism had also attracted serious concern among the new middle class. As mentioned earlier, the Malaysian political system has been described as 'neither authoritarian, nor democratic' (Crouch 1993, 1996). This description suggests that while the system has the formal institutions of democracy and conducts elections regularly, yet authoritarianism is strong in practice. It was the BN government's record in relation to the judiciary in particular and the use of the draconian Internal Security Act (ISA) which allows detention without trial that has been severely criticized in recent years. The issue of the separation of powers and the 'checks and balances' between the executive, legislature (parliament) and the judiciary, was thrown into sharp relief, especially following the sacking the independent-minded Lord President, Tun Salleh Abbas, in May 1988 following the UMNO split in 1987 (Tun Salleh Abas 1989). The judiciary's independence has again been strongly questioned ten years later in 1998 following the sacking of Anwar Ibrahim, his long-drawn-out court trial and the subsequent 15-year prison sentence imposed upon him for charges of corruption and sodomy. The trials of the Lord President and Anwar were both perceived as politically motivated, leading to charges of executive interference in the judiciary. This has resulted in the loss of public confidence in the independence of the latter, a fact admitted by the new Chief Justice of the Malaysian Federal Court, Tan Sri Mohamed Dzaiddin Abdullah, who took over the post of the top judge from Tun Eusoffe Chin on 20 December 2000.[10]

For this study, the author tried to establish some empirical evidence by examining how these issues were perceived by the new Malay middle-class respondents. How independent is the Malaysian judiciary in their eyes? From the study, it was found, rather unexpectedly, that only a quarter of the respondents maintained that the judiciary was independent and that there was no political interference in its conduct and decisions. The overwhelming majority had a completely different perception. To them, executive interference in the judiciary was a reality, with about half of them feeling this strongly to be the case. The fact that this perception was already formed well before the Anwar trials, which lasted from late 1998 until August 2000, shows that there were serious doubts in the eyes of the public about the integrity of the judiciary even then, a concern which increased during and after the high-profile Anwar trials.

Another major concern to the respondents was the implications of the BN continuing to have a more than two-thirds majority in Parliament. Though this was considered necessary by some to ensure a strong government and stable political climate, others believed this situation could lead to abuses of power. As was the case with the perception of the judiciary, only about one-quarter of the new Malay middle-class respondents maintained that the BN government's strong majority had not resulted in the abuse of power, while the rest felt that such abuses had taken place. As might have been expected, the feelings were strongest among respondents in Kuala Terengganu and Kota Bharu.

To check the abuses of power by the ruling party, most new Malay middle-class respondents saw the importance of voting for a strong parliamentary opposition. While it was expected that this view was most strongly expressed in Kuala Terengganu and Kota Bharu, in the Klang

Valley, a substantial proportion of the respondents (38.4 per cent) also felt that a strong opposition was good for the country. The demand for a strong parliamentary opposition was in keeping with their desire for greater democratic space in the country's political system. Only a minority (about a quarter of the respondents) felt that a strong parliamentary opposition was not necessary, implying that they did not mind some kind of one-party rule.

Various attitudes of the new Malay middle-class respondents discussed above suggest that they wanted democracy, an independent judiciary, and a strong opposition in Parliament to help check abuses of power, reflecting a desire for greater democratization and the growth of civil society. In fact, such stances were conducive to the evolution of a two-party political system. The emergence of Barisan Alternatif (Alternative Front) – the loose coalition of four opposition parties (PAS, Keadilan, DAP, and Parti Rakyat Malaysia) formed before the 1999 general election to contest against the ruling BN (Abdul Rashid Motem 2000) – though immediately spurred by the political twists and turns following the Anwar saga, must have benefited from these favourable conditions that preceded the crisis.

However, the democratic stances of the new Malay middle-class respondents contained a paradox, and were not thoroughgoing. For example, when they were probed deeper on a wider range of issues, including workers' rights and individual freedom, their commitment seemed somewhat less resolute. When asked whether they agreed that workers could launch industrial action in an industrial democracy to fight for their interests vis-à-vis their employers, a very small number gave unqualified support, while the majority (slightly less than two-thirds) would only agree to a certain extent or depending on circumstances, and over a third were opposed to it. It is significant to note that voting against the ruling party does not necessarily translate into support for basic workers' rights. This is clear from the responses of the new Malay middle-class respondents in Kota Bharu and Kuala Terengganu. While support for the opposition was strongest in these two provincial towns, the proportion opposed to workers launching industrial action was also largest.

Like their views regarding workers' rights, their views on the Internal Security Act were also in consistent with their other apparently democratic stances. When asked whether they would agree that the ISA be continued, only a very small minority opposed it outright, while about one-quarter took the opposite stand – that is, strongly in favour of its continuation. The majority (about two-thirds) hesitated to give unreserved support but were willing to support its continuation, depending on circumstances. This suggests that new Malay middle-class respondents had mixed views about the ISA. There have been cases, which the author detected through interviews, of some respondents who opposed the ISA, but only selectively. For example, they would not oppose the ISA if it was applied only to certain non-Malay or communist elements, whom they regarded as 'chauvinists' or 'extremists', though they would oppose it if they saw there was a clear abuse of the act. They would, however, not hesitate to oppose it if it was applied to Malays and Muslim organizations (for example, the action against members of the Arqam movement). (For a write-up on the Arqam movement, see Sharifah Zaleha 1997, 1999.)

These apparently contradictory stances were not peculiar to members of the new Malay middle class, for they cut across classes and ethnic groups. As shown below, such apparent paradoxes were also seen among Malay, Chinese and Indian workers, as well as among members of the new Chinese and Indian middle classes, with differences largely a matter of degree. From our study among Malay workers in Kuala Lumpur in 1997, it was found that their views on the ISA were almost identical with those of the new Malay middle-class respondents – only 10.5 per cent opposed it, 29.3 per cent supported it fully, while another 60.2 per cent gave it qualified support. However, among the Chinese and Indian working-class and middle-class respondents, the responses were slightly different. A much larger proportion of Chinese and Indian working-class respondents opposed it, but the majority still fully or partially supported it. The stances of the new Chinese and Indian middle class against the ISA were stronger than among respondents from the new Malay middle class, but somewhat softer compared to the stances of the Chinese and Indian working-class respondents.

Conclusions: is civil society in the making?

Civil society is a contested concept, though many freely use it, while adducing different evidence in support of their claims. Sloane (1999: 202) argues that in Malaysia, 'Paradoxically entrepreneurship is presented as evidence that Malaysia *has* produced a modern civil society, defined as social and economic arrangements that counterbalance the power of the state by providing an alternative source of power and prestige to the state itself.' She criticizes this thesis by contending that entrepreneurship as presently constituted in Malaysia is very state-dependent. For her, Malay entrepreneurship serves the needs of the state by aligning and organizing Malay political loyalty and justifying its system of economic rewards; as a result, a picture of Malaysianized civil society as comprised of social and economic arrangements or networks which counterbalance the power of the state is only an illusion (Sloane 1999: 203). Her observations – based on an in-depth ethnographic study of a group of Malay entrepreneurs in Kuala Lumpur – seem to correspond with Gomez's study – on a more general level – of the interconnections between Malay business interests and UMNO and the state (Gomez 1994, 1996).

The findings in my study of the new Malay middle class, however, do not present such a monolithic picture. At least two trends have emerged among the new Malay middle class. On one hand, many seemed to accept the overall BN government framework, tolerating its authoritarianism in return for order and stability. They wanted the UMNO-led BN to continue ruling the country, because of its development record of having narrowed the gap among ethnic groups and between rich and poor as well as its success in maintaining national unity. These achievements had been attained within the context of political stability over the last few decades. Despite its repressive nature, respondents seemed to see the ISA as a means of ensuring political stability. To them, the system was not only effective, but also had legitimacy. This was in contrast to the situation noted by Scott in the 1960s that 'What the system lacks in legitimacy it makes up for by its effectiveness' (Scott 1968: 166). While the contemporary new Malay middle class may be different from the westernized bureaucrats of the early post-independence years of the 1960s, many had not made an ideological leap from the 'tutelary democracy' that Scott (1968: chapter 10) found to be upheld by the latter then.

On the other hand, an increasing number among the new Malay middle class have become critical of the BN government. In recent elections, they have voted for the opposition, and asserted their political and ideological independence from the state. A smaller number have also been active in political NGOs. Though these forces were small, they were growing, constantly providing critical voices, and have served as a restraint upon the state itself. Besides them, we must also take into account other critical voices – that is, those who were not members of any NGO or political party, as well as those within UMNO who were in favour of opening up a larger democratic space. This means that, overall, the forces advocating democratization and the growth of civil society could be much stronger. The existence of these forces is quite consistent with the findings in Saravanamuttu's study in the late 1980s (Saravanamuttu 1989) that the middle class was a force to be reckoned with in opposing creeping state authoritarianism and in promoting civil society. This suggests that the 'democratization' thesis is, to a certain extent, valid among the new

Malay middle class in Malaysia. Nevertheless, as shown in this study, it is not embraced by the whole of the new middle class, but only by its progressive component.

However, things are dynamic and constantly changing. While being ideological, consciousness is also historically contingent. The growth of civil society often begins with the beliefs and activities of small groups before drawing support from a larger number in society. It sometimes requires an 'exogenous' fillip to carry this process forward more rapidly. This seems to have happened to members of the new Malay middle class almost two years after the fieldwork was done, when many came out in support of the reform movement triggered by the sacking in early September 1998 of Anwar Ibrahim, the Deputy Prime Minister and previously anointed successor of Prime Minister Dr Mahathir Mohamad, an issue we will touch upon in the concluding chapter (see Chapter 10).

9
The New Malay Middle Class and *Melayu Baru*

Introduction

In the preceding chapters, I have analysed the phenomenon of the new Malay middle class, using a combination of quantitative data from my own survey and official statistics. I have shown that the new Malay middle class, although relatively affluent, is of recent origin and still in the process of formation. Mostly products of the NEP, members of the new Malay middle class – managers, professional and administrators – have appeared on the historical scene during the last three decades of Malaysia's rapid economic growth. A considerable number of individuals from this class have 'graduated' to become big Malay capitalists, heading a number of public listed companies. The presence of the Malay capitalist and new middle classes has had a significant impact on the course of contemporary Malaysian history. Their presence has not only redefined the class structure and altered the class map, but has also promoted the agenda of modernization and transformation of Malay society, and, by extension, Malaysian society. To complement the earlier discussion of middle-class formation and the character of the new Malay middle class in this study, I propose, in this chapter, to take another route to examine the phenomenon of the new Malay middle class by presenting a qualitative analysis regarding issues of the formation of this class from the viewpoint of the redefined agenda of modernization and transformation of Malay society expressed in the concept of *Melayu Baru* (the New Malay).[1]

The concept of *Melayu Baru*, advanced by Malaysia's Prime Minister Dr Mahathir Mohamad in his presidential address at the UMNO general assembly in November 1991 (Mahathir 1991b), has sparked off a debate among scholars, who have offered quite different, though not necessarily unrelated viewpoints. One school of thought dismisses it as a political gimmick rather than a people's movement, suggesting that it is a political construct, a phantom which has no basis in reality. Other critics suggest that it is a move by the UMNO leadership to create and expand the Malay capitalist and the new middle classes to achieve inter-ethnic parity, while a third group regards it as an attempt to work out a redefinition of the Malay personality in line with the imperatives of the new age. While not necessarily disagreeing with the above viewpoints, I am adopting a slightly different position. My argument here will be that although Mahathir's *Melayu Baru* can be seen as an attempt at a typological redefinition of the Malay character and is meant to enhance the growth of the capitalist and the new middle classes in order to expand the Bumiputera commercial and industrial community, the whole issue is not *solely* about the creation of these classes. Essentially, the *Melayu Baru* is a project directed to the transformation and modernization of the Malay society, with its emphasis currently on the creation and expansion of the Malay capitalist and the new middle classes, and the development of a work culture and ethics in keeping with the demands of the work regime of a rapidly industrializing society. The project, envisioned by early Malay nationalists and propelled by Malay nationalism, has assumed different forms and emphases during different historical periods. In the Mahathir era today, it has assumed a distinctly pro-business character because of the ideological orientation of its champion, who believes that the future of the Malay community lies in the development of Malay capitalism. In fact, Mahathir's *Melayu Baru* discourse is intended to serve as an ideological mould shaping the world view and work ethic not only of the Malay capitalist class, but also of the new Malay middle class, whose emergence and expansion I have discussed in the earlier chapter of this book.

For analytical convenience, this chapter is divided into four parts. First, there is an explanation of the historical context in which the concept of *Melayu Baru* emerged, dealing especially with how Mahathir problema-tized the Malay dilemma and the need for Malays to undergo reformation by becoming *Melayu Baru*; second, we offer a brief analysis of the perceptions and meanings of *Melayu Baru*, as understood and defined by a few Malay middle-class informants I have interviewed; third, an overview of the ensuing debate in the academic discourse since Mahathir's espousal of the concept is given; and fourth, I outline my own views and comments on the problem.

Melayu Baru: statement of the problem

The concept of *Melayu Baru* was first advanced by Mahathir at a critical juncture in Malaysian history. It was espoused soon after the official ending of the New Economic Policy (NEP) (1971–1990) and the launching of the National Development Policy (NDP) (1991–2000). It also came soon after Mahathir's Vision 2020 speech made in February 1991 in which he stressed the need for the creation of a united *Bangsa Malaysia*, or Malaysian nation. In the speech, he envisioned that Malaysia would become 'a fully developed industrial country ... in our own mould' by the year 2020, and he argued that to achieve this vision, the first and most fundamental challenge Malaysia must overcome is 'establishing a united Malaysian nation with a sense of common and shared destiny' in which the various ethnic groups are 'integrated, living in harmony and full and fair partnership, made up of one *Bangsa Malaysia* with political loyalty and dedication to the nation' (Mahathir 1991a: 2–3).

The official ending of the NEP and its replacement with the NDP and Vision 2020 indicated that the Malaysian government under Mahathir had embarked on a new development strategy. The recent policy changes – already preceded by such measures as privatization, deregulation and Malaysia Incorporated implemented since 1983 – marked a strategic shift from state intervention, characteristic of the NEP era, to more private and free market-based expansion, involving selective economic liberalization. In order to benefit from such changes, Mahathir enjoined Malays to transform their culture, value system and work ethics by undergoing 'reformation' to become *Melayu Baru* so that they can enhance their competitiveness in an increasingly market-driven world. It is in this context that Mahathir defines *Melayu Baru* as new Malays who 'possess a culture that is in keeping with the times, who are capable of meeting all challenges, able to compete without assistance, learned and knowledge-able, sophisticated, honest, disciplined, trustworthy and competent' (Mahathir 1991b). He also invokes Islam when he enjoins all UMNO members to regard the struggle for the emergence of twenty-first century new Malays and other Bumiputera as a *jihad* (crusade), a glorious struggle to save the faith and the religion of the Malays, thus indirectly saving other Muslims as well.

Mahathir's advocacy of *Melayu Baru* came slightly more than two decades after the 13 May 1969 communal riots in Kuala Lumpur and the publication of his controversial book *The Malay Dilemma* in 1970, in which he attempted, among other things, to explain the cause of the 13 May incident. In the book – considered by some as 'the definitive document of post-Merdeka, pre-NEP Malay nationalism' (Khoo 1995: 25) – he presented what he considered the essence of the Malay dilemma, which was that although the Malays were the definitive people of Malaysia, they faced dispossession in their own land. Arguing that the Malay dilemma was multifaceted (economic, political, cultural and psychological), Mahathir was singularly pessimistic about the capacity of the Malays to compete with the non-Malays, particularly the Chinese. To quote:

> [A]lthough the Malays managed to enter the economic field, they have never been able to, and can never hope to catch up with the Chinese. Even as Independence brought the Malays increased opportunities, it has brought the Chinese even greater opportunities which have propelled them so far ahead as to make the entry of the Malays into business almost ridiculously insignificant. The Malay economic dilemma is still unsolved and seems likely to remain so. The Malays' feeling of frustration continues to deepen. (Mahathir 1970: 51)

The same view was echoed equally forcefully in a working paper Mahathir presented at a seminar in Australia in 1971. On this occasion, he said that:

> As growth in commerce is usually by geometrical progression, the result is that no matter how the Malays tried they could never catch up with the non-Malays. This is the problem. The Malays will feel insecure for so long as they are left behind in the mainstream of Malaysian life. The years tend to whittle down their political dominance but they seem as far as ever from achieving parity in the other field with the non-Malays. To achieve parity and real progress they are required to rid themselves of the habits and values that they, with reasons, cherish. This is not an easy process. It takes time. But time in turn works against them for no matter how they spurt forward, the other went ahead faster. (Mahathir 1994c: 80)

He concluded that their inability to compete economically, coupled with the threat of weakened political power, had increased the Malay sense of insecurity: 'And when the Malays are insecure the nation itself cannot be secure' (Mahathir 1994c: 80).

What was the root cause of Malay backwardness and their inability to compete with the non-Malays, and what was the solution to this problem? In Mahathir's view, the Malay lack of progress was due to a mix of hereditary and environmental factors, especially the Malay character, as well as their culture and value system, including their code of ethics (Mahathir 1970). To overcome the dilemma, he suggested a two-pronged strategy. First, the Malay problem had to be treated as part of the Malaysian problem. Arguing that 'the Malays cannot solve their problem unless all Malaysians are willing to help solve them' (Mahathir 1971: 80), he suggested that the government must pursue 'constructive protection', given the fact that the Malays were the definitive people of Malaysia (Mahathir 1970). Second, among the Malays, there must be some kind of 'revolution'. As he put it,

> To complete the rehabilitation of the Malays there is a need for them to break away from custom or *adat* and to acquire new ways of thinking and a new system of values. Urbanisation [of the Malays] will do this to a certain extent, but there must also be a conscious effort to destroy the old ways and replace them with new ideas and values. The Malays must be confronted with the realities of life and forced to adjust their thinking to conform with these realities. (Mahathir 1970: 113)

He maintained that 'If they [the Malays] admit this, and if the need for change is realized, then there is hope; for as in psychiatry, success in isolating the root cause is in itself a part of the treatment. From then on planning a cure would be relatively simple' (Mahathir 1970: 173). These ideas, propagated three decades ago, constituted the ideological precursor to Mahathir's concept of *Melayu Baru*.

When Mahathir became Malaysia's fourth Prime Minister in 1981, some quarters were apprehensive about whether he still maintained the views he had espoused in *The Malay Dilemma,* and whether he would pursue the same policies he had proposed in it. Mahathir then admitted that he still maintained his views, but acknowledged that certain things had changed compared to the situation in the late 1960s when he wrote the book.[2] However, in May 1997, after more than 15 years in power, Mahathir went on record saying that he had revised some of his views. He said that the views expressed in the book about the inability of the Malays to succeed had been proven wrong. As he put it:

> *I no longer believe what I wrote in* The Malay Dilemma ... *The Malays are not inferior to others... in fact, we are now a model to many other races.* ('Dr. M: Views in *The Malay Dilemma* proven wrong', *New Straits Times*, 12 May 1997, p. 2; italics added)

His speech at the UMNO general assembly in November 1993 summed up his pride in successful Malays:

> Today we have Malays and Bumiputera as heads of departments, scientists, actuaries, nuclear physicists, surgeons, experts in the fields of medicine and aviation, bankers and corporate leaders. In fact, some are already managers of major conglomerates with assets worth billions of ringgit and are able to acquire bigger companies in the open market or participate in mergers and acquisitions which are complex and sophisticated. (Mahathir 1993)

He was all the more impressed since some of them came from humble backgrounds. He was of the opinion that the success of Malays and Bumiputera in the economic field was 'extraordinary' and well beyond 'expectations' (quoted in *Utusan Malaysia*, 17 April 1997, pp. 1–2). In short, to Mahathir, the Malay dilemma was over since it had more or less been overcome because the *Melayu Baru* he had once dreamt of have been born, thus ending the 'prehistory' of the Malays (Khoo 1995: 338).

The Malay dilemma and *Melayu Baru:* the perceptions of Malay managers

Before reviewing the debate on *Melayu Baru* in public and academic discourses, I will present some of the perceptions of the dilemma faced by the Malays and the meaning of *Melayu Baru* as understood and defined by a number of actors – Malay managers and professionals I have interviewed. Reflecting on the move by Malay professionals to enter the corporate sector – a change critical in the formation of the Malay new middle class – a Malay corporate figure in his early sixties, who is today chairman of a group of companies in the financial sector, expressed himself thus:

> From my experience, the transition of Malays into the private sector took place from the early 1970s. Before that, the corporate world was a mystery and alien to them, an area they were not prepared to enter. One reason was they were not really prepared to take risks. In the corporate world, you have to compete. In the government, there is job security, and you feel you are protected; in the private sector, if you don't perform, you'll get sacked. But, from that time [early 1970s], the corporate sector began to be attractive – mainly the salary, the perks, and also the prestige. The government also encouraged Malays to enter

the corporate world. Many Malays began to respond to this. So, you can see the beginning of the transition.

However, during the early years, the entry of Malays into the corporate sector was still at the professional and administrative levels, and did not entail Malays going into business. As he put it:

> But then, even when I entered the corporate world, I went in not as an entrepreneur; I was just an employee in a big foreign company. So, it was just like being a civil servant, the only difference was my *tauke* was not the government and my pay was much higher and the prestige that came with it. Later, when we set up business, we went into trading or services. In this respect, we have not entered the real world of entrepreneurship, of producing goods.

This corporate figure has been following the debate on *Melayu Baru*. He has also observed the positive and negative effects of privatization, and has reservations about a number of things. On the subject of *Melayu Baru*, while accepting the need for change, he takes a moralistic position and emphasizes the importance of assisting the small and medium-scale businessmen, and the creation of greater numbers of the new middle class.

> I don't know what criteria you use to become *Melayu Baru*, I don't understand why we should create *Melayu Baru*, and I don't know for how long one can apply the term *Melayu Baru*. What will *Melayu Baru* become, say, after 100 years or 1,000 years? Will they become *Melayu Baru baru* [new New Malay]? And then, what about *Melayu Lama* [the Old Malay]? To my mind, what is more appropriate is *Melayu mengikut zaman* [Malays who keep up with the times] irrespective of whether they are new or old. Societies change because of modernization, because of the development of science and technology, and Malays must keep abreast with that. What is important is to reduce the gap between the haves and the have-nots, and wealth should not be controlled by a tiny minority. For example, the implementation of privatization projects should be more widely distributed, we should not just create a few millionaires or billionaires. My idea is that the country should have more of the middle class and upper middle class ... As I see it, in the corporate world, there are three types of corporate players. First, you have the professionals such as engineers, accountants, and so on; they don't manufacture products but provide services. Second, the technocrats and managers – they are like civil servants in

the government, but they work in the private sector and they don't own the firms. Third, the entrepreneurs, big and small. To me, the small *usahawan* (entrepreneurs) must be given more assistance. The big ones, they have become giants – some become greedy, arrogant and often forget their roots. This is my worry.

While his scepticism about *Melayu Baru*, dismissing it as a symbol of modern materialistic Malays, is shared by a number of other Malay managers and professionals, many others see it in a more positive light. They share to varying degrees Mahathir's definition of *Melayu Baru* as modern, sophisticated and competitive Malays who are prepared to take risks. As they put it, *Melayu Baru* consist of modern, progressive Malays who are not dependent on the government, who can stand on their own feet, and who take other ethnic groups and peoples in the advanced nations as examples to learn from. However, they also emphasize that *Melayu Baru* must retain their identity and should not be greedy and materialistic. These perceptions can be detected in the views of another respondent, a Malay corporate figure in his forties, in charge of an organization meant to assist Malay entrepreneurs to set up their businesses and train and nurture them with entrepreneurial skills and ethics. To him, the *Melayu Baru* Mahathir talks about refers mainly to owner-managers, the new Malay entrepreneurs with a serious commitment to their business duty, and who possess sophisticated skills, extensive networks, and strong religious ethics.

We already have many successful Malay professionals, [some of whom] later became big corporate figures and very rich. But, many professionals are not owner-managers. This is what Malays have to become – entrepreneurs, owner-managers. But to become genuine entrepreneurs, they must have several important criteria: management skills, experience, good self-image, integrity and trust, communication skills, clear vision and commitment. ... I stress these criteria because once they become successful, they quickly develop inflated ego, with their ego becoming so big. To control that, we instill Islamic values. So, we ensure that they participate in an orientation programme for about a week, including participating in *qiamullai* (activities at night devoted to collective prayers). This is important so that they remember Allah, God the Almighty, and when they succeed, they must always remember where their *rezeki* [good fortune] comes from. We also stress team-building so that they will help each other, and not only care for themselves.

Fund management is an important field of business activity in which Malay managers feel that they have created an impact and changed perceptions of other Malaysians. Many fund management companies have been set up, some by the government – for example, the Majlis Amanah Rakyat (MARA), the Permodalan Nasional Berhad and a number of other funds set up by the state governments. Several such companies have also been set up by Malay bankers and other financiers on their own, while others have joined hands with non-Malay partners. The manager of a large fund management company had this to say:

> We have been able to manage Bumiputera funds. They place their savings and invest in our unit trust schemes. Now, non-Bumiputera also have faith in us, and invest their money in our funds, for example, in our property unit trust. Ten or twenty years ago, they thought Malays could only be politicians and government servants – that was supposed to be their forte. But not today – now they have changed their perceptions; they have accepted us as managers and financiers just as they accept non-Bumiputera managers and financiers. This means that we have gained the trust and confidence of *Malaysians*. To me that's very important.

However, this manager set his sights beyond Malaysian shores, eyeing the international market. Consistent with Mahathir's views of *Melayu Baru*, he felt his company has sufficient financial muscle, sophisticated managerial skills and confidence to become an effective international player. As he put it:

> But we are not going to stop here. We are working towards the next step – to gain the trust of the international community. We do not want to manage funds belonging to Malaysians only; we want to become an international fund manager, and would like to be seen as such. So we must improve ourselves. It just won't do if we merely benchmark against local standards, we're going beyond by benchmarking in the international market. We're stressing this to our managerial and professional staff. They must continuously improve their performance.

One major psychological block among Malay professionals in the 1970s perceived by our first informant quoted above was their reluctance to take risks. Today, this situation has changed. Besides the importance of networking, they recognize that one must be prepared to take risks.

Another manager expressed the view this way: 'Though we must be prudent, we must dare to take risk. As the saying goes, no pain, no gain. To me in the corporate world, daring to take risk is the name of the game.'

Daring to take risks, seizing new opportunities and turning around an unfavourable situation to become favourable to one's company is considered an important characteristic consistent with Mahathir's *Melayu Baru*. Referring to the financial and economic crisis that erupted in July 1997 and how his company managed the crisis, the manager of the fund management company interviewed above regarded it as an opportunity to make new investments and increase their equity in several companies due to the falling value in their stocks. Through taking such action, his company increased stakes in a number of conglomerates that have a proven track record. However, he stressed that such activities should be selective and conducted prudently, preceded by thorough up-to-the-minute market surveys.

Melayu Baru: an overview of the debate

The definitions and perceptions of *Melayu Baru* in the eyes of Malay managers quoted above stress three qualities: professional skills, vision, and ethics. In stressing these aspects, they directly or indirectly accept Mahathir's redefinition of the agenda of modernization and transformation of the Malays, and as managers, they perceive that their role is to execute it.

However, among scholars and other intellectuals, the *Melayu Baru* debate takes place on a different, more analytical and even critical plane. The rejectionist critics, contra Mahathir, argued that the latter's idea of *Melayu Baru* is a 'political gimmick and not a people's movement' (Husin Ali 1993). In fact, quite a few raise doubts about the appropriateness of the term *Melayu Baru*. Their argument is that if there are *Melayu Baru*, then, by implication, there must be *Melayu Lama* (the Old Malays), and queried what was so wrong with *Melayu Lama* to require them to change to become *Melayu Baru*? (On this, see Abu Bakar Hamid 1992.) The *Melayu Baru* concept has also been criticized as an abstraction, a mere political construct 'which has no reality because there is no basis for its existence, there is no process for its emergence, and there is no practice for its perpetuation' (Zainal Kling 1993: 1). It is regarded as nothing but a 'phantom born from the imagination of a desperate and frustrated Malay leadership because of the latter's failure in bringing progress to the race [Malays]' (Zainal Kling 1993). Arguing that the *Melayu Baru* campaign was actually aimed to benefit corporate Malays at the expense of the Malay masses, the critics regarded 'new' Malays as a new breed of vulgar, greedy, materialistic and westernized corporate businessmen. They maintained that the emergence and expansion of the ranks of these *homo economicus* who were divorced from their own cultural roots would widen existing economic and cultural gaps, and hence exacerbate class and status divisions within Malay society. They also felt that it would engender new ethnic tensions since the campaign would divert various ethnic groups from forging a *Bangsa Malaysia Baru* (new Malaysian Nation) into championing *Cina Baru* (New Chinese), *India Baru* (New Indian), *Iban Baru* (New Iban), *Kadazan Baru* (New Kadazan), and so on (Husin Ali 1993).

In addition to the rejectionist position above, a less polarised approach by some other scholars invokes a class viewpoint, while a rather 'soft' approach adopted by others considers a typology of desired new personality traits in the Malay character, or from the viewpoint of the transformation and modernization of Malay society. Taking a class approach in his intellectual biography of Mahathir, Khoo Boo Teik considered *Melayu Baru* as signifying the successful rehabilitation of the Malays and the end of the Malay dilemma. He argued that Mahathir's *Melayu Baru* does not refer to the Malays as a whole, but only to the new class of 'Malay entrepreneurs and the (non-government) Malay professionals who broadly make up the *Bumiputera* commercial and industrial community' (Khoo 1995: 337). Quoting Mahathir, Khoo drew attention to the latter's speech at the UMNO General Assembly in November 1993 (cited above) in which he expressed pride in the achievements of the Malays and Bumiputera who have become leaders in various fields which Malays would not have dreamt of being able to excel in only a generation earlier. In Mahathir's view, these achievements are significant symbols and testimony that the Malays 'have arrived' and that they can be as successful as anybody else, as long as they not only accept '*Malaysia boleh*' ('Malaysia can do it'), but more importantly, '*Melayu boleh*' (Malays can do it) (*Utusan Malaysia*, 17 April 1997, p. 2).

However, Khoo observed that while the Malay business and professional classes 'lie closest to Mahathir's *Melayu Baru* heart', there is no place in Mahathir's *Melayu Baru* scheme of things for the Malay royalty, Malay peasants and agriculturalists, or for the Malay working class – the latter being, 'the unsung hero of the NEP' (Khoo 1995: 336–7). According to him, Mahathir's *Melayu Baru* is all about the creation and expansion of Malay capitalism, and Mahathir 'knows no other class [than the business and professional classes] to whom the Malay future can be entrusted'. Khoo noted that Mahathir's identification with the Malay cause has always been characterized by a marked rejection of 'Malayness'. Thus, for Mahathir, the emergence of *Melayu Baru* signals the end of the 'pre-history' of the Malays, which, in turn, marks the beginning of Malay history and, by extension, the history of *Bangsa Malaysia* (Khoo 1995: 338).

Sharing Khoo's view, Shamsul (1997: 256) argued that Mahathir's *Melayu Baru* is a community of completely rehabilitated Malays, who have undergone a mental revolution and a cultural transformation, leaving behind feudalistic and fatalistic values. To Shamsul, the creation of *Melayu Baru* involves a reconstitution of the concept of 'Malayness', a move which 'interrogates' and compromises 'the pillars of Malayness' (such as Malay royalty, Malay culture and language). He is critical of the exclusivist nature of *Melayu Baru*, which refers only to the business and (non-government) professional classes, while the new Malay proletariat – born out of and the basis for Malaysia's rapid industrialization and capitalist transformation through the NEP – is excluded. By implication, Shamsul is arguing that the Malay proletariat, a crucial component of the new Malay industrial society, should be accorded a proper place in future society if *Melayu Baru* is to be at all inclusive. With their inclusion, the new Malay industrial society would definitely be a larger community than presently envisaged (Shamsul 1997: 258–259). In a later article, Shamsul (1999: 92) said that while 'from the top down the *Melayu Baru* consist of the corporate players, political elites and the professional middle class', we should also examine it from the viewpoint of the grass roots. Taking what he called the 'cultural construction' approach, he suggested that, viewed from the grass roots, the term *Melayu Baru* is used 'as a phrase or cliché to "make fun of others" [the new rich persons], both negatively (*perli, giat, kutuk* – as an expression of ridicule) and positively (*puji, sokong, ampu bodek* – an expression of praise)' (Shamsul 1999: 92).[3]

While the class approach considers *Melayu Baru* as collectivities, the typology approach focuses on the personality traits of the individual, although the latter is not necessarily divorced or isolated from the collective. As argued by its proponent Syed Hussein Alatas (1995), the problem of 'New Man' has been found in many societies throughout the world during various historical epochs. When societies are confronted with new and different sets of problems, they attempt to solve it through the creation of the 'New Man'. History has seen this happening in Japan since the Meiji Restoration of the late nineteenth century, and in China, where the idea of the 'New Chinese' has been advanced since the beginning of the twentieth century. Similarly, the Malays, who have faced their own different problems at different historical stages, have also tried to redefine their personality and what they want to preserve and consolidate. With these historically informed views, Alatas put forward a typology of personality traits of the 'New Malay', as rational, moral and selective, and, to a certain degree, universal human beings. As he put it, the 'New Malay' views the world in a more rational manner, using reason, calculation and plans: 'He does not subscribe to merely rationality, but it is rationality combined with certain universality. Malays are Muslims and being Muslims, they participate in certain universality by belonging to a world religion having a universal system of values' (Alatas 1995: 8–9). But very importantly, Alatas stressed that the 'New Malay' 'is not a new or sudden creation, without continuity with the past. ... [In fact, the] "New Malay" is a new breed ... continuous with the past' (Alatas 1995: 6).

Melayu Baru as a project of transformation and modernization of Malay society

The preceding arguments bring us to the fourth strand of thought, which considers *Melayu Baru* as an agenda or project of modernization and transformation of Malay society. To my mind, all the aforementioned approaches have their own merits, with each one informing a particular dimension of a larger historical phenomenon. However, I would like to offer another approach which is not necessarily exclusive of, or in disagreement with, the above views, but which attempts to locate the phenomenon of *Melayu Baru* in a broader historical perspective, by seeing its present advocacy in a modernization trajectory, but not a linear one. I am suggesting here that *Melayu Baru* is at once a concept, an idea and a movement of modernization and social transformation; that though the term may be of recent origin and is associated with Mahathir and the UMNO leadership, *Melayu Baru* as an idea and a project of modernization and transformation of Malay society has old historical roots. It is an idea that has historically set things in motion and still has compelling power today.

My approach here is not new. A similar approach has already been advanced by Rustam Sani, whose views I shall deal with briefly here. According to Rustam, the term *Melayu Baru* actually has the potential of becoming a concept, provided it is theoretically informed (Rustam 1992, 1993, 1997; Abdul Rahman 1994). Benefiting from insights offered by the Weberian thesis on the transition from tradition to rationality and modernity, Rustam posits that *Melayu Baru* is the latest expression of the idea of renewal or renaissance of Malay society in the present historical juncture. Critical of what he called the mainstream 'economistic and quantitative' approach adopted by the UMNO leadership, which emphasizes the creation of a predetermined number of Malay entrepreneurs, he is of the opinion that *Melayu Baru* should be treated as a movement of transformation, involving the sociocultural modernization of Malay society, to complete the unfinished agenda of Malay nationalism. Such a transformation would require an attack on two fronts, viz. a thoroughgoing reform of the educational system, and a concerted effort at nation-building for the formation of *Bangsa Malaysia*. Educational reform, according to him, is absolutely necessary to enhance the cultural literacy, modernity and competence of the Malays so that they will overcome what he termed the cultural and intellectual crisis besetting them, while the establishment of *Bangsa Malaysia*, based on Malaysian nationalism, is a critical factor for the consolidation of the nation-state, undermined by the forces of globalization.

As explained above, the problem of the 'New Man' is not something peculiar to Malay history and society. Neither is the idea of the 'New Malay' or *Melayu Baru,* since it has a long historical pedigree beginning in the nineteenth century with Abdullah Munshi, considered the 'forefather of *Melayu Baru'* (Harper 1996: 242). However, the inseparable symbiotic relationship between man and society needs to be more clearly stressed, since creating the 'New Man' cannot happen in a vacuum, but must occur in the context of society, with all its various institutions and structures. Thus, to this idea of *Melayu Baru* as the 'New Man' should be added the larger idea of Malay reformation and the emergence of a new kind of modern society which would emancipate the Malays from the shackles of feudalism, servitude, blind religious faith (*taqlid buta*) and moral degradation. Such ideas, for example, had already been mooted in the writings of Abdullah Munshi, a pioneering Malay reformist thinker of the first half of the nineteenth century. Abdullah could be described as an archetype of *Melayu Baru,* but, more importantly, he was propounding a vision of a new society as implied in his critique of Malay feudalism. In his visit to the East Coast states of Peninsular Malaysia in 1837/1838, he made critical observations of Malay society which he wrote of in *Kisah Pelayaran Abdullah* [Travels of Abdullah]. To him, the poverty among Malays which he saw was not due to indolence, but feudal oppression, which had killed the people's incentive and their will to work. Abdullah explained: 'To my mind, this is the cause of [Malay] poverty in Pahang. All the subjects live in constant fear of the injustice and greed of the ruling house and their nobles' (Abdullah 1964: 44).[4] Abdullah attributed such injustice and the general weakness of the Malay states to the poor education of their rulers and aristocrats, and also because of their deviation from the true teachings of Islam (Abdullah 1964: 123). He wanted the transformation of such a society, which he believed could only be achieved through education and reform of Malay beliefs, appreciation by Malays of their own language and modern learning[5] as well as changes in their attitude towards Islam. The social change advocated by Abdullah already contained the germ of the project of the transformation and modernization of Malay society.

However, Abdullah's modernization project was too futuristic and revolutionary for a society deeply entrenched in feudalism, and thus found little support for over half a century. But, in the period from the beginning of the twentieth century to the Second World War, with the awakening of Malay nationalism, the project gathered momentum and manifested, for example, in the writings of a diverse group of people such as Syed Sheikh Alhadi;[6] Zainal Abidin bin Ahmad (Za'ba);[7] Abdul Rahim Kajai (or Kajai for short);[8] and Ibrahim Yaacob[9] and Ishak Haji Mohamad.[10] In the post-war years, with Malay nationalism on the upsurge, the modernization project gathered greater momentum in sociocultural, political, and economic movements urging for the reform of Malay society and political independence (Ariffin Omar 1993). The birth of Malay-based political parties and movements, such as Parti Kebangsaan Melayu Malaya (PKMM) in 1945, the United Malays National Organisation (UMNO) in 1946, the radical youth movement Angkatan Pemuda Insaf (API) in 1946, the women's movement Angkatan Wanita Sedar (AWAS) also in 1946, and the various political, economic and cultural congresses held during the pre-independence period were all part and parcel of this growing modernization movement to bring Malays to the fore in the modern world. The pre-independence modernization project was not couched in class terms; it was, instead, more populist in nature, involving the whole 'race' (Malays), and not merely a particular class(es) or fraction of it, unlike the emphasis on the Malay capitalist and the new middle classes in contemporary discourse as espoused by Mahathir. The project grew from below, from the small, but vocal, intelligentsia, or members of the incipient middle class, with a vision for a modern Malay society that could be built only with the attainment of the country's independence.

Why was the Malay modernization project then more populist in nature? In part, it was because Malay society at this time, although increasingly differentiated, could still maintain a certain degree of internal homogeneity, given the relatively low level of urbanization and industrialization. There were no substantial Malay business and professional classes to speak of, unlike today (see Chapters 3 and 4). At the same time, there were clear 'boundaries' between them and the non-Malays as well as the British colonial masters, thanks to the existence of a Furnivallian plural society and the colonial 'divide-and-rule' policy (Furnivall 1956; Saunders 1977). Besides, the fact that political power was in the hands of the British, and not in the hands of the Malays, meant that it was impossible to implement the Malay modernization agenda, and that in order to achieve it, the Malays had to remain as one to gain the country's independence through the mobilization of the Malays as a whole.

The situation had changed dramatically with *Merdeka* (independence), more so with the social engineering of the NEP. Economic development through industrialization, modernization and rural development, as well as the democratization of education over the last four decades, more so during the recent two and half decades, had transformed Malaysian society, especially Malay society, from being basically traditional, rural and agrarian into being predominantly urban and modern. The transformation has brought about marked internal differentiation, especially within Malay society, characterized particularly by the ascendance of the capitalist and middle classes, and the decline of the traditional rural-based classes.

With political power in the hands of Malay leaders who shared it through consociational arrangements with the non-Malays in the UMNO-led BN government, the post-independence project of the transformation and the modernization of Malay society had been both state-sponsored and state-led. However, it should be remembered that the leaders were responding to the modernization impulse and demands 'from below', namely from members of the small Malay middle class, who pressed for Malay economic, cultural and social modernization. The demands grew louder with independence. For example, the Malay economic congress of 1947 was followed during the post-independence years by the two Bumiputera economic congresses in 1965 and 1968, whose demands were incorporated into the NEP; the struggle for Malay language, culture and education of the pre-independence years continued with greater vigour in the 1960s and 1970s, resulting in the establishment of the National Language Policy, the National Education Policy, and the National Culture Policy, and so on and so forth. What the state leaders did was to appropriate the demands emerging in the struggle, use them as their political platform by tempering them with their ideology and inclinations, and translate some of them into policy programmes, thus making the modernization agenda as something being 'pushed from above'.[11]

The role of the state in modernization and transformation is not peculiar to Malaysia or to Malays. Japan's modernization, for example, initiated during the Meiji Restoration of the late nineteenth century, was state-sponsored and state-led (Kunio 1988). Malay modernization – hampered by centuries of colonialism and Malay feudalism – required the synergic force of the state to carry it through, which it did through various policies, the most important being the NEP. (For further details, see Chapter 3.)

The earlier phase of post-independence Malay modernization, especially under the second Prime Minister Tun Abdul Razak Hussein (1970–1976), was clearly in response to the movement from below, a movement that expressed sharp dissatisfaction with the slow progress the Malays made under the first Prime Minister, Tunku Abdul Rahman (1955–70). The NEP -modernization project involved the Malay masses, aiming to unrelease them from the shackles of poverty, illiteracy, ignorance, and rural backwardness so that they could participate in the modern economy. During a period of about two decades (1971–90), it had produced new social classes and groups – especially the Malay capitalist and the new middle classes – and had generally broken down the psychological impasse, characterized by a lack of confidence and insecurity previously found among the Malays. The affirmative action carried out by the state had ensured a certain degree of achievement of this earlier phase of the modernization agenda, and today, the modernized Malays – better educated, urbanized and placed in better positions and statuses in the social hierarchy – have generally rid themselves of their inferiority complex and emerged with greater self-confidence and assertiveness. This new sense of confidence could clearly be gleaned from the narratives of the interviews with the Malay managers presented earlier in this chapter.

However, despite these changes, Mahathir was still unhappy. As argued in the preceding section, he continued urging Malays to change themselves and become *Melayu Baru* in the mould he defined. There are several reasons for this. In order to respond to the ongoing changes in the regional and global scenario, and manage it effectively, Mahathir set the Vision 2020 agenda for Malaysia to become a fully developed industrial nation within a matter of one generation. Though Malaysia and the Malays had achieved some successes, he warned that 'we cannot be satisfied with ordinary successes' for, in order to catch up with the advanced nations, we 'have to run faster than them', otherwise we run the danger of being 're-colonised by a new form of colonialism' (Mahathir 1997: 6). To catch up with the advanced nations, he again stressed the importance for Malays to learn from and adopt the work culture of the advanced countries, especially their commitment to work, their critical attitude towards their own achievements, and their efforts at enhancing quality and strengthening resilience. At the same time, he called for a reform of Malay views and approach to Islam, by giving greater prominence to its substance, rather than to rituals.

What was recently advocated by Mahathir thus constitutes the latest and most articulate expression of the idea and movement of Malay modernization and transformation, and it is clear that the idea now has a greater force of action because of his leverage as Prime Minister and President of UMNO since 1981. The *Melayu Baru* project today becomes a distinctively pro-business movement because it is stamped with the ideology and vision of the Prime Minister who believes that the salvation of the Malays lies in the development of full-blown Malay capitalism. In keeping with his overall belief in privatization, deregulation and Malaysia Incorporated, Mahathir believes that the Malays' future cannot be centred around the state. Rather than becoming routinized bureaucrats who feel secure in their posts, or salaried middle-class employees with limited purchasing power, or even traditional rural producers, Malays must look to become entrepreneurs and corporate professionals in the private sector.

Nevertheless, to be fair to Mahathir, new social categories are also being included in his version of *Melayu Baru*. Having focused on the creation of the big corporate figures as part of an emerging Bumiputera capitalist class through various privatization projects, in early 1997 Mahathir turned his attention to creating small capitalists, or what he termed as 'a Malay/Bumiputera entrepreneurial middle class', consisting of small- and medium-scale Malay/Bumiputera businessmen, whom he also wanted to be part of the Bumiputera commercial and industrial community. The shift was in part a response to the growing dissatisfaction among small capitalists who felt that they had been 'left out of the game'. The Federal Ministry of Entrepreneurial Development and specialized institutions such as the Perbadanan Usahawan Nasional Berhad (PUNB) (National Entrepreneurs Corporation Limited) and other relevant state agencies have been entrusted with this task. In this exercise, arrangements are made to have the small Bumiputera capitalists networked with banks and Bumiputera-based corporate giants, who – as part of what is termed their 'social responsibility' – are supposed to serve as an 'umbrella' to help nurture their growth (for example, through the vendor system). The results of this programme are yet to be seen, but it is clear that the inclusion of small capitalists has not dramatically changed the strongly pro-big business orientation of Mahathir's *Melayu Baru*.

Melayu Baru **and cultural modernization**

As argued above, *Melayu Baru* is a modernization project that has been propelled by Malay nationalism, but the project has experienced changes during different historical periods, with its content determined largely by the ideological orientation and vision of the Malay leaders in power at these times. Needless to say, the changes at the level of ideas need to reflect the changes occurring in the economy and society, and these ideas should be sufficiently advanced and visionary to provide guidance and direction to the changes. This explains why certain long established beliefs of Malay nationalism have been redefined during different historical periods. Mahathir's *Melayu Baru* project, in fact, involves a redefinition of Malay nationalism to give it new relevance for Malaysian nation-building and globalization.

In an obvious rebuttal to his critics who argued that Mahathir's *Melayu Baru* project has 'sacrificed' Malay language and culture at the altar of market forces by giving prominence and pride of place to English, Mahathir maintained that *only* when Malays are successful economically would the Malay language be respected. In his presidential address at the UMNO General Assembly in September 1997, he redefined what, to him, is a nationalist.

> True nationalists are those who work so that their race can progress and will be capable of competing successfully with the advanced nations. True nationalists are people who are respected because they hail from a successful race... True nationalists are those who ensure that their race gains respect and emulation of others due to their excellent achievements. (Mahathir 1997)

Mahathir is consistent in maintaining this view. In his end-of-year interview with *Bernama* on 26 December 2000, he again stressed that, '... a nationalist is someone who has acquired all the knowledge and mastered all the skills and is capable of contesting against the rest of the world' (Mahathir 2000: 9).

'Competitiveness', 'success', and 'achievements' – the key words running through Mahathir's thinking – refer to the economic realm, but the route to success is not merely through economic or financial means, but, more importantly, through culture, for, to him, 'culture is the determinant of achievement'.[12] He maintained that the new culture that the Malays need to inculcate, including the mastery of English, would not make them any less Malay. To drive home the point, he posed the rhetorical questions:

> Will we lose our identity, the identity of our race if we rectify our values so that we can build a new culture and civilisation; a culture and civilisation which is more suited for progress, and with which can redeem and establish our dignity? ... [W]ould we become less Malay, or less Iban or less Kadazan ... just because we accept certain aspects of foreign culture? (Mahathir 1997)[13]

Mahathir's formulation of *Melayu Baru* takes the instrumentalist view of culture, which is to answer the pragmatic question of 'How to bring about development?' However, an important thesis which is reasonably prominent in the development literature, especially following the Weberian tradition, is the philosophical question of 'development for what?' This is a critical dimension in the *Melayu Baru* discourse which is clearly underplayed in Mahathir's formulation, but it remains implicit in the modernist impulse of the early Malay nationalists, and in the arguments of some of the more recent critics of the state-led Malay modernization. The social-transformation approach adopted in this study hinges upon the recognition that, while culture change, namely the adoption of a new work culture, is necessary to bring about development, prosperity and wealth, the latter cannot and should not be an end or an ideal in itself. Wealth creation is a means to a larger and more noble end – that is, the creation of a modern society with a modern culture (including modern work ethic) and modern civilization in Malaysia. The latter should be characterized by a flowering of cultural activities, especially high culture, art and literature, intellectual creativity and wisdom, spiritual fulfilment, scientific invention and innovation, and the enlarging of civil society. Wealth creation, to be achieved by adopting the capitalist work ethic, can become devoid of a human soul, if it is not integrated as part and parcel of overall human development.

These noble values are actually found in Vision 2020 propounded by Mahathir (1991a), but in practice, they have not been given prominence, because the vision has been appropriated by the 'new rich' from the corporate world. Thus, there is no attempt at integrating the economic modernization agenda of the *Melayu Baru* project with the all-encompassing vision of establishing of a modern Malaysian civilization. Such integration is very necessary because the newly-created wealth enjoyed by many corporate and new middle-class Malays and non-Malays alike is neither accompanied by a flourishing culture nor by a renaissance in the social, intellectual and artistic spheres.[14] Instead, it has been accompanied by a growth of consumerism[15] and materialistic individualism.

In sum, the *Melayu Baru* project of modernization and transformation of the Malay society as advanced by Mahathir focuses only on two fronts: (i) the generation of wealth in order to be advanced economically; and (ii) the creation of the Malay capitalist and the new middle classes. However, it neglects a very important component, that is, the creation of a modern society with modern culture and civilization in which the wealth created would become a boon, because it enabled the people to enjoy the higher things in life. At the same time, in the creation of the modern classes, especially the capitalist and the new middle classes, Mahathir's *Melayu Baru* project does not stress the role of these classes as standard-bearers of modern culture and civilization in Malaysia.

Conclusions

This chapter has argued that *Melayu Baru* is a historically-based project aimed at the transformation and modernization of the Malay society, propelled by Malay nationalist aspirations. The project had been championed by various nationalist leaders at different historical stages. However, today it has assumed a distinctively pro-business character because of the ideological orientation and vision of its champion, Mahathir Mohamad, who believes that the salvation of the Malays lies in the establishment of a Malay/Bumiputera commercial and industrial community through the building of a prosperous Malaysian capitalism, and his views have found resonance among Malay capitalists, managers and professionals. To carry this through, Mahathir believes that Malay nationalism today has to be redefined to assume a more globalist and cosmopolitan outlook to be integrated with Malaysian nationalism for establishing *Bangsa Malaysia*. Nevertheless, the project is still unfolding, and whether an integrated *Bangsa Malaysia* – consisting of various ethnic groups having a common identity – will evolve is still extremely uncertain, given the undermining forces of globalization.

Based on the analysis of the various viewpoints in the *Melayu Baru* debate and of the character, changes and complexities in Malay modernization, I would like to propose, by way of conclusion, that the term *Melayu Baru* be accepted as an investigative concept in Malaysian social science. My arguments are as follows.

First, the historically-based project of the transformation and modernization of Malay society – a project which has its own specific characteristics, despite certain similarities with modernization projects elsewhere – requires a short-cut but comprehensive reference to the above-described processes. The utilization of this concept can contribute meaningfully to the universal discourse on modernization and transformation that has been the preoccupation of thinkers since the birth of the modern age and of social science generally. Viewed in these terms, the *Melayu Baru* concept is the particularization in Malaysia of the universal discourse on modernization.

Second, the *Melayu Baru* discourse shows that the modernization project is not unilinear, and that it assumes not only an anti-feudal stance as in Europe in the eighteenth and nineteenth centuries, but also an anti-colonialist position, which was not present in the European process of modernization. At the same time, the concept is informed by a complex interplay between multi-ethnicity and nation-building, for *Melayu Baru*, which began as a movement that interrogated not only feudalism (though partially) and colonialism, but also the migrant communities, today accommodates and cooperates with the latter, who are accepted as rightful partners in establishing and consolidating the independent Malaysian nation.

Third, the utilization of the concept of *Melayu Baru* also helps scholars to explore an intellectual route to a fruitful discourse on the modernization of culture and religion, which is also a major theme in social science. In Malay intellectual history, these two issues (Malay culture and Islam) had been part of the Malay modernization discourse, which posited that for Malays to succeed, there must be a reform of Malay culture as well as a critical re-examination of their orthodox approach to Islam, and that discourse is becoming increasingly vocal and pervasive today, because it is informed not only by the views of Prime Minister Mahathir, but also by those of intellectuals and the previously silent voices of Muslim women activists.

Fourth, the *Melayu Baru* discourse also helps to unravel the complex interplay between the instrumentalist role of culture in development, and culture as embodying the fine values or the higher things in life that human development should strive for. The concept thus embodies the spirit of pragmatism as well as philosophical idealism.

In short, the *Melayu Baru* as a concept is a useful and comprehensive reference to an historically-based ongoing intellectual and social-cultural movement for Malay modernization and advancement in the modern world which will continue in the twenty-first century. This modernization project is not only being pushed 'from above', but has been articulated in various forms 'from below'. Its utilization as a concept will enrich the corpus of Malaysian studies of social change, modernization and the middle classes, provided it is theoretically informed, and viewed with intellectual rigour, irrespective of the fact that its current usage has been largely due to the vigorous and often controversial espousal by a public intellectual-cum-Prime Minister, and not by some figure(s) within academia.

10
Concluding Remarks: The New Malay Middle Class and Social Transformation

In the preceding chapters, we have argued that although the beginnings of the modern classes – the capitalist, the middle and the working classes – in Malaysia could be traced to socio-economic developments since the turn of the twentieth century, their rapid expansion and development are recent phenomena, closely tied up with the policies of state-led modernization and industrialization together with capitalist expansion in post-independence Malaysia. Through the New Economic Policy (NEP) (1971–1990), the UMNO-controlled Malaysian state has sought to create a Bumiputera commercial and industrial community (BCIC), a euphemism for the Bumiputera capitalist and new middle classes, and, in the process, has also developed a Bumiputera working class. Unlike the earlier Malay middle class, which was made up mostly of administrators and school-teachers, the new Malay middle class, comprised largely of professionals and managers working in both the state and the private sectors, has emerged and expanded in the last 30 years, becoming a conspicuous presence in Malaysian cities and towns. The NEP's affirmative action programmes, however, have not precluded the growth of the non-Malay capitalist and middle classes. Nevertheless, the state's role in the formation of the non-Malay capitalist and new middle classes has been indirect. Since the state has generally been market-friendly, even when implementing the NEP's action programmes, its policies have enhanced the growth of capitalism, which provided the economically stronger Chinese community with rich opportunities to produce their own new middle class. Unlike the pre-1970 period, when the new middle class in Malaysia tended to be dominated by those of Chinese origin, the new Malaysian middle class today is multi-ethnic in composition, with the new Malay middle class constituting a major component. The changes that have taken place, which led to the emergence and expansion of a multi-ethnic new middle class, indicate that the new middle class is not a static social category, but rather a historically constituted and dynamic entity, which has emerged in the specific historical, political, economic and cultural context of the country's development. The dramatic changes in the ethnic and sectoral composition of the new Malaysian middle class is closely related to Malaysia's social transformation in the last 30 years.

We also have provided a portrayal of the new Malay middle class at close range based on our empirical study conducted in the second half of the 1990s in the metropolitan city of Kuala Lumpur and its suburb, Petaling Jaya, on the west coast, and in the two provincial towns of Kota Bharu, Kelantan and Kuala Terengganu, both on the east coast of peninsular Malaysia. Drawing comparisons with the new middle classes in East Asia, it was shown that, like their East Asian counterparts, the new Malaysian middle class, especially its Malay component, is a 'first-generation' middle class, that is, a historically new class, whose parents came from humbler class backgrounds, as farmers, fishermen, labourers, policemen, clerks, petty traders, schoolteachers, and so on, and with only a small proportion coming from the ranks of government administrators. Upward intergenerational mobility has been very much dependent upon sponsorships by the state. The 'first-generation' phenomenon – very apparent among the new middle class in the two provincial towns – was also found in the metropolitan Klang Valley.

The dynamics of the formation of the new Malay middle class – a new social formation in urban settings – has produced a kaleidoscope of cultural forms, including a complex array of adaptations, innovations and changes, and this was examined at two levels: sociocultural and political. We now present some aspects of both the social and political cultures of this class, and explore some of their implications for Malaysia's social transformation in the twenty-first century. Our discussion will take into account not only the findings already presented in the preceding chapters but also some of the developments following the 1997–98 economic and political crises in Malaysia.

The dynamics of the social culture of the new Malay middle class

First, members of the new Malay middle class in our study can be recognized by their professions as managers, professionals and administrators who work in air-conditioned offices in modern complexes, often in large organizations, earn relatively high incomes, and enjoy authority and prestige most of their parents probably never dreamt of. Many are industrious, working beyond the stipulated work-hours, often taking home urgent office work to complete, and not always using up their annual leave because of heavy work schedules – many describe themselves as 'workaholic' or 'partially workaholic'. All these suggest that many members of the new Malay middle class have undergone a cultural transformation with them developing a new work culture and ethics, indicating that they have accepted the work regime of a rapidly industrializing society. In short, they display the *Melayu Baru* work culture in the manner espoused by Prime Minister Mahathir Mohamad.

Second, many members of the new Malay middle class are generally well off, with a few being very affluent. They live in suburban housing areas, either in bungalows or terraced housing different from that experienced by earlier generations. The most affluent new middle-class fraction – small in number, but very conspicuous – have differentiated themselves from other classes by acquiring symbolic status items such as luxurious bungalows fitted with alarm systems and electronically controlled gates, moving around often in imported, sometimes chauffeur-driven, luxury cars, carrying 'gold' credit cards and mobile phones, joining golf clubs, often spending quite lavishly on themselves, regularly dining at hotels, engaging in foreign travel, often to Europe and America, shopping abroad, and sporting branded clothes and other consumer items. This small new middle-class fraction constitutes the cosmopolitan urbanites who are part of the new rich that has been created during the last three decades of rapid economic growth.

Third, unlike their parents, our new Malay middle-class respondents possess high educational qualifications, marry at a relatively later age, and practise homogamous marriage patterns, though men tend to marry lower on the social scale, and women higher, and often form dual-career families, with some having domestic maids. Their family structure is predominantly nuclear, with a strong emphasis on conjugal relations, which often involve spending leisure hours together with their children. Although there is some degree of male dominance in several families in terms of power-sharing, there is an increasing tendency towards egalitarian relationships between the spouses.

Fourth, a major concern of the new Malay middle-class respondents in this study is class reproduction. They manifest a 'fear of falling' with regard to their children's future, showing concern as to whether their children will be able to reproduce their parents' class position, or go down instead. We have shown that in Malaysia, success in education is the key avenue for social mobility. The 'credential explosion' in Malaysia over the last two decades has intensified competition among young students to enter tertiary education. Realizing that the ability of their children to reproduce their class position is not secure, new Malay middle-class parents put tremendous pressure on them to excel in their studies. At the same time, reflecting market changes in their career preferences for their children, they want them, especially male children, to work outside the government sector, either by joining the private sector or by setting up their own businesses.

The characteristics of the social culture of the new Malay middle class discussed above may be quite universal as they are also found among the new Chinese and Indian middle classes in Malaysia, and among the new middle classes in other societies. There are, however, certain aspects of their social culture that may be specific to the new Malay middle class, some reflecting innovations in their ways of adapting to new urban environments, while some others are responses to the ongoing religious movements.

First, despite being modern and highly educated, many new Malay middle-class respondents express strong preferences for, and actually have, large families – a practice commonly found in traditional societies, but today it is continued, under the influence of the Islamic *dakwah* movement as well as the government's population policy. They also maintain close links with their parents and extended kin through regular flows of remittances, by returning regularly to their birthplace to visit parents or relatives, especially during the annual *balik kampung*, and through other means of communications. Living within a network of kin and friends, the new Malay middle-class family, although nuclear, is not isolated in the urban setting. Their extended family relations are being reconstituted and reaffirmed continuously, transforming them into a modified extended family system adapted to urban conditions.[1] This characteristic is most noticeable in the two provincial towns, but it is also conspicuously present in the metropolitan Klang Valley.

Second, unlike the highly affluent new middle-class Malays who have differentiated themselves from other classes, many of our respondents are generally modest in their lifestyles. They frequent shopping outlets also patronized by the working class; they are always on the look out for 'sales' rather than for branded items. They eat out at economy restaurants and *warung*, take their families for vacations domestically, or have vacations abroad in neighbouring countries rather than in more costly far-away Europe or the United States. In short, they have adapted to urban living by trying to live within their means, a carry-over of the frugality of their humble origins.

Third, when Malays move to urban areas, they usually attempt to construct communities with *kampung*-like characteristics in new urban settings by relying on certain cultural resources they had acquired as young persons growing up in rural villages. Many also remain as 'folk urbanites', that is, urban-dwellers who operate within the domain of Malay cultural values and religious practices, and whose lifestyles are relatively modest, with strong family and community orientations. Under the influence of the Islamic *dakwah* movement, which has emerged since the 1970s, many new middle-class Malays show strong religious affinities. In fact, a major factor contributing to the construction of communities with *kampung*-like characteristics in new Malay middle-class residential areas, including in Kuala Lumpur and Petaling Jaya, is their members' commitment to religion, expressed in individual ritual performance and congregational prayers, thus revitalizing and reinforcing both the sense of community and religious identity. The *surau* is an important religious-cum-social institution which brings believers together and forms the basis of community interactions. Compared to rural areas, the *surau* as an institution in the changed material conditions of new urban environments, one in which neighbours are often strangers, becomes all the more important and pivotal in the construction of the community among the new Malay middle class. *Surau*-based religious and social activities help Malay urbanites to know each other and to interact more frequently as neighbours. This can be considered as a cultural innovation in a new environment based on traditional cultural resources. As such, the residential areas of the new Malay middle class, especially those in Kota Bharu and Kuala Terengganu, and also in many areas in the metropolitan Klang Valley, are not mere aggregations of dwellings, but communities in which many people know each other personally, interact on a regular basis, participate in *gotong royong* activities, and show concern for their neighbours when they suffer personal tragedies and so on. This suggests that many new middle-class Malays do not feel ill at ease in cities and do not consider the urban environment to be anonymous, alien and hostile to them.

Fourth, while ethnic and religious identities are strong and important among our new Malay middle-class respondents, the latter do not constitute a homogenous category in terms of their attitudes to, and relationships with, the non-Malays. Generally, new Malay middle-class respondents can be categorized into three groups: first, a small group which has close relationships with, and many friends from, other ethnic groups; they can be regarded as Malaysian and cosmopolitan in their attitudes and ways of life. The second group, which is much larger, has non-Malay friends and interacts with them, but their circles of non-Malay friends are smaller, and their interactions are rather limited. The third group, smaller in proportion, is more exclusive with its members not really having friends from other ethnic groups. They can be regarded as conducting their lives mainly within their own ethnic community and only having interactions with other ethnic groups at the marketplace.

Compared to those in Kota Bharu and Kuala Terengganu, a larger proportion of the Klang Valley new Malay middle-class respondents belong to the first category – those who have close relationships with other ethnic groups. However, in the Klang Valley there is also an almost equal proportion of new middle-class Malays who conduct their lives mainly within their own ethnic group with no circles of friends outside their ethnic boundary. This finding suggests that one's presence in a multi-ethnic surrounding (such as Kuala Lumpur or Petaling Jaya) does not automatically induce one to establish contacts with those from other ethnic groups. On the contrary, it may make one feel a greater need to keep within the same ethnic boundary. In the two provincial towns, the proportion of respondents who have non-Malay friends is smaller, as one might expect, while the majority have no friends from other ethnic groups. However, this should not be interpreted as meaning that they shun non-Malays because in these two towns, Chinese and, more particularly, Indians are tiny minorities. In fact, one may argue that in predominantly Malay areas such as Kota Bharu and Kuala Terengganu, where there are less inter-ethnic rivalries, Malays feel more secure and may be more open towards non-Malays while in the Klang Valley, where such rivalries are more common, attitudes and feelings vary from being open, secure and confident to one of being less open, insecure and even suspicious of other ethnic groups.

This comparative study of the new Malay middle class in both the metropolitan city in the multi-ethnic Klang Valley and in the two predominantly Malay provincial towns highlights not only the similarities of members of this class but also some important differences. New middle-class Malays in the three urban centres have experienced changes in their social culture, although the degree of change differs. In fact, greater proportions of new middle-class Malays in the Klang Valley exhibit a greater degree of class differentiation compared to those in both Kota Bharu and Kuala Terengganu. In the metropolitan city, the small, highly affluent fraction among middle-class Malays have developed high-status lifestyles and become, in Marxist terms, a 'class for itself'. The sense of community and community life among them, although present, are relatively weaker than in the two provincial towns.

Given the above scenario, what is the likely trend in terms of future social transformation? Does this mean that the new middle-class Malays in metropolitan cities face the danger of the demise of community, and of losing their roots because of stronger ethnic plurality, cultural heterogeneity and cosmopolitanism in the latter? These possibilities are there. This is so not only because of generational change as the 'first-generation' middle class gives way to the second, third and so forth, but also because of the Malaysian state's frenzied drive to modernize the country to achieve Vision 2020. In fact, the metropolitan city of Kuala Lumpur and its suburbs are being symbolically transformed into a cosmopolitan global city that prides itself on having numerous global icons of material modernity such as the world's tallest skyscraper (the Petronas Twin Towers), the world's longest building (the Linear City, a project derailed due the 1997–98 economic crisis), a cyber city (Cyber Jaya), the country's biggest shopping mall (the Mid-Valley Mega Mall), and so on.

There are, however, some policy 'brakes' along the way, expressed top-down in the form of the need to become a developed nation within 'our own mould' (Mahathir 1991), but these policy brakes are rather weak because what 'our own mould' is, has not been clearly defined, and its implementation has been inconsistent. Nevertheless, as this study has shown, the changed material conditions expedited by forces of globalization have induced new middle-class Malays to continuously construct and reconstruct their communities and identities. The sociocultural and religious resources held in common by them – enhanced by their desire and consciousness to 'preserve', in the face of change, some of the traditional characteristics of Malay culture and identity – are indeed vital in such construction and reconstruction. This explains the staying power of some aspects of the social culture of the new Malay middle class that appear seemingly 'traditional'. However, as argued in the study, the desire to relate to 'tradition' or 'the past' among new middle-class Malays is not 'residual' or traditional, but is itself a modern construct.

The dynamics of the new Malay middle-class political culture

What are some important political implications of being a 'first-generation' new Malay middle class that is state-sponsored? Are members of the new middle class capable of developing a certain degree of autonomy in order to exercise some restraints upon the state and market, and to become a force promoting social change, democracy and civil society in Malaysia?

While the social culture of the new middle-class Malays presents a varied picture, their political culture is also far from monolithic, reflecting acquiescence and loyalty to state authority and leadership on one hand,

and dissidence and opposition on the other. In this regard, it is worth recalling the arguments of Chandra (1979, 1998) that unquestioning acceptance of, and acquiescence to, the authority of the state and of the man at the helm of government, within a significant segment of society has been part of Malaysian, especially Malay, political culture for a long while.[2] Such a tendency is also found in this study of Malay middle-class politics, especially among the respondents in the Klang Valley. Many seem to accept the overall BN government framework, even tolerating its authoritarianism ostensibly to maintain ethnic hegemony, political stability and continued growth.

However, it was also shown that even before the outbreak of the 1997–98 crisis when the earlier phase of this study was conducted, an important, albeit much smaller, segment of the new Malay middle class was already critical of the BN government and had demanded or, at least, supported change. We have not only to look at political parties and NGOs, but also to go beyond them for such voices. Some of these middle-class elements were members of, and voted for, the opposition in the 1995 general election. A smaller number was also active in political NGOs, some were within UMNO, while others remained outside political parties and NGOs. Whatever their organizational affiliations, they constantly provided critical voices, calling for more democratic space and serving as a moral restraint upon the state and market.

The latter is part of the broader democratic force that would grow – though much more slowly – had it not been energized two years after the study, that is, in 1998, by the economic and political crisis, and the call for *reformasi* by Anwar Ibrahim, who demanded justice, democracy, transparency, good governance, and an end to corruption, cronyism and Mahathir's rule. In his campaign against the latter, Anwar openly challenged the man at the helm of the state, mobilizing tens of thousands of supporters, including many middle-class Malays – the young and women included – to participate in rallies and demonstrations calling for Mahathir's resignation. The unprecedented upsurge against Mahathir's leadership triggered by the Anwar-inspired *reformasi* movement succeeded in demolishing 'the halo of the protector' (Chandra 1998), and in giving birth to the growth and widening of multi-ethnic politics in Malaysia. In fact, it was this politics that led to the galvanizing of opposition forces into a loose multi-ethnic democratic coalition called Barisan Alternatif (Alternative Front) or BA, comprised of four opposition parties – PAS, Keadilan, Parti Rakyat Malaysia and DAP – whose leadership, particularly in the first three parties, is largely drawn from the new Malay middle class.

The disaffection and oppositional stance among the populace, including among the new Malay middle class, was clearly demonstrated in the November 1999 general election.[3] Though BN managed to secure 148 out of a 193-seat *Dewan Rakyat* (House of Representatives), the election witnessed the emergence of a Malay-led opposition in the Lower House. In this historic election, BA – though formed not long before the general election – managed to win 42 seats, with 27 going to PAS (a substantial increase from only five in 1995), five to Keadilan, and 10 to DAP.[4] Despite maintaining its two-thirds majority in Parliament BN only obtained 56.5 per cent of popular votes, while BA secured 40.1 per cent (Election Commission 2000). BN also failed to capture the Kelantan state from PAS, and lost the oil-rich state of Terengganu to the latter – altogether it lost 32 Malay-majority parliamentary constituencies. BN also lost almost one-third of the Kedah State Assembly seats, as well as many seats in Perak, Selangor, and the Federal Territory of Kuala Lumpur to BA. While unable to win many of the seats in these latter three states, particularly the Federal Territory of Kuala Lumpur, BA was able to garner large numbers of popular votes, and their defeats in many of the contested seats were quite marginal. (For details, see SIRD 2000.) BA could have won more seats in the election had the 680 804 newly registered voters, mostly young first-timers, were allowed to cast their votes in the 1999 general election.[5]

Despite statements from several party leaders and observers that the general election results were a 'wake-up' call for UMNO, and that the latter must quickly reform itself, UMNO in particular, and BN in general, could not arrest its downward slide. As shown exactly a year later in the November 2000 state by-elections, BN lost Lunas, its traditional stronghold in Mahathir's home state, Kedah, after holding it for over 40 years (Anil Netto 2000). After retaining it with a 4700 majority in the 1999 general election, BN surprisingly lost the constituency to BA by a margin of 530 votes out of more than 20 000 votes cast. With the BN's, particularly UMNO's continuing setbacks, party leaders and analysts began reminding their members that UMNO and BN could possibly face a similar fate as the Congress Party in India and the Koumintang in Taiwan which have been thrown out of office after long years in power.

In short, what has been happening in the last few years reflects a growing crisis of confidence among the people – including among new middle-class Malays – towards the BN government. The moral credibility of public institutions of governance such as the judiciary,[6] the police,[7] the Election Commission, the Anti-Corruption Agency, and mainstream media[8] has come under close scrutiny. Coupled with that is the growing dissent against Mahathir's leadership within UMNO. In fact, some UMNO leaders have openly attributed the BN's setbacks in the general election and its defeat in Lunas to Mahathir, whom they regarded as becoming a liability to the party after having been in power for two decades.[9] On the other side of the coin, the ability of the parties in BA to forge a common manifesto and to fight on the basis of multi-ethnic democratic politics, as well as the support it enjoys among many NGOs and intellectuals, is regarded as marking a 'watershed' in Malaysian political history, and the emergence of 'new politics' in Malaysia (Shamsul 2001; Syed Husin Ali 1999; Mohd Yusof Kassim 2001). This development could pave the way for the eventual emergence of an effective multi-ethnic two-coalition system in the country (Abdul Rashid 2000; Chandra 2000).

However, the Malaysian political scene is rather complex. While the Anwar incident triggered the *reformasi* upsurge, which converged with the earlier calls for justice and democracy advocated by both Malay and non-Malay parties based around the middle class, by NGOs and by intellectuals, the forces of change are rather fragmented, and the success of BA's multi-ethnic political mobilization is still very much in its early stages. Middle-class politics in Malaysia, including the politics of the new middle-class Malays, does not follow a straightforward equation of being either for or against democracy and civil society. Among these forces, the idea of change may not mean the same thing to different groups. While some may see change in terms of promoting democratization and enlarging civil society, others may see it as change in the current leadership but which, nevertheless, maintains the ruling set up with some minor adjustments. This means that their demand for change cannot automatically be taken to mean a demand for democracy and civil society, and the insistence on maintaining the current political order by some quarters does not necessarily equate to support for authoritarianism.

Nevertheless, being dynamic, the political culture of Malaysians, including the new middle-class Malays, is bound to change. It will be influenced by their continuing exposure to (and for some, participation in) the ongoing debates on, and struggles for, such issues as democracy, human rights and good governance in the country, through their contacts and comparisons with the outside world, and their access to the Internet and other media. They will most likely push for further democratization, demanding greater participation in the affairs of the country. In this respect, sections of the new Malay middle class – despite being state-sponsored – have asserted their ideological and political independence from the state.

However, the paradox in the stance of the new middle class is also noticeable. Consistent with its characteristics as a class that is security-

and consumption-oriented, the new middle class – although wanting change – is understandably rather cautious. Playing on the sense of insecurity felt by many members of this class, the BN government will continue to advance the politics of developmentalism and its patriotic appeals by raising the haunting spectre of globalization in order to win back its lost support.

But the government's ability to reaffirm its moral foundation and galvanize mass support, especially among the new Malay middle class, is hampered by several factors, particularly the erosion of confidence in the government and its key institutions, and the lack of commitment and inability of the ruling BN, in particular UMNO, to reform itself, particularly to attract new blood into the party, and to rejuvenate its leadership. People are watching to see if UMNO in particular will undertake serious changes in the direction of democratic reforms within the party, government and society. These are critical, strategic issues that UMNO and BN will have to contend with in the coming years in the light of the rising political awareness among the people, including among members of the new Malay middle class.

Malaysia has undergone deep social transformation in the last three decades and the process is an ongoing one. However, social transformation is not just change. It also involves fundamental alterations in the character of society and in social relations between classes and groups. It also involves changes in people's minds, especially in the way they look at things, and their ideology and political culture, together with changes in their ethics and lifestyles. The changes may be gradual, but they can also be rapid. The new Malay middle class, while economically still in the process of formation, is currently at a cultural and political cross-roads. The class is a product of social change, and after having reaped the benefits of change, a substantial proportion now wishes to maintain the status quo, but a growing number continues to demand social and political change. Both the social and political cultures of the new Malay middle class are evolving at their own pace, although currently the political culture is changing much faster. The character and pace of this change will have a significant impact on the contours of Malaysia's social and political transformation in the twenty-first century, and the new middle class, particularly its Malay component – despite justifiable reservations regarding the extent to which it will, and can, effectively carry through the transformation – will play an important role in this democratic transition.

Afterword: After the Crisis: the Southeast Asian Middle Classes Today

Clive S. Kessler

Studies of class groupings, especially those from the middle class broadly defined, have generally followed one of two approaches: either the empiricist and objectivist approach based upon the analysis of quantified data about individual members of class groupings; or culturalist and intersubjectivist approaches which focus upon the emergence and consolidation in action of common forms of public consciousness.

At the same time, a further dualism is apparent among the middle classes of Southeast Asia, especially since the regional economic crisis of 1997. On the one hand, many of them recognize that they have enjoyed advantages which they wish to hold onto and are reluctant to imperil, and they recognize that they owe their enjoyment of many of these benefits in a broad sense to government policies and sponsorship. At the same time, as they become more habituated to their middle-class position and its accompanying attitudes and habits of mind, the more sceptical many of them tend to become of government paternalism, even authoritarianism. Abdul Rahman Embong's important study throws light upon these core dualisms and ambivalences among the middle classes of contemporary Malaysia, and perhaps Southeast Asia more generally.

We are all familiar with a methodological puzzle or conundrum at the heart of sociological studies of class. Class, every first-year student learns to recognize, is a social phenomenon, a collective reality. Yet how do we, most of the time, study class? By conducting surveys and seeking quantifiable responses from individuals in order to assign them to classes. Then, from their imputed membership in the classes to which we have for our own purposes assigned them (which is to say from statistics about individuals), we seek to draw inferences and reach conclusions not about individuals but about classes and class experiences. It is odd that we so often, indeed routinely, fail to recognize not simply the circularity of this procedure but its vitiating reductionism.

After all, if class is not just individuals but is grounded in a social transformation of individual identities that is catalysed by collective experiences which are in turn framed within deep-seated social processes, the chances of our learning much of real value about class from a sequence of interrogations of an aggregate of isolated, atomistic individuals would seem fairly slight. So class, then, as E.P. Thompson (1963: 9 et passim) tried to make us understand a generation ago, is not a thing but an experience, a process, a happening. Class is contingent, emergent, fluctuating: not historically given and permanently available but, occasionally and usually quite problematically, historically achieved. It ebbs and flows like the tides, or the weak signals – sometimes clear, sometimes blurred, often faint, at times distorted, and sometimes even elusive or entirely absent – that we search for with our short-wave radio sets when as we seek to tap into the evidence and traces of remote, even exotic, human experience.

To speak of class in this way may seem both fanciful and heretical, and may lead to an odd coalition of strange intellectual bedfellows. After all, conventional empirical social researchers and conventional old-style Marxist sociologists can agree on very little. But one thing they might happily agree upon is that this concept of class – collective, contingent, and anything but concrete – is an affront to good sense: to the individualistic and quantifying good sense of the mainstream empiricists; and the politically correct good sense of the mechanical dichotomizers of the 'material' and 'ideal', or 'objective' and 'subjective', realities who are to be found among dutifully simplistic Marxists and their 'political economy' offspring. Such people can be expected to look askance at this more flexible concept of class and to have difficulty with it.

Class occurs and expresses itself in the lives of individuals (if it didn't, it wouldn't mean much at all). But the world in which it does so, as Durkheim rightly insisted long ago, is a world that, while built up upon individuals, does not consist solely of individuals. Individuals are the indispensable substratum of the social but not its essence nor its exclusive, even primary, manifestation. On the contrary, it is everything that emerges among individuals from out of their common association and mutual interaction, but which is not purely individual in its nature or origins, that it the quintessence or core of the 'social'. *Mutatis mutandis*, 'class'.

Classes emerge as the manifestation, and on the basis, of 'class experience', itself situated within the enabling but by no means determining context of 'class situations' in 'class societies'. But what makes class, what underlies its emergence as an actual social reality, is the articulation and crystallization of certain forms of public consciousness, usually in situations of overt or at least impending conflict. Similarly, what makes class recede, disappear or undergo transformation into something else is a reversal of that process: a weakening, a fragmentation or a transformative modification of that class-inflected *'conscience collective'*: of a longer- or shorter-lived manifestation or evanescently stable articulation of a form of public consciousness revolving around the problematics of 'class'.

In this account, class is cultural or it is nothing. Class theories which are adequate to their task are culturalist theories, not theories grounded solely in the 'objective facts' of political economy or in dutifully researched empirically ascertainable individual psychological responses to the supposed facts of political economy. Explanations of class are nothing if not culturalist. In other words, the only explanations that make any sense of class are those which actually 'make sense' of class and class experience, or seek to do so.

This comment on the nature of class and of theories of class may help clarify some dualities, antinomies or dichotomies that seem to characterize the middle classes of contemporary Southeast Asia and which therefore also run through much of the literature, especially that written since the regional economic crisis of 1997, about the political outlook, temperament and inclinations of key components of the Southeast Asian middle classes. These various theories offer contrasting, even rival, characterizations of current middle-class political sentiment in the region. Are the members of today's Southeast Asian middle classes courageous advocates of reform and partisans of 'civil society', the political sociologists now ask; or are they fearful, familistic and materialistic conformists, unconcerned with issues of the public good so long as they can enjoy the benefits of attractive share issues and access to the latest and most desired consumer goods? Which is the true picture? Will the real Southeast Asian middle class please stand up?

How is this difference, this duality, to be resolved? Yet this is not a matter which needs or should be decided one way or the other. This claim is not a matter of special pleading or exceptionalism; rather, it is in the inherent nature of class situations that they are dualistic. People situated within them are forever balancing precariously on the edge where the public class-framed consciousness of typical common experience is on the verge both of crystallizing and also refragmenting. People generally, and most strongly at moments of historical crisis and transition, experience both a powerful sense of sharing a common fate with others whose life situation is similar to their own and also an urgent, even desperate, desire to escape that promiscuously common fate, to assert an individual identity and thereby reaffirm some measure of individuality and with it a capacity for individual agency. Insistent and also widespread in the face of crisis is the human temptation to want to be 'the one who got away'. Here, class identities and allegiances are no exception.

Collective identities are always problematic, incomplete and unfinished. They are simultaneously forever both forming and dissolving, crystallizing and fragmenting – or at least undergoing kaleidoscopic reconfiguration. That is a general truth. Here, we are dealing with a situation where we need to be especially sensitive to this generic dualism and its implications. Specifically, and quite understandably, many members of today's Southeast Asian middle classes display a form of dual or divided consciousness. They are not one or the other of the two simplistic rival 'identikit' portraits which contemporary accounts of them proffer – courageous reform-minded citizens or selfish 'amoral familists' (cf. Banfield 1958) unmindful of public issues – but both of these, or more than a little bit of both, at the same time. Some, of course, may be decisively or predominantly one or the other. But many are both at the same time, even if not equally and actively so at all times. Many are about as courageous as, when it seems safe and possible and the outlook is favourable, they dare to be; while they are also as private, circumspect, and reluctant to stick their heads up as a proper and prudent concern for their own and their family's well-being might recommend.

When times are not favourable, then, is it any wonder to see not just optimism but public-spiritedness and even 'civil courage' seemingly evaporate, as people 'go to ground' or at least retreat into middle-class privacy and put their possibly dangerous aspirations 'on hold'. To activists eager to see, and therefore to promote, change this withdrawal, the ebbing of middle-class public sentiment, may be dispiriting. But before capitulating to demoralization, the partisans of 'civil society' might remember to look at the other side of that same coin. They might recall that, when circumstances again change and the pendulum begins to swing back, the other half of the divided middle-class persona is likely still to be there, ready to surface once more and to express itself in public life. This is precisely what a nonsimplistic theory of class, class identity and class politics would suggest, even in quite ordinary historical circumstances and social conditions.

We have, at the backs of our minds, a stereotype or myth about the middle class and its liberal political inclinations; one that arises from, even if it does not accurately reflect, the Western European experience. There, we know, the emerging middle classes exploded away the residues of the old feudal order, challenged the ancien régime, and forced their way into, and their interests upon, the modern state. Even for Marx and Engels, unremitting critics of the nineteenth-century bourgeoisie, the role of the European middle classes in their earlier formative period had been heroic.

As for the Southeast Asian middle classes, their origins are rather different. An earlier immigrant middle class, essentially what Weber termed a 'pariah bourgeoiie' had taken root under the colonial state but without its favour or support. Later, in Malaysia and elsewhere, post-independence governments sought as a major objective of a developmentalist public policy to create new middle classes from the majority, and paradigmatically autochthonous or indigenous, populations to rival and challenge these older immigrant commercial classes.

While the old middle class emerged in the interstices of the indifference and hostility of the colonial state, the new middle classes were created, in a project of nationalist social engineering, by the successor postcolonial régimes which inherited the colonial state apparatus. They were state-produced and state-dependent, not insurgents who successfully stormed and forced their way into the citadels of the modern Leviathan. There is nothing heroic about the origins of such a class, nor does it therefore have ingrained within its structures and common psyche the legacy of any heroically insurgent formative stance towards the state and public life within it. Whatever manifestations of independence, even rebelliousness, it displays will be more Oedipal than heroic: the ambivalent, even querulous, expression of almost familial resentments; those of children against the parent state and of younger disfavoured brothers and sisters against their more advantageously placed elder, senior siblings. By their origins, and in this respect they resemble the older immigrant middle class whose ascendancy Malaysia's Malay-dominated government created them to contest, the newer state-constructed indigenous middle classes were born of a political quietism, even servility, rather than preadapted by any older form of civility and liberal civic consciousness to an emerging 'civil society'. Neo-traditionalist in character, their contemporary political culture is one that turns upon loyalty, deference, and instrumental, even manipulative, clientship, not the virtues of '*courage civil*' or a cognate Rhenish '*Zivilcourage*' (see Kessler 1992).

It is no wonder, then, that the Southeast Asian middle classes, especially in the wake of the regional economic crisis of 1997, now display a dual consciousness, a divided politics, a split personality. They live in hope and anxiety, dependent upon the state which, they know, has been a generous, even indulgent, parent but which may also prove, especially when stressed, an irritable, punitive and unforgiving one too. The new Malaysian middle classes have now matured as grateful beneficiaries, when they look back at what they already have, and, when they look forward to what they still need and wish, as anxious supplicants of state sponsorship, initiative and largesse.

The experience of the regional economic crisis of 1997 and its aftermath seems only to have amplified both sides of this split consciousness: to have made Dr Jekyll more jackal-like and Mr Hyde more hide-bound. On the one hand, many of them recognize that they enjoy, and have become habituated to the enjoyment of, advantages which they wish to hold onto and are reluctant to imperil; and they recognize that they owe their enjoyment of many of these benefits in a broad sense to government policies and sponsorship. They have their shares and the near-tangible hopes, tantalizingly close to realization it often seems, which those shares represent; but they also have their anxieties that those hopes may yet somehow fail to materialize or fail to deliver real happiness, a real improvement in their quality of life as distinct from standard of living; and they also have their debts, often incurred to pay for those shares, which they will only be able to redeem provided economic recovery, attainable solely through government and on its terms, proves sustainable.

At the same time, as they become more habituated to their middle-class position and its accompanying attitudes and habits of mind, the more sceptical many of them tend to become of government paternalism, even authoritarianism. They hope for something not just more than but also, when differences of quantity will somehow magically transmute into one of quality, for something different from what they currently have and, on that basis alone, can imagine; for something, that is, not just different but elusively better. But they are anxiously unsure: and not only about whether they will manage to attain, whatever it may be, that 'something more'. Not accustomed to thinking in these terms, they are themselves also unsure what this 'something more' might actually mean and how it might look and feel if they had it.

They sense themselves to be on the threshold not simply of new or enlarged consumption patterns but of a new consciousness, often deflected or displaced generationally towards their children. While they may recognize that they will never themselves break out of the mindset and habits of a politically prudent quiescence, they often seem to hope that their children will not have to share, and be hobbled by, this same anxious and unadventurous conformism which has so tightly framed their own lives and personalities. They hope for all this, whatever it may prove to be, for and through their children, but are at the same unsure whether things will ever really 'loosen up' even in their children's time. So their children and their children's imagined social careers become a focus of genuine anxiety and even well-founded fear as well as of vicarious hope.

Much self-serving chatter has been heard from régime apologists about the inherently communitarian emphasis of 'Asian values'. But what has maintained and underwritten social peace throughout Southeast Asia in recent times has not been any distinctively Asian social ethic but, rather, the experience of rising economic growth, material welfare and living standards – and the expectation that they will continue to advance without serious interruption. It is for this reason that the protracted post-1997 economic reversal has posed more than simply an economic challenge, but also a social and political and cultural moment of truth as well, to the societies of Southeast Asia, not least to their new middle classes who have been the focus and fulcrum of the defining developmentalist projects of those now beleaguered state régimes.

Abdul Rahman Embong's timely analysis, conducted while the new Malaysian middle classes were hopefully, if not altogether confidently, taking shape during the mid-1990s boom years, opens a window to these processes, revealing some of the complexities and ambivalences of their common character and outlook. It sheds light upon both the sources and also the very specific limitations of the middle-class activism that, for a while, publicly flourished in Malaysia but which has now prudently lowered its sights, its expectations and its political voice. It probes the political economy and helps document social construction of their divided consciousness.

Note: This afterword draws upon a longer text entitled 'Alternative Approaches, Divided Consciousness: Dualities in Studying the Con temporary Southeast Asian Middle Classes', in a volume edited by Abdul Rahman Embong, *Southeast Asian Middle Classes: Prospects for Social Change and Democratisation* (Bangi, Malaysia: Penerbit Universiti Kebangsaan Malaysia, 2001).

References

Banfield, E.C. 1958. *The Moral Basis of a Backward Society: Amoral Familism*. Glencoe Ill.: The Free Press.

Kessler, C.S. 1992. 'Archaism and Modernity: Contemporary Malay Political Culture'. In J.S. Kahn and F.K.W. Loh (eds). *Fragmented Vision: Definitions of the Future in Malaysian Political Culture*. Sydney: Allen & Unwin, pp. 133–57.

Thompson, E.P. 1963. *The Making of the English Working Class*. New York: A.A. Knopf.

Notes

1 Introduction

1. While the 1970 and earlier census reports used the term 'Malays', later census reports combined Malay and other indigenous ethnic groups in one category, Bumiputera. However, since Malays constitute the largest proportion of the Bumiputera community, the figures for Bumiputera in later censuses are still comparable with earlier census data on Malays.
2. Middle-class studies conducted in the West are too numerous to quote here. Among those referred to in this study are Mills (1975), Giddens (1980), Edgell (1980), Abercrombie and Urry (1984), Goldthorpe (1980, 1982), Wright (1991, 1994), Vidich (1995), Butler and Savage (1995) and Lockwood (1995).
3. Among the studies of the East Asian middle class are Hsiao (1993, 1999), Robison and Goodman (1996), Hsiao and Koo (1997) and Hing Ai Yun (1997).
4. According to the Ministry of Rural Development, in Malaysia in 1995 there were 417 200 households (9.6 per cent of all households) living below the official poverty line 16.2 per cent of poor households were found in Sabah (highest), followed by Kelantan with 14.7 per cent, and Terengganu with 9.9 per cent.
5. Although this procedure may exaggerate the characteristics of the provincial new middle-class respondents because of the apparent over-sampling there, its risks are minimized since in the chapters that follow (Chapters 4 to 8), the author always analyses each of the three sub-samples on its own before making an overall comparison between the metropolitan and provincial new middle-class respondents.
6. This metropolitan and provincial divide is only for analytical purposes. It should not be seen as a dichotomy, but rather as a continuum. This is because large proportions of the metropolitan new middle class consist of 'outsiders', that is, people who have migrated to the Klang Valley from the various provincial states. They have roots in their places of origin and return to these places at times of cultural festivals and other occasions.
7. Admittedly, if the researcher concentrates only on one residential area and a sampling frame is available, a random sampling technique is more feasible. However, since the study is comparative between three different geographical areas, it would be much more costly and time-consuming if the researcher used such a technique.
8. Many instances of the lack of co-operation from residents in the Klang Valley were reported in the press when the Malaysian government conducted the population and housing census in July 2000. See, for example, the letter from one of the census-takers, Vijay Ramasamy, entitled 'A Rather Bumpy Census Exercise' (*The Star*, 24 July 2000, p. 22). In this, Ramasamy outline the difficulties he experience in trying to conduct the census among the residents of a condominium on the outskirts of Kuala Lumpur.

9. Among the proliferation of writers researching on class in the West today are Wright (1991, 1994), Marshall (1997), Marshall et al. (1988), Lockwood (1995), Edgell (1993), Crompton (1993), Vidich (1995), and Mc Nall, and Levine and Fantasia (1991). In the new industrializing countries (NICs), include Hsiao (1993), So and Hsiao (1994), Hsiao and Koo (1997) and Hing Ai Yun (1997).

10. Wright (1991) distinguishes two positions, adopted by Marxist writers: (i) the 'minimalist' position whereby some Marxist writers try to keep the concept of class structure as uncomplicated as possible, reducing it to a simple polarized vision of the class structure of capitalism; and (ii) the 'maximalist' position, whereby writers such as himself attempt to increase the complexity of the class structure concept in the hope that such complexity will more powerfully capture the explanatory mechanisms embedded in class relations (Wright 1991).

11. Referring to managers and professionals in the corporate sector.

12. Referring to administrators in the state sector, who try to run their organizations in accordance with their defined 'corporate philosophy and work ethic', and wield sufficient power in their dealings with the private sector as well as the lay public.

13. Literally meaning new rich persons, who become so through their business enterprise.

14. Literally meaning 'New Malays', a term used by Prime Minister Mahathir Mohamad when enjoining Malays to transform their work culture and ethic. (see Chapter 9).

15. To my mind, a definition is useful only as long as it delineates the entity by indicating what it is and is not, and also as long as it draws attention to objective and subjective processes leading to its formation and expansion. The working definition employed above, in some measure, not only conforms to the historically-based political economy approach that offers an 'objective' definition of the phenomenon of the new Malay middle class, but also to the 'cultural construction' approach that defines it 'subjectively', that is, from the viewpoint of the people, including members of the new middle class themselves. When reviewing the first volume in the series on the 'new rich' in Asia edited by Robison and Goodman (1996), Shamsul (1999) notes the absence of the 'cultural construction' approach in the study. He takes the contributors to task for the imprecision and elusiveness of the term 'new rich' employed by them – a fact also acknowledged by the editors. Shamsul's critique is that the volume unintentionally excludes two significant factors pertinent to the 'cultural construction' of the new rich in Asia: 'first, the changing idiom, texts and contexts of popular discourse that shape the social meaning of the new rich in the public sphere, past and present; second, the role of "cultural politics" in the formation of the new rich' (Shamsul 1999: 86–87).

16. Kahn (1991: 56), a proponent of the overriding role of the state, maintains that the Malaysian middle classes owe their existence not so much to the changing demands of capital as to the emergence of the modern state, and that the middle classes have been just as embedded in the state as in capitalist relations. In fact, he further argues that the emergence of a new middle class, at least in post-colonial Malaysia, might have as much, if not more to do with the emergence of the modern state as with capitalist development per se, and that the middle class 'is composed largely not of private, self-employed

entrepreneurs, or middle ranking employees of private enterprises, but those employed directly or indirectly by the state' (Kahn 1996b: 24) (see Chapter 3 for details).

2   A Critical Review of Malaysian Middle-Class Studies

1. An expanded version of this chapter appeared as Chapter 5 'Malaysian Middle Class Studies: A Critical Review' in Jomo (1999).
2. Due to space constraints, the review in this chapter is necessarily selective, confined to published works from 1989 to the present. Only one unpublished paper (Norani 1997) is included on the basis that it offers a different approach to the study. Shamsul's works (1997, 1999), which are published, focus specifically on *Melayu Baru*; thus they are discussed in Chapter 9, which deals with *Melayu Baru* and the new Malay middle class.
3. This view is pursued in his later works based on empirical studies in the 1990s (Saravanamuttu 2001).
4. Mohd Nor's survey focused on two questions: first, perceptions of members of the middle class concerning economic opportunities available to them through the NEP; and, second, their politics – whether tending towards moderation and compromise, or towards ethnic polarization. His sample consisting of 200 respondents – 65 per cent Malays and 35 per cent Chinese and Indians – drawn from six major towns in peninsular Malaysia (Penang, Seremban, Ipoh, Alor Star, Kota Bharu, and Kuala Terengganu) surprisingly included none any from the federal capital, Kuala Lumpur. By occupation, they consisted of white-collar employees from both private and public sectors, ranging from high-level professionals such as engineers, doctors, architects, and lawyers to administrators and schoolteachers and a few businessmen.
5. The usual argument is that since middle-class people are more educated, more open-minded and more tolerant, they therefore possess a natural inclination for democracy. Crouch, however, maintains that the middle class tends to favour democratization for different reasons. To quote:

> Because middle class people are better educated and have a certain economic security, they are more prepared to stand up for their rights and to demand participation in order to further their own interests. They support democracy not because they believe in equal rights for everyone but because democracy gives them access to political power. Thus, a middle class 'chauvinist' Malay might not be particularly commited to giving rights to Chinese or workers, but he wants a system that will be responsive to his demands. To the extent that democracy meets his interests, he will be inclined to support it. But democracy is not necessarily the only system that will meet personal requirements. (Personal communications, 20 September 1995)

3   Industrialization and Middle-Class Formation in Malaysia

1. Some writers (such as Crouch 1994) take only the first four occupational categories listed in the census – professional and technical; administrative and

managerial; clerical; and sales – as middle class occupations. Besides these four, others – for example, Johan Saravanamuttu (1989) and Abdul Rahman (1995) – also include about half the workforce in the services category. The first two categories give an estimate of the new middle class, whilst the other three give an estimate of the old middle class and the marginal or lower middle class.

2. The participation rate of the female workforce during the early decades of the twentieth century was very small, making up only about 5 per cent of the total registered workforce (Nathan 1922). Thus, we find that workforce statistics used by various studies of that period (see, for example, Hirschman 1975) often only refer to the male workforce. This chapter, which relies on these secondary sources, refers only to the male workforce for the same reason.

3. Mining activities, although normally considered part of the primary sector, are included in the secondary sector here. This is so because mining activities since the 1970s have concenrated on oil, which involves not only upstream, but also downstream, activities.

4. According to the 1991 census, urban areas are gazetted areas with adjoining built-up areas which have a combined population of 10 000 or more. Built-up areas are defined as areas contiguous to a gazetted area with at least 60 per cent of their population (aged 10 or above) engaged in non-agricultural activities and at least 30 per cent of housing units having modern toilet facilities (Malaysia 1996: 153).

5. The public universities are: Universiti Malaya (UM), Universiti Sains Malaysia (USM), Universiti Kebangsaan Malaysia (UKM), Universiti Putra Malaysia (previously known as Universiti Pertanian Malaysia) (UPM), Universiti Teknologi Malaysia (UTM), Universiti Utara Malaysia (UUM), International Islamic University (IIU), Universiti Malaysia Sarawak (Unimas), Universiti Malaysia Sabah (UMS), Universiti Perguruan Sultan Idris (UPSI), and Universiti Teknologi Mara (UiTM).

6. The 1996 Education Act allows the setting up of private universities, including branch campuses of foreign universities. The local private universities currently in operation include Universiti Multimedia, Universiti Tenaga (Uniten), Universiti Petronas, Universiti Tun Abdul Razak (Unitar), and the International Medical University (IMU), while two foreign universities – the University of Monash, Australia, and the University of Nottingham, United Kingdom – have established branch campuses in Malaysia.

7. Brown (1994) divides the development of the Malaysian state into three phases: (i) the colonial period; (ii) the period from independence to 1969; and (iii) the post-1969 period. According to him, during the colonial period, the state was the agency of British capitalist interests, mainly those in plantation and mining, so that state expenditure was focused on the infrastructural developments necessary to promote primary-product exports. During the period from independence to 1969, the state mediated between competing classes and among class fractions among the bourgeoisie, and this was reflected in the institutionalization of a governing alliance between various bourgeois class fractions. During the post-1969 period, he argues that the bureaucratic bourgeoisie gained control of the state machinery and progress-ively used this to attain dominance within the governing alliance, and to acquire access to commercial and industrial capital. As the state more clearly became the agency of the bureaucratic bourgeoisie, the stability of the alliance

was threatened, both by fractional rivalries because other bourgeois class fractions were marginalized, and by class tensions because state-based industrial development exacerbated disparities between the bourgeoisie as a whole and subordinate classes. The bureaucratic bourgeoisie then sought to employ the machinery of the state to contain and mediate resultant tensions. They did this, partly by granting political concessions, but primarily through the manipulation of ideology, particularly the ideology of ethnicity (Brown 1994: 211–12).

8. The financial and economic weakness of the Malay business and middle classes can be clearly seen in the following example. In 1964, out of a total of RM15.1 million shares allotted to Malays – in fact, practically all the 50 000 or so Malay civil servants were encouraged to buy up to RM10 000 each in company shares – only RM3.8 million shares, or 25 per cent of their allocation – were acquired because of a lack of funds (Jesudason 1989: 64–5).

9. Jomo (1986) argues that until the NEP, the role of the post-colonial state had been largely confined to administrative, supportive, and regulatory activities, and that it did not make direct and active efforts in promoting the interests of the governing group. However, according to him, with the NEP, the state no longer merely played a supportive role for private capital; it now moved to centre stage to become a medium for capital accumulation, serving the particular interests of the governing class. He suggests that, at least in this important sense, it can be argued that the statist bourgeoisie crystallized with the implementation of the NEP. He posits further that with the growth of public enterprises, political power and control over capitalist enterprise have converged in the hands of the statist bourgeoisie. Ministers, other ruling-party politicians, and senior bureaucrats in government service share control of these new instruments of class interest (Jomo 1986: 266).

4   The Making of the New Malay Middle Class

1. This applies only to the white middle class, because the black or coloured middle class is still in the process of formation in Britain and the United States (Phillips and Sarre 1995; Evans 1995).
2. For an explanation of the sample, see Chapter 1.
3. MCE or the Malaysian Certificate of Education (now known as SPM or *Sijil Pelajaran Malaysia*) is awarded to students after they have passed five secondary examinations. HSC or the Higher School Certificate (now known as STPM or *Sijil Tinggi Pelajaran* Malaysia) is awarded after passing six secondary examinations. Students are normally required to pass six secondary examinations before they can enter the university.
4. The respondents in the study numbered 520 persons, consisting of 42.1 per cent Malays, 42.1 per cent Chinese and 15.8 per cent Indians and Others. Of that number, 49.8 per cent were new middle class, 4.8 per cent capitalist class, 23.8 per cent old middle class, 11.9 per cent marginal middle class, and 4.8 per cent working class. The study, conducted in 1996, also shows a clear trend of upward intergenerational mobility among the new middle class. Nevertheless, such a trend was not confined to the new middle class alone; it was also a

general trend involving other classes, suggesting fluidity in the class structure. For example, the proportion of respondents originating from the labouring and peasant classes in the study was 40 per cent among the capitalist class, but was much higher among the old middle class (54 per cent) and the marginal middle class (54.8 per cent). This suggests at least two things. One, that a large proportion of members of the capitalist class, old middle class and new middle class were also first generation; and two, that although the class structure was rather open, and upward intergenerational social mobility was a distinct phenomenon, it nevertheless tended to be rather 'short range' in the sense that it was relatively easier to enter the old and marginal middle classes rather than the new middle class and the capitalist class.

5. In the 1970s, a Superscale G civil servant earned RM2000 a month, a Superscale A RM4000, and the Chief Secretary to the Cabinet, that is, Malaysia's top civil servant, earned RM4500 (Nordin 1976: 194). Today, based on the salary revision implemented from 1 January, 1995, their basic salary had increased considerably, with Superscale G officers earning about RM3000, Superscale A about RM7000, and the Chief Secretary to the Cabinet about RM10 000. (These figures do not include the various allowances they enjoy.)

6. For example, despite her high position and five-digit income, a financial director (a lady in her forties) of one large Malaysian conglomerate studied, planned to give up her present job to start her own company. She felt that her prospects would be better by being independent and her own boss.

7. During the interview, Tun Ismail said that at the First Bumiputera Economic Congress in 1965, he initially opposed the move by some delegates to form a Bumiputera bank (later known as Bank Bumiputra Malaysia Berhad), but that he later changed his mind. The reason why he opposed it was his reservations about the availability of a sufficient pool of Malay managers and professionals to run such a bank successfully. However, he admitted that he had no regrets for having changed his mind. After leading PNB for almost two decades and seeing the involvement of Malay managers and professionals at various levels and sectors, including in the banking sector, he became fully confident in their ability.

8. Tan Sri Geh was Tun Ismail's trusted colleague who is also a member of the PNB's Board of Directors since PNB's formation in 1978 and board member of several other companies. He was a member of the National Operations Council (NOC) set up by Tun Abdul Razak Hussein (Malaysia' second prime minister) following the May 13, 1969 riots, and also a member of the National Economic Consultative Council.

9. Interview with Tan Sri Geh on 19 March, 1996.

10. Tan Sri Khalid is currently Executive Vice-Chairman and Group Chief Executive Officer (CEO) of Kumpulan Guthrie Berhad, a large Malaysian conglomerate involved in the plantation and, property sectors among many others. He was the second general manager and CEO of PNB after Dato' Mohamad Desa Pachi. Reflecting on his experience working with Tun Ismail, Khalid – who has been dubbed as Tun Ismail's 'blue-eyed boy' – said that 'it was difficult working with Tun. With him, you've to work hard to earn his respect and trust.' (interview with Tan Sri Khalid Ibrahim on 9 February 1996).

5 The New Malay Middle-Class Family

1. Using data from national census reports, Jones (1994: chapter 3) noted the increase in the age at first marriage among Malays and highlighted the dramatic reduction in the numbers who married young. According to him, while almost 54 per cent of Malays in peninsular Malaysia between the ages of 15 and 19 were already married in 1957, the percentage of ever-married individuals in the same age group had been reduced to only about 7 per cent in 1985. Among those aged 20 to 24 years old, the percentage of those who had been married at some time in their lives fell from 90.6 per cent to 51.3 per cent over the same period.

2. The average age at first marriage among new Malay middle-class and working-class respondents in our study is comparable with that in some developed countries. In the United States, for example, women married at 20.2 years of age and men at 22.5 in the mid-1950s. In 1994, the average age of marriage for young women had increased to 24.5, and for men, to 26.7 (Shehan and Kammeyer 1997: 137).

3. In her study of families (including the middle class) in modern cosmopolitan Singapore, Quah (1990a, 1990b) noted that even highly educated women saw marriage and motherhood as major personal goals in their lives.

4. In Nordin's sample, 9.5 per cent were aged 51 and above, compared to our 4.9 per cent, while those aged 41–50 constituted 19 per cent (compared to 23.6 per cent in our study). The largest group in his sample were those aged 31–40 which made up 62.9 per cent (compared to 42.2 per cent in our sample), while the youngest (30 and below) comprised 8.6 per cent, compared to 29.2 per cent in our sample.

5. In Fatimah's study, those with no children comprised of recently married couples (three years or less). In terms of the preferred number of children per family, 16.2 per cent of her respondents preferred five or more, almost two-fifths (37.7 per cent) wanted four, while 23.4 per cent wanted three children. These figures suggest that the majority wanted large families of four or more children, which is quite consistent with our findings above.

6. Studies in western societies show that it is part of new middle-class values to prefer small nuclear families (Edgell 1980; Shehan and Kammeyer 1997). In Malaysia, this is true among the new Chinese middle class, while the new Malay middle class and, to a certain extent, the new Indian middle class prefer larger families. A recent study of the new Malaysian middle class shows that the preferred mean for the new Chinese middle class was 3.4, Indian 4 and Malays 5.2 (Abdul Rahman 1998: 258).

7. Willmott's (1969) 'symmetrical family' thesis claimed that partnership between husband and wife is expressed in three major forms. First, partnership in power, with major decisions being discussed and made together; second, partnership in the division of labour within the household as the old distinctions between men's and women's jobs (though still made) become increasingly blurred; and third, it is a partnership in social life, with couples spending more of their free time together and with their children. He concluded that despite continuing sexual inequalities, women today enjoy higher status in the family and society.

8. For non-Muslim students, Moral Education has been made a compulsory subject in the school curriculum.
9. The moral panic led to a study commissioned by the Malaysian Ministry of Youth and Sports in 1994 on *lepak* 'loafing' among youth and the ensuing *Rakan Muda* (Young Friends) programme being implemented based on the study's recommendations.
10. The nuclear family refers to any family comprising of husband and wife, and their dependent children. The extended family refers to any persistent kinship grouping of persons related by descent, marriage or adoption, which is wider than the nuclear family, comprising at least three generations, from grandparents (one or both) to grandchildren (Bell 1968).
11. Litwak (1960a, 1960b) distinguishes between the classical extended family and the modified extended family. His 'modified extended family' thesis suggests that extended family relations are possible in an urban industrial society, at least among the middle class, albeit in a modified form. The modified extended family is a series of nuclear families joined together – on an eglitarian basis – for mutual aid, not bound by demands for geographical propinquity or occupational similarity. He argues that geographical propinquity is not a prerequisite for these relationships and that such extended kin relations do not impede occupational mobility. Litwak states further that neither the classical extended family of rural society nor the isolated nuclear family is functional and suited to modern urban conditions (Litwak 1960a, 1960b; Bell 1968).

6 New Malay Middle-Class Lifestyles and Culture

1. By profession, most (62.9 percent) top-level executives and senior managers among the new Malay middle class in the Klang Valley owned luxury cars, while among middle-level managers and professionals, the percentages were much lower – that is, 29 per cent and 27.8 per cent respectively.
2. Muslims have to perform prayers five times daily, beginning with *Subuh* (prayer at dawn), *Zuhur* (afternoon prayer), *Asar* (evening prayer before dusk), *Maghrib* (night prayer immediately after dusk), and Isya' (late night prayer, normally performed an hour after *Maghrib* and before *Subuh*).
3. Some studies (for example, Tan Poo Chang et al. 1996) took the one-year period prior to the study as the cut-off point. In this study, we took a two-year period because travel and vacations are not necessarily an annual occurrence. Because of their busy work schedule or financial constraints, some respondents may not take their families on vacation this year, but may go in the next. Thus, the period of one year may not fully capture such activity.
4. Foreign travel and vacation discussed here does not include travel to perform the *Haj* or *Umrah* in Mecca (see Chapter 7 for a discussion of the latter).
5. Compare the Malaysian situation with South Korea under President Roh Tae-woo, which was dubbed 'the golf republic', although it had a much smaller number of golf courses than Malaysia. In 1991, South Korea had 60 golf courses in operation and another 118 were under construction (half of these golf courses were in the Seoul metropolitan area) (Cotton and Leest 1996: 190). In Malaysia, the metropolitan Klang Valley alone had over 130 golf courses in the

early 1990s managed by exclusive golf clubs, while there are less than 20 recreational parks for the public with a population of over two million (Norani Othman et al. 1996).

6. To gain an insight into the thinking of agencies responsible for promoting the use of Malay in government, universities, and the private and public sectors, I interviewed Tuan Haji Aziz Deraman, the Director-General of Dewan Bahasa dan Pustaka (the national language and literature agency) in 1997. In the interview, he regretted the apparent lack of commitment among members of the new Malay middle class as well as the private sector, especially those in the metropolitan Klang Valley, to join hands in promoting Malay in their daily communications as well as in commerce and industry. He saw the task of extending the usge of Malay in the private sector as an uphill struggle.

7 The New Malay Middle Class and Community

1. Some of the adaptive forms of urban living in multi-ethnic and multicultural Malaysia appear as hybridization. Here, hybridization is more than adaptation, and does not simply mean the phenomenon of cultural heterogeneity. Heterogeneity creates the conditions in which hybridization may emerge. Hybridization refers to the process of mutual influences between different cultures existing in the same milieu, with the resulting formation of something new, but still contains some elements of the originating culture(s). For example, in functions attended by an ethnically heterogeneous audience, Malay speakers usually begin the address with the Muslim salutation of *Assamu 'alaikum* (Arabic, meaning peace be unto you) to address the Muslim/ Malay crowd, followed by *salam sejahtera* (Malay, meaning 'greetings of peace') to address the non-Muslims/Malays. When Chinese middle-class families hold open houses to celebrate the Chinese Lunar New Year, and invite their Malay friends, they always assure their guests that the food served conforms with the Muslim *halal* (allowed by religion) prescriptions. Thus, the types of food comprised not only Chinese, but also Malay, and even Indian dishes. Nevertheless, in keeping with Chinese tradition, they serve mandarin oranges, and give *angpows* (monetary gifts contained in small red packets) to children. These two examples show that while elements of the originating culture(s) exist, the new cultural form is a cross or a hybrid between two or more cultures.

2. Social culture refers to the values and practices (including lifestyles) of individuals, as reflected in their relationships and interactions with other members of society.

3. These cultural resources include experiences of growing up as a village child/ adolescent and young Muslim, knowledge about the world and urban life obtained through schooling and the media, and knowledge about urban life obtained through stories about those who have been to towns and cities.

4. In the context of Malaysia, this idea of 'folk urbanites' and *kampung*-like communities is by no means original, though I cannot trace its originators. What I have tried to do here is to present the idea more systematically by relating it to social theory. I first presented this thesis – the construction by some sections of the Malay new middle class of '*kampung*-like' communities in

urban settings and some members of the Malay middle class being classified as 'folk urbanites' – in a paper at a conference on the middle class in Taipei in June 1997 (Abdul Rahman 1997a). By chance, I later met Kosaku Kunio at Universiti Kebangsaan Malaysia, and showed him my paper. He felt that there was some strength to what I was arguing and introduced me to his own work (Kosaku 1992) on Japan, in which he introduces the 'reproductionist' (or 'extensionist') theory of modern society.

5. Modernization theory often assumes that for a traditional society to be modern, it has to change its traditional culture and adopt western values and lifestyles. The literature is often filled with descriptions of the transformation process of traditional societies becoming modern, the resulting breakdown of traditional life, and the preservation of some aspects of traditional culture (see, for example, Lerner 1958, who is a pioneer in modernization studies). In this sense, as shown by Kessler (1992: 133–4), modernization theory sees tradition as 'residual': 'it is the residue of the past, that part which survives undisturbed and is accordingly, at least for the moment, preserved'. But, Kessler argues that what is preserved in modern society today is not simply 'residual' or 'traditional'.

> In this view tradition is not simply the surviving residue left undisturbed by the advancing yet incomplete modernization. Rather, it is essentially new, modern, contemporary – a recent construct. The recognition of and an attachment to the 'pastness' of certain cultural materials (what we come to call 'tradition') is itself, in this view, a product of modernity.

Kessler, in fact, takes another step beyond the 'modernity of tradition' argument, by suggesting that some aspects of the Malay *political* culture are not even residual, but inventions of tradition. However, in my discussion of the *social* culture of the Malay new middle class, I propose to limit it only to the argument of the 'modernity' of tradition.

6. Communities naturally involve networks. The concept of 'community as networks of relationships' as defined above is partially based on Barnes (cited in Frankenburg 1969: 243), who distinguishes three social fields of networks: the first is *territorial*, consisting of the locality in which people live and carry on their day-to-day existence (such as a village), with a more durable membership. The second field is *occupational*, the membership of which is not permanent but where each independent unit is temporarily linked in order to carry out its function to the full. The third field has neither unit nor boundary nor coordinating organization, but consists of all the friends whom a person requires through life, whether such ties are formed through work or at leisure, through kin or by accident. Each person sees himself at the centre of his own particular network of friends, and each friend will himself overlap into someone else's network.

7. For example, Tengku Razaleigh Hamzah, a wealthy prince-cum-businessman from Kelantan, named his mansion in Kota Bharu 'Palm Manor'.

8. As indicated elsewhere, due to time and financial constraints, my study of Malay workers was conducted only in the Klang Valley.

9. By comparison, a much higher proportion (76.2 per cent) of the Klang Valley Malay workers felt that their housing area was community-like (Table 7.1).

10. For an interesting anthropological study of how Malays in a new area organized themselves to set up a *surau*, see Zawawi Ibrahim (1998: 89–96). In this study, Zawawi shows vividly how a group of Malay labourers who came from various places in peninsular Malaysia to work in an oil palm plantation in Kemaman, Terengganu, got organized and set up a *surau*, which became the focal point of their community activities.

> The early life of the Malay labouring community was marked by a concern in maintaining a sense of community based on some cultural and social norms typical of a Malay or village way of life. The community had not yet become a political community where lower-class members felt the need to form political organizations to cater to their interests. Given this socio-cultural definition of the emerging community, the role of 'expressive leadership' assumed by the elders was therefore relevant to the existing needs of the early society. Accordingly, this form of social organization culminated in the formation of a prayer-house (*surau*), which symbolized the above ideals of Malays 'living in a community' (*hidup bermasyarakat*). (Zawawi 1998: 90)

11. In a traditional Malay village, a wedding feast was (and is) always a community affair. Relatives and neighbours are mobilized to help in its preparation, such as slaughtering the cow or buffalo, cutting up the meat, vegetables, and so on, in cooking them, as well as in seeing that guests have enough food to eat. In small urban areas such as Kota Bharu and Kuala Terengganu, this practice still continues today. In metropolitan Kuala Lumpur or Petaling Jaya, community participation in preparing the dishes has been taken over by specially commissioned caterers, and sometimes, wealthy families hold their children's weddings in hotels. However, many still hold the ceremony in the community. To ensure the occasion is a success and memorable, the host holds discussions with close relatives and neighbours on how to go about the ceremony, and their help is sought to prepare various things necessary for the occasion.

12. This is quite different from the finding by Maurice Stein (1964: 329) in his study of community in the United States. Commenting on 'the eclipse of the community', he observed that 'Community ties [in the United States] become increasingly dependent upon centralised authorities and agencies in all areas of social life' and that 'personal loyalties decrease their range with the successive weakening of national ties, regional ties, family ties, and finally ties to a coherent image of one's self'. Thus, he concludes that a series of separate but parallel 'vertical ties' to centralized decision-making bodies are replacing the 'horizontal ties' of local autonomy.

13. This trend of religious resurgence is also found in other Muslim countries. A report on neighbouring Indonesia in *Asiaweek* (29 January 1999), citing a thesis by one scholar on this topic, observes thus: The Indonesian middle class is 'both modern and pious'. They are young, professional, ethnically diverse. And the evidence of their presence is everywhere – from the explosion of Islamic-oriented tabloids and magazines (now numbering more than 40) to the popularity of Islamic music and sermons. The visible resurgence of Islam

in elite, urban culture is partly a reaction to the breathtaking economic changes the country has experienced since the 1960s. Islam becomes a way out to look at identity, where its adherents are really rooted. (See Jose Manuel Tesoro, 'Traditional Yet Modern: The Muslim Middle Class and Politics', *Asiaweek*, 29 January 1999, p. 24.)
14. Furnivall (1956: 304) defines a plural society as one with diverse groups within the same political unit who

> mix but do not combine. Each group holds by its own religion, its own culture and language, its own ideas and ways. As individuals they meet, but only in the market place, in buying and selling. There is a plural society, with different sections of the community living side by side, but separated within the same political unit. Even in the economic sphere, there is a division of labour along ethnic lines.

15. The issue of inter-ethnic relations is complex, and the survey data unfortunately does not allow us to draw firmer conclusions. This issue needs to be explored more fully by using the ethnographic approach, which I could only do partially here. From many conversations and interactions I had with several informants as well as personal observations in the three areas, I could sense that those in Kota Bharu and Kuala Terengganu had more open attitudes towards non-Malays, although they may not have many friends among them. This is also acknowledged by my Chinese informants in these two towns. In the Klang Valley, I have come across a number of Malays having such openness and multi-ethnic perspectives on various issues. At the same time, I also have come across many Malays who held strong views along ethnic lines. I have also encountered both tendencies among non-Malays in the Klang Valley. There are some middle-class Chinese and Indians who have strong views regarding ethnic issues in Malaysia, yet they have close friends among a number of Malays who they think they can trust and confide their problems.
16. The annual *balik kampung* from the Klang Valley is referred to in the media as an 'exodus' in which large numbers of people – some estimates in the mid-1990s put the figure at over one million – leave the place on homeward journeys. However, lately, the figure seems to have increased. According to a report in *Utusan Malaysia* on 26 December 2000, the highway authority, Projek Lebuh Raya Utara Selatan (PLUS), recorded that for the *Hari Raya* which fell on 27 December 2000, more than one million vehicles (mostly cars, buses and motorcyles) left Kuala Lumpur for the *balik kampung*. This means that the actual figure of the people involved could well be around two million including those who went by air and rail.
17. In a letter to the *New Straits Times* (4 February 1999), Shane L. Stone, an Australian from Darwin, wrote that 'Ramadan and *Hari Raya* are not new to me and perhaps I have tended to take the importance of these religious observances and celebrations for granted. ... Regardless of one's religious, ethnic or cultural background, *Hari Raya has become a time for celebration as a nation*' (italics added).

8   Malay Middle-Class Politics, Democracy and Civil Society

1. This introduction is, in part, based on the analysis of Malaysian middle class-politics contained in Abdul Rahman 1999.
2. Samuel Huntington, the leading advocate of the 'third wave' democratization thesis (that is, democratization of the late twentieth century), argues that rising incomes lead to changes in social structures, beliefs and culture that have been conducive to the emergence of democracy.

    > Rapid economic growth creates rapidly the economic base for democracy that slower economic growth creates more slowly. It, however, raises expectations, exacerbates inequalities, and creates stresses and strains in the social fabric that stimulate political mobilization and demands for political participation. (Huntington 1991: 68–9).

    However, we should note that there is no linear route to democracy. Some countries, such as the post-Marcos Philippines and post-Suharto Indonesia, despite their slower economic growth than Singapore or Malaysia, have a far more vibrant political life and democracy than their two Southeast Asian neighbours.
3. Those who indicated that their vote was 'secret' are assumed here to have voted mostly for the opposition (see Table 8.3).
4. Due to various constraints, the study on Malay workers was only conducted in the Klang Valley.
5. This phenomenon has not gone unnoticed by UMNO leaders. Of late, UMNO leaders have repeatedly expressed concern that many Malay youth were not joining the party and they urged the UMNO Youth to intensify campaigns to recruit them. In fact, UMNO Youth has come under strong pressure and criticisms for its ineffectiveness in attracting Malay youth, including young Malay workers. These criticisms became stronger after the November 1999 general election in which the BN, and especially the UMNO, suffered serious setbacks. Subsequently, UMNO Youth became embroiled in a leadership crisis after the BN defeat in its traditional stronghold in Lunas, a state constituency in Kedah in the November 2000 by-election, with the critics alleging that UMNO Youth had failed to prevent the youth from going over to the opposition. The debate has been going on in the mainstream media for quite some time. For example, Abdullah Ahmad, an UMNO veteran who was formerly deputy minister and a close confidante of Malaysia's second prime minister, Abdul Razak Hussein, wrote thus in his weekly column in *Mingguan Malaysia* on 17 December 2000:

    > UMNO must admit that it finds it hard today to attract Bumiputera youth though they might not be anti-government. This happens because of our [UMNO's] own doing, including the action by some UMNO leaders with strong vested interests who erect brick walls [between the party and the youth]. If UMNO fails to inspire the confidence of these youth and convince them that UMNO is not a party of the selected few, but a party of all Malays, then the youth will seek a different political alternative. There was no

alternative to UMNO before, but there is such an alternative today. If UMNO doesn't change fast enough, it will face defeat in future elections.

In another column written for the *New Straits Times* on 26 December 2000, Abdullah Ahmad stressed that UMNO Youth 'must re-invent itself' and 'be youth-friendly'.

6. This is not to deny that in the 1995 general election, Chinese voters gave greater support to the BN compared to their stand in the 1990 election, whereas there was less change among Malay voters in the Klang Valley.

7. During the acute water crisis in the Klang Valley in 1998, the Federation of Malaysian Consumer Associations (FOMCA) threatened to take the Selangor State Government and the Water Supply Department to court for their failure to provide the water supply to the public. The confrontation later cooled down after both sides entered into discussions to resolve the issue amicably, and the Selangor State Government pledged to the handle the crisis more effectively.

8. Nevertheless, of late, due to rising prices and environmental degradation, awareness of consumer rights and the need to protect the environment is growing.

9. In his study, Gomez (1996: 39–40) drew attention to the swing against the BN among rural voters in Terengganu, Kelantan and Kedah in the 1995 election, which he attributed to their frustration that government policies were exacerbating social differentiation and economic disparities in the community. In our study, except for new Malay middle-class respondents in Kota Bharu, the economic disparity issue also appears to be a major concern among a substantial number of the Malay middle-class respondents in Kuala Trengganu and in the Klang Valley.

10. In a special interview with the media, the new Chief Justice admitted that public confidence in the judiciary was at its 'lowest ebb' and that 'I fully realise that during the next two years or so there is plenty of work to do to repair the damage.' He stressed that his immediate task was 'to put our house in order' ('CJ Confident of Bringing Change', *The Star*, 22–3 December 2000).

9 The New Malay Middle Class and *Melayu Baru*

1. Over different periods of Malaysian history, the agenda of modernization and transformation of Malay society has been redefined. The debate on *Melayu Baru* that has unfolded since 1991 is the newest attempt at such a redefinition.

2. The question was posed by the former Malaysian Opposition MP, the late Dr Tan Chee Khoon, who asked whether Mahathir had modified his views contained in *The Malay Dilemma*. Mahathir acknowledged that since the book was written in the late 1960s, certain things were only valid then. However, he added that 'All the views are still held by me. But certainly some of them are still valid and where they need to be acted on, we do act' (quoted in Khoo 1995: 25).

3. Shamsul (1999: 91–3) suggested that the term is actually a replacement for *Orang Kaya Baru* (lit. the new rich person), which was already in use in everyday conversation before the 1960s:

> The term *Orang Kaya Baru* was coined and came into popular use to refer to people who had just become rich, or *orang yang baru jadi kaya*, whose behaviour is rather odd and not really like the 'real' rich people. The way it is used in this context indicates that the emphasis is on the word *Baru*, not on *Orang Kaya*, because the term as a whole refers to those who have just become rich, but who adopt behaviour that is perceived as not in the repertoire of the 'really rich'. Similarly, it is used for those who are not really rich, but who behave oddly in trying to make out that they are.

4. Abdullah's acute observations about the cause of Malay poverty and their so-called indolence are worth considering. According to Abdullah, the people only saw futility in greater striving; as they argued: 'What is the point of working hard? When we get a little bit of money or food, they attract the greed of the nobles who are sure to seize them. That's why the people remain in poverty and indolence all their lives' (Abdullah 1964: 45). Abdullah was of the opinion that

   > there has never been a country in the world in which all the subjects are complacent. If they can get the benefits of their own work and efforts, and the profits arising thereof, and feel secure at heart, and if just half of the population in the country work hard to earn their living, the country is sure to be great and rich. (Abdullah 1964: 44)
   >
   > (For a further discussion of Abdullah's views, see Shaharuddin Maaruf 1988.)

5. Abdullah criticized the Malays for their orthodox practice of only reading the Quran in Arabic without understanding its meaning. He also regretted that Malays did not study their own language seriously, and neglected the pursuit of learning. He warned that in the end, the Malays would neither acquire Arabic, nor would they be well-versed in their own language, and ultimately 'the name of Malay itself would disappear from the face of this world' (Abdullah 1964: 36–8).

6. Islamic reformist and founder of *Al Imam* in 1906, a periodical espousing Islamic reforms along the lines advocated by the Middle Eastern Islamic reformist Mohamad Abduh (Roff 1994).

7. Pioneering Malay language scholar and writer who systematized Malay grammar and wrote essays on Malay backwardness in the 1920s (Roff 1994).

8. Pioneering Malay journalist and chief editor of several Malay newspapers in the 1930s (Abdul Latiff Abu Bakar 1984).

9. A left-wing Malay nationalist who formed the first Malay political party, the *Kesatuan Melayu Muda*, or Union of Malay Youth in 1937 to fight for Malaya's independence (Roff 1994).

10. Another well-known left-wing Malay nationalist, a close comrade-in-arms of Ibrahim Yaacob.

11. See Chapter 2, especially on views of Joel Kahn (1996b).

12. This slogan, which in Bahasa Malaysia reads 'Budaya Penentu Kecapaian', was proposed by Mahathir for the 39th National Day celebration in Malaysia held on 31 August, 1996. This slogan is meant to underline the importance of developing a work culture and ethics in line with the imperatives of modern industrial capitalism.

13. Note that in the above formulation, Mahathir had widened the scope of cultural reform to include non-Malay Bumiputera (Iban and Kadazan) as well. Despite Mahathir's repeated urgings to UMNO members to discuss seriously the issue of cultural change and Islamic reform, the party has not risen to the challenge. Mahathir was disappointed that very few UMNO leaders and members took up the two issues on which he spoke at length in his presidential address at the UMNO General Assembly in September 1997. He felt that the delegates shied away from the subject (culture and religion) not only because it was 'academic' in nature but also because they were being politically cautious (*New Straits Times,* 8 September 1997, p. 6).
14. In my discussion of Malay middle-class lifestyles in Chapter 6, it was shown that the middle-class respondents did not have a strong reading habit.
15. In popular discussions, the ten years or so (prior to the financial turmoil of 1997) had been regarded not only been 'a decade of growth' in economic terms, but also 'a decade of greed' in moral-cultural terms. Some people attribute the moral backlash in the form of religious conservatism today as a reaction to such consumerism.

10 Concluding Remarks: The New Malay Middle Class and Social Transformation

1. As shown in Chapter 5, the modified extended family system is not specific to the new Malay middle class as it is also found among the new Chinese middle class in Malaysia and sections of the new middle class in advanced industrial societies. However, preference for, and practice of, having large families, while common among Malays, are not common among them.
2. Conditioned by the feudal background of Malaysian society, this relationship between ruler and ruled, which was particularly strong within the majority Malay community, was reinforced by its deep psychological need for a 'protector' to look after the community's interests in the face of the competition posed by the economically better-off Chinese minority. Invariably, it was the UMNO President and Prime Minister, who donned the mantle of 'protector'. Blind loyalty to the protector was, however, not just a product of a feudal psychology. As in other political systems, what assured the protector of the loyalty of his followers were the perks and positions he could provide. (Chandra 1998)
3. The disaffection of the middle class towards the UMNO-led state has been due to a whole gamut of factors, including Mahathir's handling of the Anwar incident, the state's tendency towards excesses and extravagance, the high-handed attitude and the lack of an engaging approach by the state towards dissent, and the leadership's loss of touch with the gras roots, especially with the young and women.
4. Three other seats went to Parti Bersatu Sabah or PBS which is neither in BA nor in BN.
5. Though the voters registered themselves in April and May 1999, the Malaysian Election Commission ruled that they could only cast their votes after their names had been verified, an exercise which the Commission said, would normally take nine months to complete (*New Straits Times*, 15 September 1999,

p.4). Since the tenth general election took place in November the same year – that is, seven months after the voter registration – the new voters were thus denied their democratic rights in the 1999 general election.

6. In an interview with the new Chief Justice of Malaysia, Tan Sri Mohamed Dzaiddin Abdullah, who took over as head of the judiciary on 20 December, 2000, he admitted that 'the credibility of the judiciary is at its lowest' and one of his main tasks was to 'put our house in order' (*The Star* 21–2 December 2000). Concurring with the views of the Chief Justice with regard to the crisis of confidence towards the institutions of governance, especially the judiciary, in a media interview on 24 January 2001 Rais Yatim, the Minister in the Prime Minister's Department in charge of Malaysia's legal and judicial administration, said that the Prime Minister's Department was preparing a report on the administration of the judiciary, the Attorney-General's Chambers, the police and other enforcement agencies 'to restore public confidence' (in these institutions). He admitted that 'we are coming under close scrutiny now and the administration of justice has come under heavy criticism. The Government cannot simply leave it at that. We must do something fast. The Government is concerned about the people's perception of the administration of justice' (*New Straits Times*, 25 January 2001, p. 1).

7. The worst incident that severely eroded the credibility of the police was the beating of Anwar Ibrahim by Rahim Noor, the then Inspector-General of Police, while the former was held in police custody after his arrest on 20 September 1998 (Royal Commission of Enquiry 1999). Thousands of Anwar's 'black eye' posters were displayed throughout the country by BA campaigners during the 1999 election campaigns, a testimony of police brutality which the BA leaders cleverly utilized.

8. One very senior journalist on the *New Straits Times*, who chaired a round-table discussion on *Bangsa Malaysia* held just before the 43rd anniversary of Malaysia's independence on 31 August 2000 (the discussion was organized by the paper in which the author was one of the panelists), admitted that the paper had suffered a serious blow to its credibility. He said that one reason why the Malaysian public was somewhat sceptical of the Malaysian government's explanations regarding the *Al Maunah* arms heist in Perak in July 2000 (in which a group of Muslim men donning army fatigues raided two outlying army camps, and carted away weapons and ammunitions) was because they were conveyed through mainstream media which had suffered a serious credibility problem among the people.

9. One UMNO Supreme Council member, Shahrir Samad, called Mahathir 'a sulking old man' always in a state of denial, and suggested that he might have become a political liability (*Asiaweek*, 15 December 2000, p. 25; *International Herald Tribune*, 16–17 December 2000, p. 5). Commenting on UMNO's current malaise, including its defeat in Lunas, UMNO Youth deputy head, Abdul Aziz Sheikh Fadzir, in an interview with the Malay weekly, *Mingguan Malaysia* (10 December 2000, p. 7) put the blame on the UMNO leadership, and cited Mahathir by name. In an outspoken style – rare under Mahathir's leadership – Aziz bluntly said that the era of not wanting to offend the party leadership 'has ended', and that UMNO must change if it wanted to remain relevant.

Bibiliography

Abdullah Ahmad. 2000. 'UMNO Mesti Segera Dekati Muda-Mudi' [UMNO Must Immediately Get Close to the Youth]. *Mingguan Malaysia*, 17 December p. 10.

Abdul Latiff Abu Bakar. 1984. *Abdul Rahim Kajai: Wartawan dan Sasterawan Melayu* [Abdul Rahim Kajai: Malay Journalist and Writer]. Kuala Lumpur: Dewan Bahasa dan Pustaka.

Abdul Majid Mat Salleh. 1989. 'Dasar Ke Arah 70 Juta Penduduk: Satu Analisis dari Perspektif Demografi' [The 70 Million Population Policy: A Demographic Analysis]. In Hairi Abdullah (ed.). *Penduduk Semenanjung Malaysia* [Population of Peninsular Malaysia]. Bangi: Penerbit Universiti Kebangsaan Malaysia.

Abdul Rahman Embong. 1994. 'Memperdalami Transformasi Budaya' [Deepening Socio-Cultural Transformation]. *Negarawan* May–June: 41–2.

Abdul Rahman Embong. 1995a. 'Malaysian Middle Classes: Some Preliminary Observations'. *Jurnal Antropologi dan Sosiologi* 22: 31–54.

Abdul Rahman Embong. 1995b. 'A Critical Review of Studies of Malaysian Middle Classes'. Working paper presented at the International Workshop on Social Transformation and the Rise of the Middle Classes in Southeast Asia, organized by the Program for Southeast Asian Area Studies (PROSEA), Academia Sinica, Taipei, Taiwan on 29–30 June.

Abdul Rahman Embong. 1996. 'Social Transformation, the State and the Middle Classes in Post-independence Malaysia'. *Southeast Asian Studies* 34 (3) December: 56–79.

Abdul Rahman Embong. 1997a. 'Cultural Transformation of the Malay Middle Class in Malaysia'. Working paper presented at the International Workshop on the Southeast Asian Middle Classes in Comparative Perspective, organized by the Program for Southeast Asian Area Studies (PROSEA), Academia Sinica, Taipei, Taiwan, 6–8 June.

Abdul Rahman Embong. 1997b. 'Malaysian Middle Class Studies: A Brief Overview'. Paper presented at the First International Malaysian Studies Conference, organized by the Malaysian Social Science Association, University of Malaya, 11–13 August.

Abdul Rahman Embong. 1998. 'Malaysian Middle Class: a Study of the "New" Middle Class in the Klang Valley, Malaysia'. In *Proceedings I – Conference on Social Stratification and Mobility: Newly Industrializing Economies Compared,* organized by the International Sociological Association Research Committee 28, in Academia Sinica, Taipei, Taiwan, 7–9 January.

Abdul Rahman Embong. 1999. 'Middle Class Politics, Democracy and Civil Society in Malaysia'. Universiti Kebangsaan Malaysia, Mimeo.

Abdul Rahman Embong. 2000. *The Culture and Practice of Pluralism in Post-independence Malaysia* (IKMAS Working Paper Series No. 18, September). Bangi, Malaysia: Institute of Malaysian and International Studies (IKMAS), UKM.

Abdul Rahman Embong. 2001. 'Beyond the Crisis: The Paradox of the Malaysian Middle Class'. In Abdul Rahman Embong (ed.). *Southeast Asian Middle Classes: Prospects for Social Change and Democratisation.* Bangi, Malaysia: Penerbit Universiti Kebangsaan Malaysia.

Abdul Rashid Moten. 2000. 'The 1999 General Elections in Malaysia: Towards a Stable Democracy?' *Akademika* 57 (July): 69–88.

Abdullah bin Abdul Kadir Munshi. 1964. *Kisah Pelayaran Abdullah* [The Travels of Abdullah]. Kuala Lumpur: Oxford University Press (with introduction and annotation by Kassim Ahmad).

Abercrombie, N. and J. Urry. 1984. *Capital, Labour and the Middle Classes*. London: Allen & Unwin.

Abu Bakar A. Hamid. 1992. 'Melayu Baru: Apa Salahnya Melayu Lama?' [New Malay: What is Wrong with the Old Malay?). *Negarawan* April–May: 15–18.

Ackerman, Susan E. and Raymond L.M. Lee. 1988. *Heaven in Transition: Non-Muslim Religious Innovation and Ethnic Identity in Malaysia*. Honolulu: University of Hawaii Press.

Adam, Christopher and William Cavendish. 1995. 'Background'. In Jomo K.S. (ed.). *Privatizing Malaysia: Rents, Rhetoric, Realities*. Boulder, San Francisco and Oxford: Westview Press.

Alatas, Syed Hussein. 1972. *Modernization and Social Change in Southeast Asia*. Sydney: Angus & Robertson.

Alatas, Syed Hussein. 1995. *The New Malay: His Role and Future*. (Occasional Paper Series). Singapore: Association of Muslim Professionals.

Alisjahbana, Sutan Takdir. 1983. 'The Great Cultural Traditions in Southeast Asia and in the Arising World'. *Ilmu Masyarakat* 4 (October–December): 1–8.

Alisjahbana, Sutan Takdir, Xavier S.T. Nayagam and Wang Gungwu (eds). 1965. *The Cultural Problems of Malaysia in the Context of Southeast Asia*. Kuala Lumpur: The Malaysian Society of Orientalists.

Allen, G.C. and A.G. Donnithorne. 1957. *Western Enterprise in Indonesia and Malaya*. New York: Allen & Unwin.

Anil Netto. 2000. 'A New Era Begins'. *Aliran Monthly* 20 (9): 2–6.

Anuwar Ali. 1995. *Globalisasi, Pembangunan Industri dan Peranan Pemerintah di Malaysia* [Globalization, Industrial Development, and the Role of the State in Malaysia]. Bangi: Penerbit Universiti Kebangsaan Malaysia.

Ariffin Omar. 1993. *Bangsa Melayu: Malay Concepts of Democracy and Community 1945–1950*. Kuala Lumpur: Oxford University Press.

Azizah Kassim. 1984. 'Dasar Kependudukan Malaysia 1984' [Malaysia's Population Policy of 1984]. *Manusia dan Masyarakat* [Man and Society]. Journal of the Department of Anthropology and Sociology, Universiti Malaya, 5: 72–4.

Banks, D.J. 1983. *Malay Kinship*. Philadelphia: Institute for the Study of Human Issues.

Bell, Colin. 1968. *Middle Class Families: Social and Geographical Mobility*. London: Routledge & Kegan Paul.

Beyer, Peter. 1994. *Religion and Globalization*. London: Sage Publications.

Bourdieu, Pierre. 1977. *Outline of a Theory of Practice*. London: Cambridge University Press.

Bourdieu, Pierre. 1984. *Distinction: a Social Critique of the Judgement of Taste*. London: Routledge.

Brookfield, H. 1994. 'Transformation Before the Late 1960s'. In H. Brookfield (ed.). *Transformation with Industrialization in Peninsular Malaysia*. Kuala Lumpur: Oxford University Press.

Brown, D. 1994. *The State and Ethnic Politics in Southeast Asia*. London and New York: Routledge.

Butler, T. and Mike Savage (eds). 1995. *Social Change and the Middle Classes*. London: UCL Press.

Chandra Muzaffar. 1979. *Protector? An Analysis of the Concept and Practice of Loyalty in Leader-led Relationships within Malay Society*. Pulau Pinang: Aliran.

Chandra Muzaffar. 1987. *Islamic Resurgence in Malaysia*. Petaling Jaya: Penerbit Fajar Bakti.

Chandra Muzaffar. 1998. 'The Anwar Crisis: Political Culture and Democracy'. http://www.jaring.my/just/Polcult.html.

Chandra Muzaffar. 2000. 'Lunas and Beyond'. *Aliran Monthly* 20 (10): 12–16.

Chang, Mau-Kuei. 1994. 'Culture and Lifestyles of Taiwan's Middle Classes'. Paper presented at the International Conference on East Asian Middle Classes and National Development in Comparative Perspective, organized by the Institute of Ethnology, Academia Sinica, Taipei, 19–21 December.

Corrothers, Andra L. and Estie W. Suryatna. 1995. 'Review of the NGO Sector in Indonesia and Evolution of the Asia Pacific Regional Community Concept among Indonesian NGOs'. In Tadashi Yamamoto (ed.). *Emerging Civil Society in the Asia Pacific Community*. Singapore: Institute of Southeast Asian Studies and Tokyo: Japan Center for International Exchange.

Cotton, J. and Kim Hyung-a van Leest. 1996. 'The New Rich and the New Middle Class in South Korea: the Rise and Fall of the "Golf Republic"'. In Richard Robison and David S.G. Goodman (eds). *The New Rich in Asia: Mobile Phones, McDonalds and Middle-class Revolution*. London and New York: Routledge.

Cox, Robert. 1997. 'Gramsci's Thought and the Question of Civil Society in the Late 20th Century'. Revised version of the paper presented at the Conference on 'Gramsci, Modernity, and the Twentieth Century' held in Cagliari, 15–18 April.

Crompton, R. 1993. *Class and Stratification: an Introduction to Current Debates*. Cambridge, UK: Polity Press.

Crouch, H. 1981. *Domestic Political Structures and Regional Economic Cooperation*. Singapore: Institute of Southeast Studies.

Crouch, H. 1993. 'Malaysia: Neither Authoritarian nor Democratic'. In Kevin Hewison, Richard Robison and Gary Rodan (eds). *Southeast Asia in the 1990s: Authoritarianism, Democracy and Capitalism*. Sydney: Allen & Unwin.

Crouch, H. 1994. 'Industrialization and Political Change'. In H. Brookfield (ed.). *Transformation with Industrialization in Peninsular Malaysia*. Kuala Lumpur: Oxford University Press.

Crouch, H. 1996. *Government and Society in Malaysia*. St Leonards, NSW: Allen & Unwin.

Department of Statistics. 1995a. *Population and Housing Census 1991*, vol. 1. Kuala Lumpur: Department of Statistics.

Department of Statistics. 1995b. *Population and Housing Census 1991*, vol. 2. Kuala Lumpur: Department of Statistics.

Edgell, Stephen. 1980. *Middle Class Couples: a Study of Segregation, Domination and Inequality in Marriage*. London: George Allen & Unwin.

Edgell, Stephen. 1993. *Class*. London and New York: Routledge

Election Commission. 2000. *Keputusan Pilihan Raya Umum Malaysia Ke-10, 1999* (Results of the Tenth General Elections in Malaysia). *His Majesty's Government Gazette*, vol. 44, no. 2, 20 January 2000. Kuala Lumpur: Percetakan Nasional Malaysia.

Evans, Arthur S. Jr. 1995. 'The Transformation of the Black Middle Class'. In Arthur J. Vidich (ed.). *The New Middle Classes: Lifestyles, Status Claims and Political Orientations*. London: Macmillan.

Evers, H.D. 1973. 'Group Conflict and Class Formation in Southeast Asia'. In H.D. Evers (ed.). *Modernization in Southeast Asia*. Singapore: Oxford University Press.

Fatimah Abdullah. 1994. 'Urbanisasi dan Kekeluargaan: Satu Kajian Kes Kelas Menengah Melayu di Kuala Lumpur' [Urbanization and Family. A Case Study of Malay Middle Class in Kuala Lumpur]. PhD thesis submitted to the Department of Anthropology and Sociology, University of Malaya.

Frankenburg, Ronald. 1969. *Communities in Britain: Social Life in Town and Country*. Harmondsworth: Penguin Books.

Furnivall, J.S. 1956. *Colonial Policy and Practice*. New York: New York University Press.

Gans, H.J. 1962. *The Urban Villagers: Group and Class in the Life of Italian-Americans*. New York: Free Press.

Gerke, Solvay. 1995. 'Symbolic Consumption as a Way of Life: The New Indonesian Middle Class'. Paper presented at the International Seminar on Cultural and Social Dimensions of Market Expansion organised by the Goethe Institute, Jakarta, in Labuan, Malaysia, 16–18 October.

Giddens, A. 1980. *The Class Structure of the Advanced Societies*. London: Hutchinson.

Giddens, A. 1991. *The Consequences of Modernity*. London: Polity Press.

Goldthorpe, J. 1980. *Social Mobility and Class Structure in Britain*. Oxford: Clarendon Press.

Goldthorpe, J. 1982. 'On the Service Class'. In A.Giddens and G.McKenzie (eds). *Social Class and the Division of Labour*. Cambridge: Cambridge University Press.

Gomez, E.T. 1991. *Money Politics in the Barisan Nasional*. Kuala Lumpur: Forum.

Gomez, E.T. 1994. *Political Business: Corporate Involvement of Malaysian Political Parties*. Townsville, Queensland: Centre for Southeast Asian Studies, James Cook University.

Gomez, E.T. 1996. *The 1995 Malaysian General Elections: a Report and Commentary*. Singapore: Institute of Southeast Asian Studies.

Gomez, E.T. and Jomo K.S. 1997. *Malaysia's Political Economy: Politics, Patronage and Profits*. Cambridge, UK: Cambridge University Press.

Harper, T.N. 1996. 'New Malays, New Malaysians: Nationalism, Society and History'. *Southeast Asian Affairs*: 238–55.

Hefner, Robert W. 2000. *Civil Islam: Muslims and Democratization in Indonesia*. Princeton and Oxford: Princeton University Press.

Held, David, James Anderson, Bram Gieber, Stuart Hall, Laurence Harris, Paul Lewis, Noel Parher and Ben Turok (eds). 1983. *States and Society*. Oxford: Basil Blackwell.

Heng Pek Koon. 1992. 'The Chinese Business Elite of Malaysia'. In Ruth McVey (ed.). *Southeast Asian Capitalists*. New York: Cornell University Press.

Hing Ai Yun. 1997. 'Industrial Restructuring and the Reconstitution of Class Relations in Singapore'. *Capital & Class* 62: 79–118.

Hirschman, Charles. 1975. *Ethnic and Social Stratification in Peninsular Malaysia*. Washington DC.: American Sociological Association.

Ho Khai Leong. 1988. 'Indigenizing the State: The New Economic Policy and the Bumiputera State in Peninsular Malaysia.' PhD dissertation submitted to the Graduate School of the Ohio State University, USA.

Ho Khai Leong. 1997. 'Political Indigenization and the State in Peninsular Malaysia'. In H.M. Dahlan et al. (eds). *ASEAN and the Global System*. Bangi: Penerbit Universiti Kebangsaan Malaysia.

Hsiao, H.H.M. (ed.). 1993. *Discovery of the Middle Classes in East Asia*. Taipei: Institute of Ethnology, Academia Sinica.

Hsiao, H.H.M. (ed.). 1999. *East Asian Middle Classes In Comparative Perspective*. Taipei: Institute of Ethnology, Academic Sinica.

Hsiao, H.H. M. and Hagen Koo. 1997. 'The Middle Classes and Democratization'. In Larry Diamond et al. (eds). *Consolidating the Third Wave Democracies: Themes and Perspectives*. Baltimore and London: The Johns Hopkins University Press.

Hsiao, H.H.M. and A. So. 1999. "The Making of the East Asian Middle Classes: the Five Propositions'. In H.H.M. Hsiao. *East Asian Middle Classes in Comparative Perspective*. Taipei: Institute of Ethnology, Academia Sinica.

Hua Wu Yin. 1983. *Class and Communalism in Malaysia: Politics in a Dependent Capitalist State*. London: Zed Books.

Huntington, S. 1991. *The Third Wave: Democratization in the Late Twentieth Century*. Norman and London: University of Oklahoma Press.

Husin Ali, S. 1984. 'Social Relations: Ethnic and Class Factors'. In S. Husin Ali (ed.). *Ethnicity, Class and Development – Malaysia*. Kuala Lumpur: Persatuan Sains Sosial Malaysia.

Husin Ali, S. 1993. 'Melayu Baru: Gimik Politik atau Gerakan Rakyat?' [New Malay: Political Gimmick or People's Movement?]. Speech presented at the forum on 'Melayu Baru' at the Chinese Assembly Hall, Kuala Lumpur, 7 October.

Husin Ali, S. 1999. 'For Justice and Democracy'. *Aliran Monthly* 19 (5) June: 15–16.

Husin Mutalib. 1990. *Islam and Ethnicity in Malay Politics*. Singapore: Oxford University Press.

Ishak Shari. 1995. 'Industrialization and Poverty: the Malaysian Experience'. *Jurnal Antropologi dan Sosiologi* 22: 11–29.

Jesudason, James V. 1989. *Ethnicity and the Economy: the State, Chinese Business, and Multinationals in Malaysia*. Singapore: Oxford University Press.

Jomo, K.S. and Ahmad Shabery Cheek. 1992. 'Malaysia's Islamic Movements'. In Joel S. Kahn and Francis Loh Kok Wah (eds). *Fragmented Vision: Culture and Politics in Contemporary Malaysia*. Sydney: Allen & Unwin.

Jomo, K.S. 1986. *A Question of Class: Capital, the State, and Uneven Development in Malaya*. Singapore: Oxford University Press.

Jomo, K.S. 1994. *U-Turn? Malaysian Economic Development Policies after 1990*. Townsville: Centre for East and Southeast Asian Studies, James Cook University of Northern Queensland.

Jomo, K.S. 1999. 'A Malaysian Middle Class?: Some Preliminary Analytical Considerations'. In K.S. Jomo (ed.). *Rethinking Malaysia*. Kuala Lumpur: Malaysian Social Sciences Association'.

Jomo, K.S. (ed.). 2001. *Malaysian Eclipse: Economic Crisis and Recovery*. London and New York: Zed Books.

Jones, Gavin W. 1994. *Marriage and Divorce in Islamic South-East Asia*. Kuala Lumpur: Oxford University Press.

Kahn, J.S. 1991. 'Constructing Culture: Towards an Anthropology of the Middle Classes in Southeast Asia'. *Asian Studies Review* 15 (2), November: 50–7.

Kahn, J.S. 1992. 'Class, Ethnicity and Diversity: Some Remarks on Malay Culture in Malaysia'. In J. S. Kahn and Francis Loh Kok Wah (eds). *Fragmented Vision: Culture and Politics in Contemporary Malaysia*. Sydney: Allen & Unwin.

Kahn, J.S. 1994. 'Subalternity and the Construction of Malay Identity'. In Alberto Gomes (ed.). *Modernity and Identity: Asian Illustrations*. Bandoora, Victoria: La Trobe University Press.

Kahn, J.S. 1996a. 'The Middle Class as a Field of Ethnological Study.' In Muhammad Ikmal Said and Zahid Emby (eds). *Critical Perspectives: Essays in Honour of Syed Husin Ali*. Kuala Lumpur: Malaysian Social Science Association.

Kahn, J.S. 1996b. 'Growth, Economic Transformation, Culture and the Middle Classes in Malaysia'. In Richard Robison and David S.G. Goodman (eds). *The New Rich in Asia: Mobile Phones, McDonalds and Middle-class Revolution*. London and New York: Routledge.

Kessler, C. 1992. 'Archaism and Modernity: Contemporary Malay Political Culture'. In J.S. Kahn and Francis Loh Kok Wah (eds). *Fragmented Vision: Culture and Politics in Contemporary Malaysia*. Sydney: Allen & Unwin.

Khasnor, Johan. 1984. *The Emergence of the Modern Malay Administrative Elite*. Singapore: Oxford University Press.

Khoo Boo Teik. 1995. *Paradoxes of Mahathirism: an Intellectual Biography of Mahathir Mohamad*. Kuala Lumpur: Oxford University Press.

Kosaku, Yoshino. 1992. *Cultural Nationalism in Contemporary Japan: a Sociological Enquiry*. London and New York: Routledge.

Kunio, Yoshihara. 1988. *The Rise of Ersatz Capitalism in South-East Asia*. Singapore: Oxford University Press.

Kunio, Yoshihara. 1994. *The Nation and Economic Growth: the Philippines and Thailand*. Kuala Lumpur: Oxford University Press.

Lee, D. and Howard Newby. 1994. *The Problem of Sociology*. London and New York: Routledge.

Lee, Hye-Kyung. 1995. 'NGOs in Korea'. In Tadashi Yamamoto (ed.). *Emerging Civil Society in the Asia Pacific Community*. Singapore: Institute of Southeast Asian Studies and Tokyo: Japan Center for International Exchange.

Lerner, D. 1958. *The Passing of Traditional Society: Modernising the Middle East*. Glencoe, Ill. and New York: Free Press.

Li Dun Jen. 1982. *British Malaya: an Economic Analysis*, 2nd revised edition. Kuala Lumpur: INSAN.

Litwak, Eugene. 1960a. 'Geographic Mobility and Extended Family Cohesion'. *American Sociological Review* 25: 9–21.

Litwak, Eugene. 1960b. 'Occupational Mobility and Extended Family Cohesion'. *American Sociological Review*. 25: 385–94.

Lockwood, David. 1995. 'Introduction: Marking Out the Middle Class(es)'. In Tim Butler and Mike Savage (eds). *Social Change and the Middle Classes*. London: UCL Press.

Loh Kok Wah, Francis. 1997. 'Developmentalism in Malaysia in the 1990s: Is a Shift from the Politics of Ethnicism Underway?' Paper presented at the First International Malaysian Studies Conference organized by the Malaysian Social Science Association, at the University of Malaya, 11–13 August.

Mahathir Mohamad. 1970. *The Malay Dilemma*. Singapore: Donald Moore Press.

Mahathir Mohamad. 1991a. *Malaysia: the Way Forward*. Kuala Lumpur: Institute of Strategic and International Studies.

Mahathir Mohamad. 1991b. 'Jihad UMNO untuk Bangsa Melayu Baru' [UMNO's Struggle for a New Malay Race]. Speech by UMNO President Dato' Seri Dr Mahathir Mohamad at the UMNO General Assembly on 8 November 1991. The text of the speech was published in *Utusan Malaysia*, 9 November 1991.

Mahathir Mohamad. 1993. 'UMNO Pembawa Perubahan' [UMNO, Agent of Change]. Speech by UMNO President Dato' Seri Dr Mahathir Mohamad at the UMNO General Assembly on 4 November 1993. The text of the speech was published in *Utusan Malaysia*, 5 November 1993.

Mahathir Mohamad. 1994a. 'Malay Problems in the Context of Malaysian Problems'. *Sari* (Journal of the Malay World and Civilization). Institut Alam dan Tamadun Melayu (ATMA) 12 (July): 77–86.

Mahathir Mohamad. 1994b. 'Hapuskan Segera Politik Wang' [Immediately Eradicate Money Politics]. Speech by UMNO President Dato' Seri Dr Mahathir Mohamad at the UMNO Extraordinary General Assembly on 19 June 1994. The text of the speech was published in *Utusan Malaysia*, 20 June 1994.

Mahathir Mohammad. 1994c. 'Malay Problems in the Context of Malaysia [*sic*] Problems'. *Sari*, Journal of the Malay World and Civilisation, Universiti Kebangsaan Malaysia, 12 (July): 77–86.

Mahathir Mohamad. 1997. 'Menebus Maruah Bangsa' [Redeeming the Self-respect of the Race]. Speech by UMNO President Dato' Seri Dr Mahathir Mohamad at the UMNO General Assembly on 5 September 1997. The text of the speech was published in *Utusan Malaysia*, 6 September 1997.

Mahathir Mohamad. 2000. 'PM: Decisions Made by Cabinet'. End-of-year interview with Dato' Seri Dr Mahathir Mohamad with Bernama on 26 December 2000, published in *New Straits Times*, 29 December 2000.

Malaysia. 1971. *Second Malaysia Plan 1971–1975*. Kuala Lumpur: Government Printing Department.

Malaysia. 1991. *Second Outline Perspective Plan 1991–2000*. Kuala Lumpur: Percetakan Nasional Malaysia Berhad.

Malaysia. 1996. *Seventh Malaysia Plan 1996–2000*. Kuala Lumpur: Percetakan Nasional Malaysia Berhad.

Malaysia. 1999. *Mid-Term Review of the Seventh Malaysia Plan 1999–2000*. Kuala Lumpur: Percetakan Nasional Malaysia Berhad.

Marshall, G. 1997. *Repositioning Class: Social Inequality in Industrial Societies*. London: Sage Publications.

Marshall, G.,David Rose, Howard Newby and Carolyn Vogler. 1988. *Social Class in Modern Britain*. London: Unwin Hyman.

Mc Nall, Scott G., Rhonda F. Levine and Rich Fantasia (eds). 1991. *Bringing Class Back In: Contemporary and Historical Perspectives*. Boulder: Westview Press.

McVey, Ruth (ed.). 1992. *Southeast Asian Capitalists*. Ithaca, NY: South East Asia Program, Cornell University.

Mills, C.W. 1975. *White Collar: the American Middle Classes*. London: Oxford University Press (first published 1951).

Mittelman, J. (ed.). 1996. *Globalization: Critical Reflections*. Boulder and London: Lynne Reinner Publishers.

Mohd Nor Nawawi. 1991. 'Dasar Ekonomi Baru, Perpaduan Nasional dan Kelas Menengah' [New Economic Policy, National Unity and the Middle Class]. In Khadijah Muhamed and Halimah Awang (eds). *Dasar Ekonomi Baru dan Masa*

Depannya [The New Economic Policy and its Future]. Kuala Lumpur: Persatuan Sains Sosial Malaysia.

Mohd Yusof Kasim and Azlan Ahmed (eds). 2001. *'Politik Baru' dalam Pilihan raya Umum 1999 di Malaysia* ['New Politics' in the 1999 General Elections in Malaysia]. Bangi, Malaysia: Penerbit Universiti Kebangsaan Malaysia.

Muhamad Ikmal Said. 1995. 'The State, Industrialization and the Middle Classes in Malaysia'. Paper presented at the International Workshop on the Social Transformation and the Rise of the Middle Classes in Southeast Asia, organized by the Program for Southeast Asian Area Studies, Academia Sinica, Taipei, Taiwan, 29–30 June.

Nair, Sheila. 1999. 'Constructing Civil Society in Malaysia: Nationalism, Hegemony and Resistance'. In K.S. Jomo (ed.). *Rethinking Malaysia*. Kuala Lumpur: Malaysian Social Science Association.

Nathan, J.E. (compiler). 1922. *Census of British Malaya (The Straits Settelements, Federated Malay States and Protected States of Johore, Kedah, Perlis, Kelantan, Trengganu and Brunei). 1921.* London.

Norani Othman, Abdul Rahman Embong, Rustam A. Sani and Clive Kessler 1996. 'Pembangunan Sosial dan Pembentukan Budaya Kemodenan Budaya di Kalangan Golongan Kelas Menengah Moden di Malaysia' [Social Development and the Creation of a Culture of Modernity among the Middle Class in Malaysia]. Technical Report Submitted to the Ministry of Science, Technology and Environment, Malaysia. IRPA Project No. 5–07–03–028.

Norani Othman. 1997. 'The Formation of the "New Middle Classes" and the Creation of "a Culture of Modernity" in Contemporary Malaysia'. Working paper presented at the International Workshop on the Southeast Asian Middle Classes in Comparative Perspective, organized by the Program for Southeast Asian Area Studies (PROSEA), Academia Sinica, Taipei, Taiwan, 6–8 June.

Nordin Selat 1976. *Kelas Menengah Pentadbir Melayu: Satu Kajian Perkembangan Gaya Hidup* [The Malay Administrative Middle Class: a Study of the Development of Lifestyle]. Kuala Lumpur: Penerbit Utusan Melayu (M) Bhd.

Phillips, Deborah and Philip Sarre. 1995. 'Black Middle-Class Formation in Contemporary Britain'. In Tim Butler and Mike Savage (eds). *Social Change and the Middle Classes*. London: UCL Press.

Puthucheary, J.J. 1979. *Ownership and Control in the Malayan Economy*. Kuala Lumpur: University of Malaya Co-operative Bookshop. (First published in 1960 by Eastern Universities Press in Singapore.)

Quah, Stella R. 1990a. 'Marriage and Parenthood as Personal and Social Goals'. In S.R. Quah (ed.). *The Family as an Asset: an International Perspective on Marriage, Parenthood and Social Policy*. Singapore: Times Academic Press.

Quah, Stella R. 1990b. 'Family as Hindrance or Asset? An Overview of Current Controversies'. In S.R. Quah (ed.). *The Family as an Asset: an International Perspective on Marriage, Parenthood and Social Policy*. Singapore: Times Academic Press.

Quah, Stella R. 1994. *Family in Singapore: Sociological Perspectives*. Singapore: Times Academic Press.

Rahimah Aziz, Abdul Rahman Embong, Hairi Abdullah and Mohammed Salleh Lamry. 1998. 'Kelas Menengah Malaysia: Perkembangan dan Peranannya di Malaysia' [Malaysian Middle Class: Its Development and Role]. Technical report submitted to the Ministry of Science, Technology and Environment, Malaysia. IRPA Project No. 07–02–02–021.

Robertson, Roland 1992. *Globalization.* London: Sage Publications.

Robison, R. and David S.G. Goodman (eds). 1996. *The New Rich in Asia: Mobile Phones, McDonalds and Middle-class Revolution.* London and New York: Routledge.

Rodan, Garry, Kevin Hewison and Richard Robison (eds). 1997. *The Political Economy of Southeast Asia.* Melbourne: Oxford University Press.

Roff, William. 1994. *The Origins of Malay Nationalism,* 2nd edition. Kuala Lumpur: Oxford University Press. (First published in 1967.)

Royal Commission of Enquiry. 1999. *Report of the Royal Commission of Enquiry to Enquire into the Injuries of Dato' Seri Anwar Ibrahim Whilst in Police Custody,* Vol. 1. Kuala Lumpur: Percetakan Nasional Malaysia Berhad.

Rugayah Mohamed. 1995. 'Public Enterprises'. In K.S. Jomo (ed.). *Privatizing Malaysia: Rents, Rhetoric, Realities.* Boulder: Westview Press.

Rustam A. Sani. 1992. '*Melayu Baru*: Beberapa Persoalan Sosiobudaya' [*New Malay*: Some Sociocultural Questions]. Kuala Lumpur: Institute of Strategic and International Studies (ISIS).

Rustam A. Sani. 1993. *Melayu Baru: Tradisi Cendekia and Krisis Budaya* [New Malays: Intellectual Tradition and Cultural Crisis]. Kuala Lumpur: Utusan Publications.

Rustam A. Sani. 1997. 'Transformasi Budaya' [Cultural Transformation]. *Utusan Malaysia,* 10 September, p. 6.

Saliha Hassan. 2000. 'Organisasi Bukan-kerajaan dan Penyertaan Politik di Malaysia' [Non-governmental Organizations and Political Participation in Malaysia]. In Abdul Rahman Embong (ed.). *Negara, Pasaran dan Pemodenan Malaysia* [State, Market, and Modernization in Malaysia]. Bangi: Penerbit Universiti Kebangsaan Malaysia.

Saravanamuttu, Johan. 1989. 'Kelas Menengah dalam Politik Malaysia: Tonjolan Perkauman atau Kepentingan Kelas?' [Middle Class in Malaysian Politics: Communalism or Class Interests?]. *Kajian Malaysia* 7 (1 and 2), June/December: 106–26.

Saravanamuttu, Johan 1994. 'Peranan Kelas Menengah dalam Politik di Malaysia' [The Role of the Middle Class in Malaysian Politics]. Working paper presented at the Seminar on Managing Political Change and Facing Challenges of the 21st Century in Malaysia held in Penang, 3 October.

Saravanamuttu, Johan. 2001. 'Is There A Politics of the Malaysian Middle Class?' In Abdul Rahman Embong (ed.). *South East Asian Middle Classes: Prospects for Social Change and Democratisation.* Bangi, Malaysia: Penerbit Universiti Kebangsaan Malaysia.

Saunders, Graham E. 1977. *The Development of a Plural Society in Malaya.* Kuala Lumpur: Longman.

Scott, James C. 1968. *Political Ideology in Malaysia: Reality and the Beliefs of an Elite.* New Haven and London: Yale University Press.

Senu Abdul Rahman et al. 1971. *Revolusi Mental* [Mental Revolution]. Kuala Lumpur: Penerbitan Utusan Melayu.

Shaharuddin Maaruf. 1988. *Malay Ideas on Development – From Feudal Lord to Capitalist.* Singapore and Kuala Lumpur: Times Books International.

Shamsul, A.B. 1994. 'Religion and Ethnic Politics in Malaysia'. In C.F. Keyes, L. Kendall and H. Hardacre (eds). *Asian Visions of Authority: Religion and the Modern States of East and Southeast Asia.* Honolulu: University of Hawaii Press.

Shamsul, A.B. 1997. 'The Economic Dimension of Malay Nationalism: the Socio-historical Roots of the New Economic Policy and its Contemporary Implications'. *The Developing Economies* 35 (3) (September): 240–61.

Shamsul, A.B. 1999. 'From *Orang Kaya Baru* to *Melayu Baru*: Cultural Constructions of the Malay "New Rich"'. In Michael Pinches (ed.). *Culture and Privilege in Capitalist Asia*. London: Routledge.

Shamsul, A.B. 2001. 'The Redefinition of Politics and the Transformation of Malaysian Pluralism'. In Robert W. Hefner (ed.). *Southeast Asian Pluralisms: the Politics of Multiculturalism in Malaysia, Singapore and Indonesia*. Honolulu: University of Hawaii Press (forthcoming).

Sharifah Zaleha Syed Hassan. 1997. 'Constructions of Islamic Identities in a Suburban Community in Malaysia'. *Southeast Asian Journal of Social Science* 25 (2): 25–38.

Sharifah Zaleha Syed Hassan. 1999. 'The Dakwah Phenomenon: Islamic Oppositional Discourses in Malaysia'. *Sari*, Jounal of the Malay World and Civilization, Universiti Kebangsaan Malaysia, 17 (July): 19–36.

Shehan, C.L. and K.C.W. Kammeyer. 1997. *Marriages and Families: Reflections of a Gendered Society*. Boston: Allyn & Bacon.

Sieh Lee Mei Ling. 1992. 'The Transformation of Malaysian Business Groups'. In Ruth McVey (ed.). *Southeast Asian Capitalists*. Ithaca, NY: South East Asia Program, Cornell University.

SIRD. 2000. *Dilema UMNO: Analisa Pilihanraya Umum 1999* [UMNO's Dilemma: An Analysis of the 1999 General Elections]. Petaling Jaya, Malaysia: Strategic Into Research Development.

Sloane, Patricia. 1999. *Islam, Modernity and Entrepreneurship among the Malays*. London: Macmillan.

So, Alvin and H.H.M. Hsiao. 1999. 'The Making of the Middle Classes in East Asia: the Five Propositions'. In Hsin-Huang Michael Hsiao (ed.). *East Asian Middle Classes in Comparative Perspective*. Taipei: Institute of Ethnology, Academia Sinica.

Stein, Michael. 1964. *The Eclipse of Community*. New York: Harper & Row.

Tan Poo Chang, Ng Sor Tho, Rahman Embong, Tey Nai Peng, Jamaluddin Mohd Yunos and Chwee Geok Leng. 1996. 'Survey of the Middle Class in the Klang Valley, Malaysia'. Technical report submitted to the Program for Southeast Asian Area Studies (PROSEA), Academia Sinica, Taipei, Taiwan.

Tham Seong Chee. 1977. *Malays and Modernization: a Sociological Interpretation*. Singapore: Singapore University Press.

Tönnies, F. 1957. *Community and Society*. New York: Harper & Row. (First published 1887.)

Townsend, P. 1957. *Poverty in the United Kingdom*. Harmondsworth: Penguin.

Tun Salleh Abas (with K. Das). 1989. *May Day for Justice*. Kuala Lumpur: Magnus Books.

Vidich, Arthur J. (ed.). 1995. *The New Middle Classes: Life-Styles, Status Claims and Political Orientations*. London: Macmillan.

Weber, M. 1971. *The Protestant Ethic and the Spirit of Capitalism*. London: Unwin University Books.

Willmott, P. 1969. 'Some Social Trends'. *Urban Studies* 6: 286–308.

Willmott, P. and M. Young. 1960. *Family and Class in a London Suburb*. London: Routledge & Kegan Paul.

Wirth, L. 1938. 'Urbanism as a Way of Life'. *American Journal of Sociology* 44 (1): 1–24.

World Bank. 1993. *The East Asian Miracle: Economic Growth and Public Policy*. New York: Oxford University Press.

World Bank. 1997. *The State in a Changing World. World Development Report, 1997.* Washington DC : World Bank.

Wright, E.O. 1985. *Classes.* London: Verso.

Wright, E.O. 1991. 'The Conceptual Status of Class Structure in Class Analysis'. In S.G. McNall, R.F. Levine and R. Fantasia (eds). *Bringing Class Back In: Contemporary and Historical Perspectives.* Boulder: Westview Press.

Wright, E.O. 1994. 'The Middle Class in Marxist and Weberian Class Analysis'. Working paper presented at the International Conference on East Asian Middle Classes and National Development in Comparative Perspective, organized by Academic Sinica, Taipei, Taiwan, 19–21 December.

Wright, E.O. 1999. 'The Middle Class in Marxist and Weberian Class Analysis'. In Hsin-Huang Michael Hsiao (ed.). *East Asian Middle Classes in Comparative Perspective.* Taipei: Academia Sinica.

Yamamoto, Tadashi. 1995. *Emerging Civil Society in the Asia Pacific Community.* Singapore: Institute of Southeast Asian Studies and Tokyo: Japan Center for International Exchange.

Yang, Jonghoe. 1999. 'Class Culture or Culture Class? Lifestyles and Cultural Tastes of the Korean Middle Class'. In Hsin-Huang Michael Hsiao (ed.). *East Asian Middle Classes in Comparative Perspective.* Taipei: Institute of Ethnology, Academia Sinica.

Young, M. and P. Willmott. 1957. *Family and Kinship in East London.* London: Routledge & Kegan Paul.

Young, M. and P. Willmott. 1973. *The Symmetrical Family.* London: Routledge & Kegan Paul.

Zainah Anwar. 1987. *Islamic Revivalism in Malaysia: Dakwah among the Students.* Petaling Jaya: Pelanduk Publications.

Zawawi Ibrahim. 1998. *The Malay Labourer: By the Window of Capitalism.* Singapore: Institute of Southeast Asian Studies.

Index